IRISH STUDIES
A General Introduction

Ireland: Political and Administrative Divisions

CONTENTS

LIST OF MAPS

ACKNOWLEDGEMENTS

Our thanks to Seamus O'Grady, Administrative Director of the University College Galway Summer School, for his support and encouragement throughout this project; to Mary Cawley for advice on the maps; to Siobhan Comer for drawing them; and to Marie Boran who compiled the index. Our thanks also to the *alumni* of the UCG Summer School who unwittingly have played an important rôle in determining the structure and content of this book.

T.B., C.C., R. O'D., G. O'T.

NOTES ON CONTRIBUTORS

Tom Bartlett is a lecturer in history in University College, Galway. He was born and educated in Belfast and obtained his Ph.D. from Queen's University, Belfast. His writings on eighteenth-century Irish politics and civil disturbances have been published in a number of scholarly journals. During 1982-83 he was a Fulbright Fellow at the University of Michigan, Ann Arbor. He is currently joint editor (with S. J. Connolly) of *Irish Economic and Social History* and is director of the history programme in the University College Galway Summer School.

Tom Boylan lectures in economics in University College Galway. He was educated at University College Dublin and at Trinity College Dublin and has taught courses in economic theory and economic development at universities in Britain and the USA. His research and publications are mainly in the areas of industrial and economic development, econometrics and, more recently, in the history of economic ideas.

Mary Cawley is a lecturer in geography at University College Galway. She holds a Ph.D. degree from the University of London and was a Visiting Fulbright Fellow at the Pennsylvania State University in 1985. Her research interests include historical and rural geography on which she has published widely.

Chris Curtin was born in Co. Clare and graduated from University College Galway where he now lectures in sociology. He obtained a Ph.D. in social anthropology from Hull University. His current research interests include community development, sociology of the family and agrarian politics. He has published in sociological and anthropological journals and has taught a wide range of courses in sociology and political science. He is programme director for Irish Society in the University College Galway Summer School.

Gerald Dawe, poet and critic, was born in Belfast but now lives and works in Galway. His publications include *Sheltering Places* (1978), *The Younger Irish Poets* (1982), *Across a Roaring Hill: The Protestant Imagination in Modern Ireland* (1985, with Edna Longley), and *The*

Lundy's Letter (1985). He was awarded the Macauley Fellowship in literature in 1984 and a Hawthornden Fellowship (1987).

Luke Gibbons was born in Co. Roscommon and graduated from University College Galway with B.A. and M.A. degrees in philosophy. He is a lecturer in communications at the School of Communications, NIHE, Glasnevin, Dublin. Among his research interests are the media and Irish society, sociology of culture, and aesthetics and politics. He has published (with Kevin Rockett and John Hill) a study of the cinema in Ireland.

Michael Laver is Professor of Politics and Sociology at University College Galway. He is the author of *Invitation to Politics* and has published widely on Irish elections.

Noel McGonagle was born in Derry City and educated in Northern Ireland. He obtained his Ph.D. in Celtic languages and literature from Queen's University Belfast. He is a specialist in Gaelic literature with particular reference to Ulster authors and his publications include four books and numerous articles in Gaelic literary and linguistic journals.

Gearóid MacNiocaill is Professor of History in University College Galway. He has published extensively on medieval Irish history and his works include studies of the Cistercians in Ireland (1959), the medieval Irish borough (1964) and editions of the *Red Book of The Earls of Kildare* and (with Sean Mac Airt) the *Annals of Ulster* (1983).

D.E.S. Maxwell was educated at Trinity College Dublin. He has taught in Ireland and in Africa and is currently Professor of English at York University, Toronto. His publications include a study of the poetry of T.S. Eliot (1952) and a book on American fiction (1963). He has also published *Modern Irish Drama* (Cambridge University Press 1983).

Liam O'Dowd is a lecturer in sociology at Queen's University Belfast. A graduate of University College Galway, he obtained his Ph.D. from Southern Illinois University. His research interests include Irish urbanisation, contemporary socio-economic development in Northern Ireland and social ideology in both Northern Ireland and the Irish Republic. He is editor (with P. Clancy, S. Drudy, and K. Lynch) of *Ireland: A Sociological Profile* (1986).

Riana O'Dwyer was educated at University College Galway, Université de Lausanne, and McMaster University, Ontario where she was awarded her Ph.D. for a study of James Joyce. A lecturer in English at University College Galway, she has also taught at universities in Canada and has published on various literary topics, including Joyce, modern Irish drama and contemporary fiction. She is director of the Anglo-Irish literature programme in the University College Galway Summer School.

Seán Ó Tuama is Professor of Modern Irish literature in University College, Cork, and has been a visiting Professor in the universities of Harvard, Oxford, and Toronto. His publications include two books of his own verse and four plays, as well as literary criticism and literary history. *An Grá in Amhráin na nDaoine* (1960), *Caoineadh Airt Uí Laoghaire* (1961), *Filí faoi Sceimhle* (1979) are amongst his most notable academic works, while *An Duanaire, Poems of the Dispossessed* (1981) — a bilingual anthology done in conjunction with Thomas Kinsella — attracted widespread acclaim.

Gearóid Ó Tuathaigh was educated at University College Galway, where he now lectures in history, and at Peterhouse, Cambridge. He has lectured extensively in Britain, Europe, the USA and Canada as well as in Ireland. During 1987 he was Visiting Professor of Celtic Studies at Saint Michael's College, University of Toronto. His publications include *Ireland before the Famine; Thomas Drummond and the Irish Administration 1835-41; Community, Culture and Conflict in Ireland;* and (with Joseph Lee) *The Age of de Valera;* as well as numerous articles in journals and books mainly on aspects of nineteenth- and twentieth-century Irish and British history. Gearóid Ó Tuathaigh is academic director of the University College Galway Summer School.

Patrick F. Sheeran studied at University College Dublin and the Sorbonne, and now teaches at University College Galway. His publications include *The Novels of Liam O'Flaherty* and many articles on Irish literature and culture. He is currently co-editing a volume of essays entitled *The Ire of Peripheries: Culture and Colonialism in Ireland, Poland and Norway,* for Oslo University Press.

INTRODUCTION:
WHAT IS IRISH STUDIES?

DURING the past twenty years or so there has been a remarkable quickening of interest in Irish Studies as an integrated, multi-disciplinary programme of learning. This has been particularly noteworthy in the United States where the increase in the number of institutions offering courses in Irish Studies has been remarkable. To a large extent, this increase can be attributed to the missionary endeavours of the American Committee for Irish Studies which has sought, over a period of more than twenty years, to promote all branches of Irish Studies in the United States. Growth in Canada has been more modest, but steady, while in Australia, there has been a recent awakening of interest in Irish (or, more properly, Irish-Australian) studies. Nearer home, the British Association for Irish Studies has held several successful annual conferences, and Irish Studies courses are currently on offer at a number of British universities. In Ireland itself, the concept of 'Irish Studies' as an integrated cultural/humanistic programme at second level has been on the agenda in discussions concerning curricular change and development for more than fifteen years, and there are at last encouraging signs of movement on this front. Moreover, Summer Schools devoted to 'Irish Studies' and directed primarily at the North American student are held in almost every university in Ireland; and in several Irish universities graduate programmes in Irish Studies are available.

The reasons for this surge of interest are complex but a number of key factors can be identified. The strong revival of ethnic identity among various communities in the United States from the later 1960s has obviously been an important stimulus to a renewed interest in the history, literature, and general culture of the 'donor' societies in the making of modern America. This interest in ethnicity, which was exploited at the popular level as a fashion (if not passion) for 'roots', took many forms. One can point to the revival of interest in Ireland's musical heritage among young Irish-Americans, and to the increase in Irish dancing and Irish language classes in urban America as clear illustrations of the ethnic resurgence among the 'Irish' in the United States. There was, of course, more to the growth of Irish Studies programmes than popular fashion. Interest in Irish writers such as Yeats,

1

Joyce, Synge and O'Casey had remained constant and immune to the vagaries of fashion in the literature departments of American universities. Indeed, it is not too much to say that for many American universities 'Irish Studies' was essentially about the study of key texts from major writers such as these. Furthermore the emergence of a new generation of writers since the 1950s, including Heaney, Friel, Montague and Kinsella, helped rekindle interest in 'Irish Studies' in America. More importantly, perhaps, recent trends in social history and sociology, as well as stressing the importance of immigrants in the social, economic and cultural development of modern America, have emphasised their varied experience in the New World.

Many of the same popular and academic impulses lie behind the growth of interest in the 'Irish dimension' in Australia, Canada, and latterly in Britain. The descendants of Irish immigrants in these societies desire to know more about the history and culture of the country from which their forbears emigrated; to a greater or lesser extent many descendants of immigrants have a sense of being 'Irish' (even in a hyphenated way) and are anxious to have a more precise understanding of what this may mean, or has meant in the past, in terms of 'personality' and 'identity', whether national or individual. A second major source of the interest in Irish Studies lies in the more specifically educational attractions of the Irish experience as a case-study for students of post-colonial states and societies, especially those concerned with development economics or with the dynamics of social conflict. Indeed all students with an interest in the manifold sociological implications of a society undergoing belated and uneven industrialisation and urbanisation — a society, moreover, unusually sensitive or vulnerable to external forces (economic, cultural and ideological) — will find the Irish experience particularly appropriate to their needs. As that relatively rare bird, a European post-colonial state, the Irish experience of the past sixty-five years has an understandable interest for those working in the academy of the social sciences. Anthropologists in particular have been drawn to Ireland, especially the West of Ireland, because of that society's unique blend of the archaic and the new and the survival in that region of traditional practices and customs even in an ostensibly modern environment. Indeed, so popular was the West of Ireland as a study area for anthropologists that at one time in the early 1970s it seemed that no village was complete without its resident anthropologist to log the movements of the inhabitants, present them with questionnaires, and jot down their conversations. Similarly, for those whose interest is primarily in the domain of language (language change, bilingualism, the relationship between language and identity) or in literature, the Irish experience is an especially — in some respects a uniquely — fruitful area of study: an ancient vernacular with a rich

2

literature being eclipsed, in the course of conquest and colonisation, by a new language, which in the course of time became widely adopted as the main vernacular. Issues of continuity and discontinuity — in speech and in literature; duality or schizophrenia in cultural experience; matters of essence and authenticity in discussing a 'national' literature: these are but some of the issues which arise directly from a study of the languages and literature of Ireland. What is 'Irish' literature? Is it language-bound, and if so, what are we to call literature written in English by Irishmen either in Ireland or out of 'the Irish experience', and how, in any case, are we to recognize the cultural specificity of this 'Irish experience'? These are questions which have preoccupied scholars not only of Irish and Anglo-Irish literature (with Yeats and Joyce as, perhaps, the two major *foci* of this scholarly interest), but also scholars concerned with many other comparative aspects of literary history, theory and criticism.

Perhaps the most immediate and specific factor which has led to the growth of academic and general interest internationally in the Irish experience has been the conflict in Northern Ireland during the past two decades. The mass media, notably television, have brought this conflict into the homes and the consciousness of scores of millions throughout the world, the majority of whom had no connection or previous concern (ancestral or intellectual) with Ireland. The Northern Ireland conflict has raised issues of great concern in the modern world, not just the fashionable question of terrorism and the appropriate response of the modern state but the perennial problem of the constitutional options to resolve conflict in a divided society, a society moreover with several conflicting versions of identity and political legitimacy. Inevitably, many of those whose concern with the Northern Ireland conflict went deeper than mere superficial interest have felt the need to explore the more complex long-term historical forces which have shaped, and which continue to propel, the communities in Northern Ireland along the path of division and conflict.

A final point needs to be made in respect of the origins of the concept of an integrated programme of Irish Studies. The obvious inspiration for this idea in the Irish educational debate came from the development in the 1960s of area-based programmes of interdisciplinary or multi-disciplinary studies in universities and institutions of higher learning in the United Kingdom. While the subject/discipline remained 'the primary unit of production' in most institutions, the emphasis in programme/course development was on finding the appropriate mix of disciplines to constitute a coherent, multi-disciplinary programme of study (e.g. Russian Studies, European Studies, Peace Studies, Women's Studies). In Ireland there was a particular impatience with the compartmentalisation of key areas of the school curriculum, notably in language and literature.

3

The experience of the past twenty-five years has taught us much about the virtues and problems entailed in this kind of academic course development. But the basic commitment to a more integrated curriculum remains intact. It is this commitment which prompted the editors to undertake this volume on Irish Studies.

Our understanding of Irish Studies is broad: we are concerned with exploring key aspects of the Irish experience in its historical and contemporary settings. We have sought to adopt an interdisciplinary approach, the various disciplines providing points of departure from or access to this Irish experience, and we have attempted through this method to arrive at a multi-disciplinary analysis. In some chapters, most noticeably perhaps in that on emigration, this approach is more pronounced than in others: but the book as a whole was conceived as an integrated work, not simply a number of chapters on various aspects of Ireland but as an inter-linked series of essays that taken together would help towards a definition of Ireland and the Irish experience.

This process of defining Ireland begins with Mary Cawley's chapter on the geographical setting and the physical and geological make-up of the island. She stresses the importance of climate, topography and terrain — in a word, habitat — for an understanding of the shifting settlement patterns in Ireland from the dawn of history to more recent times. The attempt at definition continues with two overtly historical chapters.

Gearóid MacNiocaill identifies the enduring consequences of a thousand years of cultural interaction between natives and newcomers and he delineates some of the complex ways in which newcomers became native. Thomas Bartlett's chapter on themes in Irish history attempts to survey those areas of the Irish historical experience which have most engaged the attention of historians. Political union, achieved in 1600 or thereabouts, was in fact accompanied by increasing religious, ethnic and linguistic diversity and this ensured that division rather than peaceful encounter would provide the dynamic of Irish history. A notable casualty of these confrontations in the seventeenth century was the Gaelic-speaking Irish, and their complex response to their 'shipwreck' over the next two hundred years forms the subject of Sean Ó Tuama's chapter on the Gaelic world in crisis. Notwithstanding the collapse of the Gaelic order and the decline of the Gaelic language, the image, if not indeed the myth, of a lost Gaelic world embodying purity, innocence, heroism (and deference) has remained a particularly potent one among nineteenth- and twentieth-century writers and poets, as can be seen from Noel McGonagle's survey of later writing in Irish. This image was not however, equally embraced by all Irishmen and the divisions of the period 1850 to 1920 are explored by Gearóid Ó

4

Tuathaigh. For every Irishman who remained in Ireland in 1900 there were two abroad, and the centrality of emigration (or exile) in Irish life and letters over the past one hundred years is emphasised in the chapter by Riana O'Dwyer, Chris Curtin and Gearóid Ó Tuathaigh.

As noted above, literature in English has provided a common approach route to Irish Studies, and yet it embodies in itself a central paradox of Irish history: the clash of languages, cultures, and traditions. In what sense does literature in English represent an Irish tradition? Does it express an Irish cultural reality? Is it simple and unitary, or complex and multiple? Questions such as these are addressed by Patrick Sheeran, and applied in particular to the nineteenth century novel. Riana O'Dwyer's account of literature in the period 1700-1900 suggests that before 1800 writers who addressed themselves in English to the subject matter of Ireland did so in the context of an English literary identity. During the nineteenth century, as McGonagle points out, studies of Irish texts, artefacts, music and folktales mediated Gaelic culture to the English-speaking public and ultimately laid the foundations for the Irish Literary Revival. The subsequent achievements of the great Irish modern writers, and the many others who responded to the stimulation offered by the Abbey Theatre, the literary movements, and the experimental and exploratory mood of the times are discussed by Gerald Dawe, D.E.S. Maxwell and Riana O'Dwyer.

How the two Irish states evolved in the decades after partition, the political institutions which grew up north and south, the economies that successive governments sought to fashion, and finally the types of society that emerged: these topics are all addressed in the chapters by Tom Boylan, Chris Curtin, Liam O'Dowd and Michael Laver. Their theme — if in fact a common theme can be identified — is that in these years, north and south, there was an increasing divergence between aspiration and reality, between what the two states claimed to stand for and what they actually represented. The catalyst in exposing this contradiction was the new-found economic prosperity of the 1960s which paradoxically helped to bring about great social changes in the south and also helped to fuel conflict in the north. In almost every way the 1960s was a watershed decade; and in a concluding chapter Luke Gibbons explores how the 'media' — in the widest sense — both reflected and inspired further change.

Inevitably the question arises as to what is the proper province of enquiry or discussion for Irish Studies. Do we explore equally the experience of those who have lived or who continue to live on the island of Ireland, whatever their sense of national identity or however intense or complex their sense of cultural affiliation? And what of the large and far-flung community of Irish emigrants, whose affection for

5

and attachment to the homeland (or ancestral land) has often been extremely strong, but whose 'version' of Ireland (its past, its current predicament, its prospects) has often diverged seriously from that of those who actually live in Ireland at any moment in time, with consequences which have been serious and problematic for the Irish both at home and abroad? There are no easy answers to these questions. The nature of Irish Studies remains a subject of debate and its limits are fluid rather than fixed. Our objective in this volume has been to explore not only, in Estyn Evans's classic formulation of the personality of Ireland, 'the habitat, history and heritage' of the island and its people, but also the dynamics of social change and the structures of the economy and society in the recent past and in contemporary Ireland. We are not concerned with divining the 'uniqueness' of the Irish experience; obsession with uniqueness can inhibit useful and illuminating comparisons. However, we have sought to elucidate the particularity of the Irish experience, while remaining conscious all the time that Ireland as a case-study invites fruitful comparisons with patterns of development in other states and societies. In short, our hope is that readers of this volume will not merely be better informed about Ireland and the Irish experience over time, but will also be able to formulate interesting questions about other societies, and in particular about their own society.

T. Bartlett, C. Curtin, R. O'Dwyer, G. Ó Tuathaigh
Galway, January 1988

1
IRELAND: HABITAT, CULTURE AND PERSONALITY

Mary Cawley

IRELAND IN CONTEXT

THE key to understanding much of Ireland's physical habitat and personality lies in its geographical location. Now a relatively small island located on the north-west edge of the European mainland, between 51.5 and 55.5 degrees north latitude and 5.5 and 10.5 degrees west longitude, Ireland was once part of that larger land mass. As a result, its geological structure and surface landforms share many features in common with the neighbouring island of Great Britain and with north-western France. Ireland remained connected to Britain by a landbridge at the end of the last major Ice Age when Britain remained similarly joined to continental Europe. The land link with Britain disappeared beneath the rising level of the Irish Sea some time after 10,000 years ago. Britain's link with mainland Europe survived slightly longer but it too was eventually submerged. The breaking of the land link with Britain brought to an end the overland migration of flora and fauna to Ireland. Many species of plants and some animals which subsequently reached Britain from mainland Europe failed to arrive in the more westerly island.

Geographical position has also been a determining factor in the climatic regimes experienced in Ireland at various stages in the past, as it is today: global temperature changes are of major underlying significance in this regard, however. The temperature changes that are of most note in the context of understanding the contemporary landscape are those that took place within the last 1.7 million years. During that period of time, Ireland experienced two major glacial advances which served to mould the surface topography of the island. The erosive work of the moving ice contributed to the creation of the many lakes, valleys and passes that intersect the mountain masses. The material eroded from the uplands was later deposited in the lowlands in a variety of surface forms.

Climate was the dominant factor in the development of the natural vegetation of Ireland in post-glacial times. Regional patterns of contemporary agricultural production are also constrained in large part by the climatic criteria of rainfall, temperature, sunshine, wind speed

7

and direction, and the incidence of frost. A moist maritime regime is experienced throughout the island with few extremes of either heat or cold. Rainfall decreases in an easterly and southeasterly direction whereas average temperatures and sunshine increase. Livestock grazing is almost universal, but grain crops, notably barley and wheat, grow most successfully only in the east and southeast.

Location in relation to mainland Europe is important in understanding Ireland's cultural history. As a peripheral island requiring travel by sea for the initial occupiers to arrive, Ireland received its first settlers relatively later than the remainder of Western Europe. Peripherality also saved Ireland from conquest by the Romans who had reached Britain; but Viking raiders arrived several centuries later. Insularity and geographical position delayed the arrival of various colonising groups, but proximity to Britain served to ensure that many cultural influences were filtered through that island, particularly from the twelfth century on when Ireland became a colony of Anglo-Norman England.

PHYSICAL HABITAT

The rock skeleton

The island of Ireland contains a wide range of physically diverse landscapes, in terms of geological structure and surface forms, within a relatively limited geographical area. Ireland is a mere 83,000 square kilometres in area and measures, at its greatest extent, 486 kilometres from north to south and 275 kilometres from east to west. Yet within that area there are geological formations which vary very markedly in age and structure. These include the ancient hard Pre-Cambrian rocks of Counties Donegal and Wexford, the bare limestone pavement of the Burren of Co. Clare, deposited in warm seas some 320 million years ago, and the columnar basalt of the Giant's Causeway of the Antrim Plateau formed when molten lava cooled rapidly on the surface during a period of intense volcanic activity in the geologically recent Tertiary period (Map 1, Table 1).

The major contrast in physical relief within Ireland is that between the coastal uplands which for the most part stand at altitudes of 700-1000 metres above sea level and the central lowlands where undulating relief rarely exceeding 122 metres dominates (Map 1). Bordering the Carboniferous Limestone lowlands are a number of limestone plateaux in Counties Clare, Sligo, Fermanagh, Leitrim and Kilkenny, the latter two of which have limited coal deposits present. The central lowlands open to the sea along the east coast between Dundalk and Dublin giving a level coastal plain. Volcanic activity in Caledonian times, some 400 million years ago, when the great rift valley of Scotland was formed, served to produce the uplands of

8

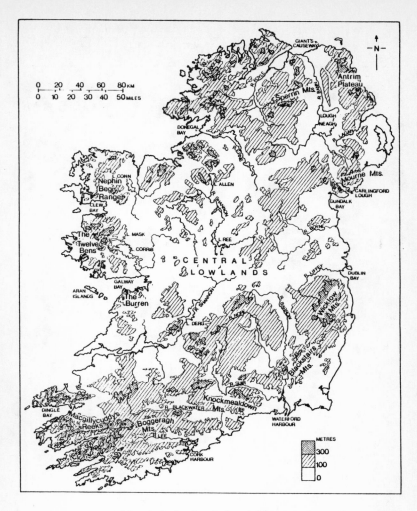

Map 1: Ireland: relief and drainage

Table 1. Simplified table of geological succession for Ireland		
TIME	**ENVIRONMENT**	**EARTH MOVEMENTS**
Present **12 000**	**Post-Glacial**	
1.7	ICE-AGE	
65	Oscillating climate TERTIARY	Volcanic activity in northeast creates framework of Mourne Mts. and Antrim Plateau
100	Chalk seas cover Ireland	
200	Sediments accumulate in various basins	Shales and clays form in northeast
300	Erosion of limestone begins	ARMORICAN framework of east-west ridges of south formed
400	Warm seas in which limestone forms flood land CARBONIFEROUS	
		CALEDONIAN intrusion of granite in Wicklow, Galway, Mayo and Donegal
500	Sediments accumulate in marine basins	
Pre-600	PRE-CAMBRIAN	Very old rocks of Donegal, Connacht, Wexford metamorphosed

Millions of Years before Present

Galway, Mayo, Donegal, Wicklow and Down which have a characteristic north-east to south-west orientation (Table 1 and Map 1). Molten lava from deep in the earth's crust was intruded into the overlying sedimentary rocks (limestones, sandstones and shales) and cooled slowly to give a highly crystalline and acidic granite. Because of the intense heat and pressure that accompanied the volcanic action, overlying sediments were metamorphosed significantly. The sandstone, for example, was changed into quartzite which forms the heart of the Twelve Bens of Connemara and gives such highly distinctive conical peaks as Croagh Patrick in Mayo, Slieve League in Donegal and the Sugarloaf in Wicklow. Limestone sediments were transformed locally into veins of marble as in west Galway where the presence of serpentine gives a distinctive green colour. Because of their resistance to erosion through natural weathering processes, their exposure to high rainfall and steepness of slope, the coastal uplands are of very limited agricultural potential and their lower slopes are for the most part peat covered.

The sandstone ridges of the south of Ireland, notably in Counties Cork, Tipperary and Waterford, present a gentler type of landscape and contain more fertile land than does the granite and its associated matamorphosed structures (Map 1). However, this is less marked in Co. Kerry where the relief is higher. Kerry has the highest point on the island, at Carrantoohill in the Macgillycuddy's Reeks, which stands 1040 metres above sea level. The southern mountains are orientated east-west in conformity with uplands of similar age in south-west England and north-west France from which the name Armorican is derived. Uplift and folding were associated with a period of earth plate movement in Central Europe approximately 300 million years ago (Table 1). A number of sandstone ridges occur in isolation in the south midlands also but they betray a north-east to south-west trend because of their location on the edge of the Caledonian formations.

Apart from possessing the Giant's Causeway, the north-east of Ireland also contains two other distinctive areas of upland. These are the Sperrin hills of Co. Tyrone which consist of old and very hard grits and mica schists now covered with peat, and the Mourne and Carling-ford mountains of Co. Down which are formed of granite intruded during the Tertiary period when the Antrim Plateau was formed.

The island's mantle

Few areas of bare rock occur in Ireland, with the exception of the limestone pavement of the Burren and the tops of the quartzite peaks. Elsewhere a cover of clay or peat material clothes the landscape. This mantle developed over a prolonged period of time and reflects the influence of underlying rock structures as well as natural and human processes. The work of ice has been a major factor in determining the

11

basic constitution of the soil cover. Rock fragments eroded from the uplands through a variety of chemical and mechanical processes were carried by glaciers into the lowlands, and became mixed with material derived from other locations, to be left as a surface deposit when the ice cover melted in response to rising temperatures. This surface material dates to the last glacial phase, except in areas of the extreme south which remained ice-free at that time and have a cover of older deposits present. The deposited material is generally known as glacial drift or boulder clay from its two main constituents. It forms the soil cover of the island at depths ranging from 60 metres or more in Co. Meath to a few centimetres in east Co. Galway. In a belt extending from Clew Bay in Co. Mayo to Carlingford Lough in Co. Down, the drift material has been deposited as gently moulded oval structures known as drumlins separated by peat or lake-filled hollows. Extending across the centre of the island, from Galway to Dublin, long sinuous sand and gravel ridges or eskers occur where running water within the ice carried away the lighter clay components.

The surface of the island is dissected by a dense network of rivers and lakes which enhance the diversity of the landscape. These include the longest river in the British Isles, the River Shannon, and the largest lake, Lough Neagh (Map 1). The major rivers and lakes pre-date the most recent ice phases: many were modified as a result of ice action by having their courses interrupted or deepened, notably in the more easily eroded limestone strata of the central lowlands. All of the major lakes, except Lough Neagh, occur in limestone (calcium carbonate) structures which are water soluble. Islands formed of harder strata which have withstood solution are characteristic of all the midland lakes and the associated deciduous vegetation includes remnants of the primeval oakwoods which once occurred widely on the deeper drier soils.

The soil cover throughout most of Ireland developed under a forest vegetation in post-glacial times. With some modifications, notably the decline of elm due to the joint effects of disease and the clearance of land for agriculture during the neolithic period, and the decline of pine in low lying areas as peat development occurred, this cover would still remain, dominated by oakwoods, were it not for man's inter-ference. An effective human impact in forest clearance to produce agricultural land dates to the introduction of iron implements app-roximately 2,200 years ago and gained momentum with the coming of the Anglo-Normans who brought commercial agriculture in the twelfth century. Most of the native forest cover was absent when Arthur Young, an English advocate of agricultural improvement, toured Ireland in the late eighteenth century. Grassland dominated then as it does today except in marshy areas of the central lowlands and on mountain slopes where an accumulation of peat was present.

Raised peat bogs (so called because of their convex surface when viewed in profile) began to form in post glacial lakes and hollows of the central lowlands approximately 9,000 years ago, through the accumulation of plant material, and now reach depths of up to 10 metres in some locations. The blanket peat of the mountainous west coast is shallower and is primarily a response to acidic rock structures and high rainfall. The peat bogs apart, which serve mainly as a source of fuel and provide some summer grazing, Irish soils reflect the influence of local rock structures, climate, relief, vegetation, time and man. Over thirty different soil types may be identified which divide into two major regions in terms of potential use: those of the south-east and east including east Connacht are generally well drained, fertile soils derived from calcareous material; the soils of the west and north are characterised by poor drainage, high acidity and low productivity.

MAN'S IMPACT

The considerable diversity of physical topography that exists within the island and the location of major waterways influenced strongly past patterns of population movement and the types of economy practised. In turn, human occupation served to modify the natural landscape. The earliest human occupation for which we have evidence occurs in the north-east and suggests that the first settlers crossed the narrow straits from south-west Scotland and became established along the lower River Bann where they practised a hunter-fisher-gatherer economy approximately 9,000 years ago. Pieces of worked flint were used as tools; examples have been found also on the shores of Lough Neagh and on the north-east coast. Evidence of a similar type of economy is available from a site in Co. Offaly some hundreds of years later. The navigable tributaries and cultivable soils of the Boyne Valley had become the focus of a sophisticated culture which built monumental burial mounds at Knowth, Dowth and Newgrange in Co. Meath about 4,500 years ago. Tara, in the same locality, was the seat of the Irish high kings in the Celtic period and the first footholds of Christianity were established in the same general area. The level reaches of the east and south coasts offered sheltered harbourage to the Viking fleets on their voyages from Scandinavia to the Mediterranean from the eighth century on and the settlements established at Dublin, Arklow, Wexford, Youghal and Cork include some of the major urban centres of the present day.

In the twelfth century, Anglo-Norman settlers from south-west Britain also established their strongest footholds in the east and south-east. Topography and soil conditions were highly suitable for commercial grain and livestock production; inland navigation was

13

possible along the rivers Lee, Blackwater, Barrow, Nore, Suir and Boyne, facilitating the collection of produce from the interior; and natural harbours existed at the mouths of these rivers where large ships from Britain could anchor. The extensive pattern of crop and livestock production on large estates, introduced by the Anglo-Normans, became entrenched in east Leinster and south-east Munster and provided the basis for a large farm economy with an emphasis on grain production which persists to the present day. The feudal practice of primogeniture, introduced by the Anglo-Normans, served to perpetuate large farm structures, to discourage early marriage and thereby to avoid overpopulation which reached insupportable proportions in areas of the west in the nineteenth century. A framework of towns established by charter, with rights relating to the marketing of produce, was a major legacy of the Anglo-Norman presence.

The Tudor conquest of the sixteenth and seventeenth centuries, undertaken to prevent Ireland from functioning as a base of operations for the enemies of England, extended the sway of rule and order into the midland counties of Leix and Offaly initially, then into Munster and Ulster and finally to Connacht. The introduction of tillage farmers from England and the building of towns accompanied the plantations, notably and most successfully in Ulster. The political and religious distinctiveness of contemporary Ulster is in large part a product of the presence of English 'undertakers' who arrived as overseers of the plantation and of Scottish Presbyterian farmers who came to work the land throughout the seventeenth century.

The mountains of Tyrone and Donegal and the less fertile areas in general became the refuges of the Irish in Ulster as they did later in Connacht following the mid seventeenth-century campaign of Oliver Cromwell, the Lord Protector. Older traditions survived here as they did in peripheral locations in Munster, notably the Irish language, the Catholic religion in a somewhat degraded form, partible systems of land inheritance and open-field rundale agriculture. By the end of the eighteenth century the farm cluster, or clachan, had emerged as the main settlement unit. Potato cultivation which provided high yields from small acreages of land permitted subdivision of farms to take place from the early eighteenth century on, a system that was tolerated and sometimes encouraged by landlords and their agents who stood to gain financially from the increased rents that accrued.

By the early eighteenth century the transfer of large areas of land from Irish Catholic to English Protestant ownership had been completed and peace reigned. During the eighteenth century there was considerable development in Irish agriculture and in industry (notably linen and provisions) and communications (roads and canals) were improved. Large estate houses, some constructed according to the

14

best neo-classical designs of the day, appeared in the landscape surrounded by formal gardens or parkland and enclosed by high stone walls. Castletown House and Carton House in Co. Kildare are two of the best examples of Irish Palladian architecture. Dublin city reached its apogee as a national capital and seat of parliament. Merrion Square and St Stephen's Green with their surrounding terraces of red brick houses were laid out, and such notable public buildings as the Parliament House (now the Bank of Ireland, College Green), the Four Courts and the Custom House were built. The River Liffey was enclosed within quays as was the River Lee in Cork. Agricultural output increased in response to the growing demand from Britain for food in the late eighteenth and early nineteenth centuries. Many wealthy and enlightened landowners developed planned towns and villages on their estates for the marketing of produce. The enclosure of land through the building of clay banks, frequently surmounted by hedgerows, gathered momentum during the eighteenth century, notably in the east of Ireland.

The eighteenth century was also a period of marked population growth, a response in part at least to the growing importance of the potato as a nutritious and high yielding food source. By 1780, the population of the island is estimated to have reached four millions; it was to double to eight millions by 1841. In the east, emigration relieved this pressure of population from the late eighteenth century, but in the west population growth continued up to the eve of the Great Famine of 1845-7.

PERSONALITY

Man's impact on the landscape, within the constraints imposed by the physical environment, has served to produce a series of marked regional contrasts within the island. Most notable are a broad east-west divide and the special identity of north-east Ulster which is the product of a series of exceptional cultural, economic, and political circumstances.

A combination of factors, including the underlying resource base, the climatic regime, the history of colonisation, demographic patterns and farm structures have given rise to a basic dichotomy between areas of small-scale farming of the west of Ireland especially along the west coast and in the River Shannon lowlands, and large-scale commercial production in the east and south-east. Commercialisation of production had of course reached areas of the west by the late nineteenth century and these areas were not bereft of large landlord estates. Similarly, even in the more prosperous east, colonisation of mountain slopes and bog margins occurred in response to population increase in the early nineteenth century. Nevertheless, the broad contrast retains considerable validity even to the present day and it remains closely associated with the inherent productive capacity of the land, farm size structures and the relative availability of off-farm employment. The strength of the disparities that exist between east and west is underlined by the repeated measures that have been undertaken towards their alieviation, expecially in the independent Irish state since 1922. The small farm problem has assumed less importance in the more heavily industrialised Northern Ireland state.

Overpopulation of land notably in areas along the western seaboard in Counties Donegal, Mayo, Galway, Clare, Sligo and Kerry, but including inland locations in Counties Roscommon and Leitrim, received attention from the Congested Districts Board (CDB) established in 1891. The CDB introduced various measures orientated towards the creation of consolidated holdings from formerly unenclosed rundale strips and the movement of population from congested localities to newly created farms on estates purchased specifically for that purpose. Fishing in coastal locations and craft-type enterprises elsewhere were supported with a view to supplementing the low incomes available from farming. Notwithstanding such measures, large-scale outmigration of the younger members of communities continued. By the early 1950s the effects of long-term outmigration, of females in particular, were apparent in the elderly age structure of the population in many western localities and in the growing incidence of bachelorhood. Little incentive for agricultural improvement existed and more than half the farms were less than twelve hectares in size.

Against this background remedial measures were taken in the form of an industrial policy introduced under the terms of the Underdeveloped Areas Act of 1952. Provision was made for attracting industrial investment to twelve western counties (the seven coastal counties plus Roscommon, Leitrim, Cavan, Monaghan and Longford) through a system of very generous cash grants and other incentives. Through industrial development it was hoped to reduce outmigration from the region and so reconstitute population structures. The policy enjoyed only limited success and special measures were subsequently designed for the Gaeltacht areas where Irish-speakers dominate, and for the Shannon Airport complex. A comprehensive national industrial policy was introduced by the Industrial Development Authority in 1973 but western areas still receive preferential grants. Much of the west of the island is also scheduled as 'handicapped' or 'severely handicapped' under the terms of the Disadvantaged Areas Scheme of the European Economic Community and resident farmers are eligible to receive payments up to a specified monetary limit for each head of beef and sheep livestock maintained on their farms.

16

The three western counties of Ulster (Londonderry, Fermanagh and Tyrone) contain one large urban agglomeration, namely the City of Derry. The historical pattern of landscape development in these three counties and the contemporary rural economy display many features in common with the western fringe of the Republic. Indeed, the term 'west of the Bann' in Northern Ireland has many of the same connotations of agricultural underdevelopment as 'the West' has in the Republic. Catholics form a larger proportion of the population in west than in east Ulster. The Sperrins of Co. Tyrone and other upland areas functioned as refuges during the seventeenth century, and rundale agriculture and clachan settlement survived longer than in the east. Small farms dominate, towns are small in size and few in number and much of the area is scheduled as under-developed.

Belfast's location on a deep-water port in east Ulster and its proximity to northern England and Scotland which facilitated the import of iron ore and coal, contributed to the growth of industry in the city and its environs. A shipbuilding industry developed there in the early nineteenth century. The population of Belfast grew from 20,000 in 1800 to 350,000 in 1901 and reached almost half a million people by 1951. Belfast is essentially a Victorian city although its origins lie in the Anglo-Norman period. The inner city with its major municipal buildings and gridiron street pattern reflects the influence of Georgian concepts of town planning. However, the main expansion of dense working-class housing took place in the second half of the nineteenth century in the vicinity of the shipyards and factories. Industrialisation was based initially on linen and cotton manufacture. Linen had begun as a cottage industry on the small well-managed farms of east Ulster in the eighteenth century where security of tenure and tenant rights apparently became established earlier than else-where in Ireland.

The Ulster Plantation, and the cultural diversification which it established more strongly than previous colonisation efforts else-where in the island, is undoubtedly of major importance in explaining the distinctive cultural and political character of the Northern Ireland state today. Some commentators argue, however, that the dis-tinctiveness of Ulster is of a much more ancient origin. Contacts between the north-east of the province and south-west Scotland have always been strong, stronger indeed than contacts with other parts of Ireland. The drumlin belt with its intervening marshes posed an effective barrier to movement until woodland clearance took place in the early seventeenth century. Even today, the drumlin country of Counties Cavan, Monaghan and south Armagh functions mainly as a frontier zone, with a mixed population of Catholics and Protestants, Nationalists and Unionists. Few major routeways cut through the area and the dense network of minor roads presents patrol problems for customs officials and security forces alike.

RETROSPECT

Ireland's peripheral position in Western Europe has influenced its cultural, social and economic history in many ways. So also has the relative location of upland and lowland within the island and the fact that the coastal lowland between Dundalk and Dublin gives easy access to the central plain. During the pre-historic era substantial periods of time elapsed before cultural influences emanating from mainland Europe reached Ireland. Many of the early immigrants entered through the north-east and east coasts and the Boyne Valley became the centre of a highly developed culture by approximately 2500 B.C., an importance which it retained into the Celtic period. Christianity also was diffused from east to west in Ireland and the Viking raiders from the eighth century on made landfall along the east and south coasts. The effective colonisation of Ireland from Britain beginning in the twelfth century followed an east-southeast to west-northwest trajectory due, in part at least, to the greater ease with which settlement could be established and protected in the central lowlands.

The east-west divide which has its origins in the physical geography of the island and in the paths of colonisation was further strengthened during a period of agricultural advance in the eighteenth century which was more marked in Leinster and east Munster than elsewhere. Older ways of life, open-field agriculture, clachan settlement and marked population growth, survived in Connacht, west Ulster and west Munster into the nineteenth century. Emigration overseas which gathered momentum at the time of the potato famine of the 1840s continued until the early 1960s in the west and has revived in the mid 1980s. Ulster, and the six counties of Northern Ireland in particular, possesses a distinctive identity that is associated with strong religious and political pluralism. The origins of pluralism lie in the Ulster Plantation, yet many observers see the separateness of Ulster as having origins deeper in the past. The greater Belfast area differs from other cities in the island also in being the only nineteenth-century industrial centre of note.

Broad patterns of habitat and history undoubtedly assist in understanding key aspects of the personality of contemporary Ireland. Interaction between man and his environment over prolonged periods of time has served to produce distinctive identities at many levels within the island down to that of the townland, the smallest administrative unit. It is this additional diversity which gives the island yet another dimension of personality.

FURTHER READING

F.H.A. Aalen, *Man and the Landscape in Ireland*, London 1978.

E.E. Evans, *The Personality of Ireland*, Belfast 1981.

G.L. Herries Davies and N. Stephens, *The Geomorphology of the British Isles: Ireland*, London 1978.

C.H. Holland ed., *A Geology of Ireland*, Edinburgh 1981.

F. Mitchell, *Shell Guide to Reading the Irish landscape*, Dublin 1986.

W. Nolan ed., *The Shaping of Ireland: the geographical perspective*, Cork 1986.

A.R. Orme, *The World's Landscapes: Ireland*, London 1970.

J.B. Whittow, *Geology and Scenery in Ireland*, Harmondsworth 1975.

2
THE LEGACY OF THE MIDDLE AGES

Gearóid MacNiocaill

THE earliest Irish traditions reflect in some measure the life of the first five centuries after Christ: the tales of the Ulster cycle, with Cú Chulainn and Conchobar Mac Nessa, portray an heroic society in which raiding, fighting and feasting play a leading part. It is, however, a picture which mingles, like the Greek epic *The Iliad*, elements from remote centuries, such as chariot-fighting (unknown in historic times), and head-hunting, with the conflicts between the Ulaid and others whose reverberations were still being felt at the dawn of historic times. Of what must have been a period of agrarian expansion in the third and fourth centuries, as attested by fossil pollen evidence for the clearance of woodland and the cultivation of food crops, little or nothing appears in such eighth-century tales as *The Driving of the Bull of Cooley*, which focus on the more mobile wealth of cattle and horses, in the possession of which the upper classes of the historic period took pride, despising the mere cultivator. We have a society which thus spills over into the historic period, when feasting and fighting and raiding were still the preferred pastimes of the nobility, the two frequently going hand-in-hand. For example in the tale of *Mac Da Thó's Pig*, of about 800 A.D., there figures a boasting contest at the feast given by Mac Da Thó for the Connachtmen and Ulstermen, which ends in a bloody battle. These archaic traditions, in that period, were preserved after generations of transmission and perhaps garbling by word of mouth and memory, by a new class practising the written word, and professing abstinence and turning the other cheek — the men of the church.

Christianity had already, by the fifth century, been seeping into this society, though perhaps more at its lower levels, among the slaves lifted in raids on Britain, than elsewhere: the earliest Christian words in Irish, such as *Cáisc* ('Easter'), *cruimther* ('priest') and *caille* ('veil'), are held to be borrowings from Latin pronounced in the British fashion. From the fifth century in particular there are indications of the spread of Christianity at other levels under the prodding of obscure missionaries such as Patrick in the north-east, Declan in the south-east, Auxilius in the east, and no doubt others of whom we know even less. The four or five generations down to the second half of the sixth century are those in which Christianity became respectable — the missionaries had in any case to seek the permission of local rulers to stay in their territories, and the obvious tactic was to direct efforts at conversion towards the leaders of society. When members of ruling families began to take up the religious life, as with Colmcille in the sixth century, Christianity had arrived: a cleric automatically had status, a bishop even more. It was, of course, a time when the old religion and the new co-existed in men's minds, a period which saw the successful christianisation of the old pagan feasts of May Day and Samhain (1 November). But Christianity had the advantage of possessing a set of clearly defined and definable beliefs, while the pre-Christian beliefs of Ireland seem to have been vague, fluid, and local, with rivers such as the Boyne treated as goddesses. Pre-Christian customs, backed by a feeling that it was unwise to offend the old gods even when they were reduced in rank to fairy-folk, have persisted to the present day.

The second gift of the church, a religion of a book (the Bible), was writing — adopting the Latin alphabet to express Irish on parchment and stone. Before long, it was used not only for the Bible and the liturgy but also to record the secular saga traditions, the laws and genealogies which had been the preserve of the lay learned class whose business it was to hand on these oral traditions. Not that this class and the church were mutually exclusive: one of the earliest Irish poets whose compositions have survived, albeit in fragments, one Colmán son of Léiníne, was also the founding saint of Cloyne, and Colmcille at his death was lamented in the Amra Choilm Cille by the poet Dallán Forgaill.

The traditions of the heroic past set down by the churchmen had a direct relevance to the life of their own time. Among them are to be found origin-legends, explaining the rise of a dynasty, such as that of the three Collas from whom the Airgialla claimed their origin, recounting how they conquered their lands from the Ulaid, once the masters of present-day Ulster but subsequently pressed back to the area east of the Bann. These legends provided both an explanation and, as important, a title to the land. Matter of this kind is common enough in the huge mass of genealogies which still survive. These trace back the ruling lineages of the sixth and seventh centuries to the dim threshold of memory in the fifth and fourth centuries; further back we have to deal with the names of gods, perhaps, or heroes — and pre-Christian Irish religion, like early Greek religion, probably drew little if any distinction between them. For the ruling lineages it was important to have an impressive pedigree framing them against a heroic background; for a parvenu dynasty, it was desirable to have one concocted as rapidly as possible. Such a link was concocted between the recent Dál gCais dynasty in Thomond and the historic and proto-historic Eoganacht rulers of Cashel, in order to legitimate the newcomers' dominance of Munster under Brian Boru. It was important to know one's lineage: kingship, the rule of a given people or territory, was an attribute of the blood of the ruling lineage; and in this early period it still had divine qualities. The early Irish *Testament of Morand*, a mythical law-giver, sets out explicitly the ways in which the just king benefits his people — the women are fertile, the crops abundant, the cows always in milk, fish swarm in the rivers and the country is at peace. (Needless to say, should war break out, victory is assured over the enemy.) Similarly, an unjust king brought disaster (defeat, famine) on his people.

Fertility is a notion which long remained attached to kingship, and the relationship between king and people was thought of as a kind of marriage, the inauguration of a king being described as the 'wedding-feast of kingship'. Victory over enemies was equally desirable, and in a society and country where there was no central authority the virtues of the warrior were essential. Nobody has been able to calculate with precision how many kingdoms there were in Ireland in the seventh century. They ranged, for example, from the great provincial over-kingdoms such as Connacht or Leinster down to the petty kingdoms which were, until the eleventh century, largely absorbed by the greater, and sometimes downgraded in the process, as the early kingdom of Luigne (in Co. Sligo) was to rule a mere chief. What is clear, however, is that these kingdoms were as often at odds with one another — frequently over territory — as at peace; and the emergence later of an over-kingship (the so-called 'high kingship') did little to minimise the fighting, since it was an institution that existed in spasms, and frequently with substantial opposition.

Within these kingdoms such as that of the Osraige (approximating to the modern diocese of Ossory) society was crudely divided into kings, lords, and commoners: a king by virtue of his lineage, and perhaps some measure of ruthlessness; a nobility whose standing depended on having a following of clients, which in turn depended on the noble's having sufficient surplus wealth in land or cattle to attract and retain clients; and commoners ranging from the independent farmer down to the serf tied to the land, and slaves. It was a society in which standing — 'honour-price' — was all-important in law, and standing depended in the last analysis on property. There was no apparatus of state to enforce and defend individual rights, and there-fore the small man, in order to survive, would be well advised to place himself in the dependence of a greater. Admittedly the church had made a considerable impact in terms of property — the greater monasteries such as Clonard, Armagh, and Clonmacnois could speak on equal terms with kings — but its progress in 'christianising' the behaviour of the members of that society was less apparent. Thus, the church's commitment to monogamy was cheerfully disregarded by those who could afford polygamy, serially or in parallel; and within the church itself there was a consciousness that the patriarchs of the chosen people had not been monogamous. There were of course spiritual penalties for bloodshed; but one may suspect that the temporal penalties, in the form of compensation to the injured or their kin, weighed more heavily. Finally, it was essentially a patriarchal society, in which women had rights in law only insofar as they owned property and were independent of father, husband, brother or grown son, and in which legitimacy depended entirely on paternity and nothing else. Admittedly, a woman could repudiate her husband as readily, and for roughly the same reasons, as he could divorce her; but once divorced, she returned to her own, male-dominated, kin-group.

In this slow-moving but not static society, a few general trends are perceptible between the seventh and the twelfth centuries. The Church, having grown rich between the sixth and the eighth centuries, experienced a reform movement, that of the Culdees. The Culdees, led (but not directed) by Maelruain of Tallaght (†792), sought a return to the ascetic standards of the sixth century, and looked to Colmcille of Iona and Comgall of Bangor and their contemporaries as their exemplars. But they lacked organisation and they failed to impose their views on the wealthy monastic churches. From the ninth century on they existed as subgroups within the church carrying out on its behalf the ascetic renunciation and mortification which the church as a whole preferred to by-pass.

The greater kingdoms profited by their various opportunities to absorb or subordinate the lesser, so that by the twelfth century the political map is somewhat simpler than in the seventh century; and in society as a whole there was a parallel process whereby the independent commoner was reduced in numbers to the point where, by the twelfth century, the dependent commoner was taken to be the type; a kind of proto-feudalism. The inroads of the Vikings from the end of the eighth century had little permanent effect, apart from a small number of loan-words in Irish. They were too few in number to carve out for themselves, as they did in tenth-century Normandy, a durable state; they supplied, of course, fighting men to the native Irish kings when convenient and profitable, making and breaking alliances with the greatest aplomb. But their outstanding contribution to the country was to establish the seaports of Dublin, Wexford, Waterford and Limerick, centres of trade and channels of wealth; for before then, Ireland had had neither towns — if one rules out the often substantial settlements around the larger monasteries — nor coinage. In the excavations of Wood Quay, in Dublin, can be traced the growth of their settlement from a mere encampment into a wealthy trading centre with a commerce in slaves and furs and hides as far afield as Rouen in Normandy.

Into this society two revolutionary forces irrupted in the twelfth century: the reform movement in the church, and the Anglo-Normans from England. The church in Ireland by the twelfth century had, time out of mind, been a monastic church, without dioceses save in the Norse seaport towns such as Dublin, and even these were of eleventh-century vintage, owing allegiance to Canterbury. It was, moreover, a church which had long since reached a comfortable accommodation with its secular neighbours, liable to such secular burdens as billetting troops (which it evaded when possible), and dominated in many instances by local lineages: for example, the monastery of Killaloe in the eleventh and twelfth centuries was just as much under O'Brien control as the secular lordships around it. The Gregorian reform of the late eleventh century was opposed not only to lay investiture in the Empire, France and England, but reached as far as Ireland, where local rulers such as Toirdhealbhach Ua Briain and his son Muircheartach were urged by Gregory VII and Lanfranc and Anselm to support reform of the church. By this was meant that it should be freed from lay influence and that continental norms should apply in Ireland as elsewhere, both in morals and administration. Changes affecting personal behaviour were accepted reluctantly, if at all, particularly in marital matters; but such administrative changes as the establishment of dioceses, through the councils of Rath Breasail in 1111 and Kells-Mellifont in 1152, were rather brisker. They gave the country an ecclesiastical structure of the common European kind, with four archbishoprics and a primate in Armagh, Tuam, Cashel and Dublin. The new bishoprics of necessity grew at the expense of the monasteries, some of whose lands were in due time taken over by the bishops.

The establishment of this new structure had repercussions elsewhere. At a stroke it eliminated the direct influence of Canterbury and its claims to primacy over the Irish church, or any part of it; and it is no coincidence that soon after, at the Council of Winchester in 1154-5, attended by Theobald, Archbishop of Canterbury, a project for the conquest of Ireland was mooted. Nothing substantial came of it at the time, for Henry II had other and more pressing problems; but soon after, Theobald's secretary, John of Salisbury, left for Rome to contact an old friend, now Pope Adrian IV, whom he persuaded to grant Ireland to Henry II 'to promote the Christian faith there'. The grant was left dormant, but proved useful when Henry II visited Ireland in 1171, in the wake of Strongbow's expedition, to persuade the Irish churchmen to accept Henry's authority.

The Anglo-Norman invasion of 1169-71 had even more drastic effects than the movement for church reform. It affected the Church, which since the end of the eleventh century had been trying to disburden itself of lay influence, by bringing it under the Anglo-Norman system of royal influence. (Fearful of dispossession, the church hastily sought confirmation of its possessions from the new rulers.) It affected large numbers of local rulers who, piecemeal, found themselves stripped of their lands over the three or four generations down to the mid thirteenth century. It brought into the country substantial numbers of settlers, heaviest in Leinster, heavy in Munster, relatively light in Connacht and Ulster, and these brought with them new languages and new institutions. From the thirteenth century onwards, Marshalls, Butlers, Fitzgeralds, Powers, de Verdons and Pippards and de Burgos loom as large on the Irish political scene as any O'Briens, O'Connors or O'Neills.

It created a new orientation of outlook: down to the twelfth century, the Irishman aware of a country other than his own was as likely to think of France or the Empire (or perhaps of the Irish monasteries there) as of England or Scotland; but from the thirteenth century, England looms largest on Irish mental horizons. The evidence is in the borrowings. From the thirteenth century onwards, Irish began the process of heavy borrowing from English that continues to this day, though at the time Anglo-Norman contributed its share: such terms as *seomra* ('room'), *garsún* ('boy'), *páiste* ('child') began life as Anglo-Norman. As the use of this dialect of French declined, the void was filled by English, which itself had drawn on it and became the standard second language and transmitter of new concepts. The borrowings are not only of the commonplace, but include technical terms of law; for example, the Irish term *finné*, 'a witness', came from Anglo-Norman *visné* 'the view of neighbours, a jury'; *baránta*, 'a warrantor', is another borrowing; *(g)iúistís*, 'a justice', yet another; and of course *cúirt*, 'a court'. The dominance attained by English ways and standards in the thirteenth century is illustrated even in penmanship: for a brief period in the middle of the century the Annals of Boyle in Roscommon abandon the Irish script and write Irish in a version of English gothic hand, as do the Annals of Inisfallen in Kerry.

All in all, it is no surprise that a group of southern bishops in 1276-80, on the assumption that English rule and dominance were an irreversible process, offered Edward I a large sum of money to buy for the native Irish the right to use English law. The fact is significant: for overall the native population was not entitled to use English law, and indeed had few rights under it. An Irishman seeking redress of injuries from an Englishman would have his plaint rejected unless he had evidence of his right to use English law; and for a period in the second quarter of the century the Dublin administration had operated a conscious policy of excluding Irishmen from posts of power and influence in the church. The policy had been opposed by the papacy when complaints were received, and lapsed in any case as the area of English control and settlement stabilised: within them, Englishmen (or Anglo-Irish) were normally elected to bishoprics or abbacies; outside, Irish were chosen. By the fourteenth century, native Irish monasteries within those areas, such as Mellifont, had become anglicised; outside, 'English' monasteries such as Granard were absorbed by the native Irish. By the late thirteenth century, all the lowlands of Leinster and Munster had been heavily settled and were as effectively under the control of the Dublin administration as any part of a medieval lordship ever was; in Connacht, matters were less clear-cut, but while the De Burgo earls of Ulster held it, it gave Dublin little trouble; and even Ulster, with very little Anglo-Irish settlement, was usually quiescent.

The stabilisation and beginning of the decline of the Anglo-Irish lordship in the late thirteenth and early fourteenth centuries was accompanied by some measure of assimilation of the 'two nations', to the extent that some principles of Irish law were adopted by the settlers — for example, to pay compensation for homicide is much preferable to being hanged — and some few are found as patrons of Irish poets, such as the first Earl of Desmond, whose son, Gearóid Iarla, was himself a poet in Irish. Effectively also the political structures of the country reverted to what they had been before the twelfth century, in that there was not in fact a single lordship of Ireland but rather a number of lordships, Irish and Anglo-Irish, which made war on one another or formed alliances sealed by giving daughters in marriage or sons in fosterage. The power of the Dublin administration, a simplified version of that of Westminster, with chancery, treasury and parliament, continued to shrink to a point where by the mid fifteenth century it controlled little more than a thirty-mile radius around Dublin.

Nevertheless, the mental stance of the country as a whole was focused on England: the Anglo-Irish looked to it for subsidy and support, and it was through England that most of the new literature and learning reached Ireland. Significantly, in the late fourteenth and fifteenth centuries a number of English texts were translated into Irish: pious tracts, such as the Middle English 'Charter of Peace', travellers' tales such as the fictions of Sir John Maundeville and the facts of Marco Polo, romances such as Bevis of Hampton and Guy of Warwick, classical tales such as the History of Hercules. And apart from direct translations from English, it is clear that the majority of the Latin tracts translated at the same time came through England — religious matters such as the immensely popular *Meditations on the Life of Christ* or Innocent III's tract *On the Wretchedness of Man's State*, or technical matter such as the versions of Bernard Gordon's or John of Gaddesden's medical tracts. In sum, despite stray contact elsewhere, with ships from Portugal, Flanders or Lübeck bringing wine from Bordeaux to Sligo or Flemish altar-pieces to Athenry, England remains the source for almost all that is new, and much that is old. Thus it was in architecture, in which fifteenth-century building in Ireland draws on English models of previous generations as in the case of Holycross abbey church in Tipperary, rebuilt about 1431. The east window follows an early fourteenth-century pattern; the window of one of the north transept chapels echoes one from Ducklington in Oxfordshire of about 1340. Nor is this dominance confined to literature and the plastic arts: in law itself, the backbone of native Irish society, by the sixteenth century the penetration of English common law is clearly visible, at least in land-law, down to the borrowings of legal terms such as *seicedúir* ('executor'), *sighinoidhre* ('assign') and — slavishly — *libré an tsésain* ('livery of seisin').

By the sixteenth century, then, almost all the elements were in place for a takeover of Ireland by England as complete as happened in Wales: administrative subordination, especially after Poynings brought the Irish parliament to heel; cultural dependence, though not linguistic uniformity; and in England, increasingly, both the inclination and resources to look to the lordship of Ireland which for two centuries had been neglected in the interests of adventures in France and because the economic stagnation of the fourteenth and fifteenth centuries left the rulers of England little choice.

FURTHER READING
F.J. Byrne, *Irish Kings and High Kings*, London 1973.
A. Cosgrave ed., *A New History of Ireland, Volume II: Medieval Ireland 1169-1534*, Oxford 1987
R. Frame, *Colonial Ireland, 1169-1369*, Dublin 1981
J.F. Lydon, *The Lordship of Ireland in the Middle Ages*, Dublin 1972.
J.F. Lydon ed., *The English in Medieval Ireland*, Dublin 1984
G. MacNiocaill, *Ireland Before the Vikings*, Dublin 1972
D. Ó Corráin, *Ireland Before the Normans*, Dublin 1972
J. Watt, *The Church in Medieval Ireland*, Dublin 1972.

3
GAELIC CULTURE IN CRISIS: THE LITERARY RESPONSE 1600-1850

Seán Ó Tuama

THOSE in the sixteenth century who engaged in the planning of the Tudor subjugation of Ireland may well have been unique in the attention they paid to cultural as well as to territorial conquest. The cultural philosophy espoused by English administrators was, in fact, the mirror image of that promoted by Irish nationalists in the beginning of the twentieth century. While nationalists in Ireland believed that re-establishing an Irish cultural identity was a prerequisite in any effort to undo the conquest, the English Empire builders in the sixteenth century believed that a prerequisite in any effort to carry out a successful conquest in Ireland was to undermine the native culture. Consequently as early as 1537 an act was passed in the Dublin parliament to effect linguistic change in Ireland [Ó Cuív, 1978, 509]. Young Irish noblemen and noblewomen were quite often now sent to England for schooling or to be brought up as wards of court — with the intention that they would learn to speak English and declare for the new Protestant religion. Irish professional poets as well as priests were jailed or hanged; a vast amount of Irish literature in manuscript was destroyed. Edmund Spenser, Fynes Moryson, and Sir John Davies were amongst those who philosophised at some length about measures such as these [Leersen, 1986, 40-53; Ó Fiaich, 1969, 104-5]. Spenser wrote in 1596: '... it hath ever been the use of the conquerors to despise the language of the conquered and to force him by all means to learn his ... the speech being Irish, the heart must needs be Irish ....' Moryson concurred: 'In general all Nations have thought nothing more powerful than the Community of language.' The cultural destabilisation of Ireland had progressed so satisfactorily by 1612 that the English attorney-general, Sir John Davies, declared: 'We may conceive and hope that the next generation will in tongue, and heart, and every way else, become English; so as there will be no difference or distinction but the Irish sea betwixt us.'

It is likely that the link being consciously forged between military and cultural conquest was not sufficiently appreciated in the early stages by the Irish themselves. In particular they did not seem to be sufficiently aware of the new English determination to bring about language change. That position is quite understandable. There had been an acceptance of English as a spoken language in many areas of Ireland for several centuries previous to this. Entering into alliances with English-speaking lords, who gave their loyalty to English monarchs, posed no problems for Irish chieftains or their bards. The classic weapon with which medieval Irish aristocrats intuitively countered cultural domination — in a situation where they out-numbered the colonists — was intermarriage. The Norman will to conquest had been sapped in that manner. Some forty years after the initial Norman invasion, for instance, an Irish poet was writing learned dedicatory verses in Irish for the Norman de Burgos, who having found themselves Irish wives, could now be fêted as people 'who are become Gaelic, yet foreign'. The cultural success of the medieval Irish approach was such that no substantial English-speaking (or French-speaking) enclave survived in Ireland at the time Sir John Davies was speaking enthusiastically of the future of the English language in Ireland [Bliss, 1978, 346-7]. In such circumstances, it is not strange that extreme hostility to the English language as a symbol of conquest was slow to develop.

Sir John Davies, of course, was wildly optimistic in his projection as to the time the process of anglicisation would take, but he had every reason to believe that cultural change was now bound to occur in a much more extensive manner than previously. In face of the planned policies of a strong centralist state, the old Irish medieval approach would no longer be effective. The new procedures set in train had already ensured that many Irish aristocrats could now read and write English. Some key members of aristocratic families had embraced the Protestant religion. Above all, colonisers had been sent into Ireland and would continue to be sent in such numbers that the chance of a substantial number of them being gaelicised, by intermarriage or otherwise, was very remote indeed. This was particularly so in view of the fact that only 15 per cent or thereabouts of the native Irish population remained as landowners a century or so after Tudor colonisation began.

While Irish opposition to territorial conquest was not particularly effective, opposition to cultural conquest was surprisingly so. The cultural will to survive remained both flexible and obstinate for some three centuries after the initial programme for destabilisation began. The extraordinary sense of nationality which existed traditionally in Ireland had much to do with the continuing durability of some of the main features of Irish culture. For while it may be true to say that medieval Irish aristocrats had a weak sense of *nationalism* in that (like the ancient Greeks) they saw no urgent need for political unity between their various small kingdoms in order to defend the whole land, its people and its cultural heritage, from foreign invaders — yet (again like the ancient Greeks) they had a strongly developed sense of *nationality* in that, no matter how much fratricidal political strife they engaged in, they passionately identified with the one national culture which they finally wished to maintain and defend. Resistance to conquest had always stemmed more from cultural than from political ideals, and would remain so, for the most part, during the seventeenth and eighteenth centuries.

I

Because of the extremely decentralised nature of traditional Irish society — and because of the further fragmentation brought about by the various colonial settlements from early medieval times — the response of Irish literary people to the new efforts at cultural conquest in the seventeenth century cannot always be seen as uniform. Irish literary figures in the first half of the seventeenth century did not, in general, seem to suffer acutely from the feeling that the language they were writing in was threatened with extinction. This applies in particular, one feels, to poets such as Céitinn (Keating) and Haicéad (Hackett) who were ancestrally associated with 'Old English' families who, for many centuries, had flourished in a bilingual and bicultural milieu. Indeed Céitinn and Haicéad, as well as Feiritéar (Ferriter) who lived on the remote Dingle peninsula, were amongst those who themselves probably spoke, wrote or read English. The promotion of English did not put literary figures such as these under any new pressures.

Ill-feeling towards the English language in this period seems mostly to stem from the fact that the lowly labouring classes — formerly 'unfree' or unprivileged in the old aristocratic order — were now shamelessly identifying with the language of the colonists; identifying, in fact, with the conquest, and rapidly treating with disrespect the learned Irish poetic classes. The efforts of the lower classes to ape their new masters by speaking broken English and imitating English fashions of dress and behaviour were scathingly satirised. As the century progressed the indignation expressed by the poets at this turn of events became increasingly savage [*An Duanaire*, nos. 25, 34]. About the year 1650, the learned author of a Rabelaisian prose satire *Pairlement Chloinne Tomáis (The Parliament of Clan Thomas)* ridicules grotesquely the cultural pretentiousness of the formerly submissive lower classes.

General awareness that major linguistic change was an integral planned part of the colonisation programme, and consequent hostility to the English language as a symbol of conquest, seems to have spread mostly from the second half of the seventeenth century onwards. Archdeacon John Lynch in his *Cambrensis Eversus* (1662) expresses what must have been a common bewilderment at the link that had been irretrievably made now between political loyalty and linguistic loyalty: 'For did the Welsh ever refuse to show obedience to the monarch of England by reason of the fact that they are steeped in the Welsh language? We don't see the Bretons in France or the Basques in Spain deny the authority of their kings because they happen to use a speech that differs from the language of their princes. Yet if the Irish have maintained their current and widespread ancestral speech, will they as an immediate result be said to hatch dangerous plots against their supreme prince? For I see no other reason why that language's abolition is insisted upon so vehemently' [Leersen, 1986, 320-1; trans.].

The link between political loyalty and religious loyalty had been made much more rapidly. While there had been long experience in medieval times of dealing with language problems, the Tudor attempted imposition of the Protestant religion was a new and divisive issue which was avidly seized on as a rallying point by disaffected Irish or 'Old English' aristocrats. Ironically it is quite a debatable point whether the sixteenth-century Irish religious tradition can best be described as a Christian tradition with a strong pagan substatum, or a pagan tradition with a nominal Christian overlay [Corish, 1981, 1-17; Ó Tuama, 1985, 29-32]. However one describes their religion, it is probably true that while the value system of the Irish people in general does not appear to have been particularly influenced by essential elements in Christian teaching, reverence for authority figures of the Roman Catholic Church, such as the Virgin Mary and the Pope, was probably quite intense. Consequently the Protestant demotion of these figures brought quickest reaction. 'Fúbún séanadh Mhic Mhuire/shameful the denial of Mary's son', declares one mid-sixteenth century poet [Ó Cuív, 1978, 510].

The dissolution of the monasteries, and the resultant lack of training facilities for clerical students, brought religious issues sharply into focus. Large numbers of members of 'Old English' gaelicised families, in particular — traditionally much more orthodox Catholics than the old Gaelic families — had been going abroad since the middle of the sixteenth century to study for the priesthood, or complete their clerical education. As the ability of aristocratic Gaelic families to maintain poets and scholars declined, increasing numbers from such families also sought continental education. The reformed post-Tridentine Catholic church began in fact to supplement the Irish aristocrat as patron of learning and letters [Silke, 1978, 587-633]. The immediate literary consequence of this was that a small but unique body of religious prose in Irish, advocating post-Tridentine reforms, was published abroad in the early seventeenth century. It is

31

unlikely that this new material in printed form made any great impact on Irish society. Even elitist scholars and poets do not seem to have paid any great attention. To judge by the material which scribes preserved in the more acceptable manuscript form, the main interest continued to be the more traditional categories of literature, of poetry in particular. The prose works of the early seventeenth century which seem to have attracted most interest were not religious but historical. Céitinn's *Foras Feasa ar Éirinn*, for instance, an account of the mythology, legends and history of Ireland until the coming of the Normans, was immensely popular. And it was a work, it should be noted, which sought above all else to enhance the old Irish aristocratic order, and to bewail its passing.

Céitinn was one of the large number of Irish scholars who completed their clerical studies abroad. He took a doctorate in theology in Bordeaux, and probably lectured there. Yet one feels from his work that he is much more emotionally involved with the fate and reputation of the Irish aristocratic world than with the new Catholic Reformation. What really causes him horror and dismay is that the old noble families are being overthrown and their lands annexed. Indeed a little while after the flight of the Ulster Earls to the continent, Céitinn had no hesitation in passionately putting forward the quite elitist viewpoint (a viewpoint which is echoed by other literary figures) that the way to proceed now was to winnow what was left of the noble wheat from the plebeian chaff — to gather the remaining Irish aristocrats and ferry them across the sea from Ireland [*An Duanaire*, no.23]. The idea that an Irish culture — even a somewhat more Christianised version of Irish culture — was worth maintaining without its natural leaders was unthinkable.

The passing of the old order, the loss of hereditary property and patronage, remained the *leitmotif* of seventeenth-century literature. Of the major poets, Céitinn (1580-c.1644), Haicéad (c.1600-54), Ó Bruadair (c.1625-98), Mac Cuarta (c.1647-1733), Ó Rathaille (c. 1675-1729), all shared this thematic material to one degree or another. Ó Bruadair and Ó Rathaille, in particular, worked out their reactions to the societal chaos in which they found themselves in most moving personal lyrics [*An Duanaire*, nos. 35, 38, 45, 52, 53].

Given that the land of Ireland had always been a central focus in the mythology and psychology of Irish people [Ó Tuama, 1985, 21-8], and that most Irish personal relationships depended in a special way on property arrangements, it is not at all strange that the rape of the land caused much more immediate cultural shock than the attempted imposition of the Protestant religion, or the promotion of the English language. The literary relationship which was possibly most affected was that of poet and noble patron. As ownership of property declined so did patronage. The decline of patronage was a long

32

process, however, and did not happen at the same pace throughout the country. It is noteworthy that all of the five poets mentioned above, even those of them who lived well into the first half of the eighteenth century, seem to have had some measure of aristocratic patronage. A clearer understanding of the complex and varying cultural responses resulting from the decline of the poet-patron relationship may be got from a brief consideration of the manner in which two of these poets, Haicéad and Ó Rathaille, were affected by their own associations with supportive aristocrats or institutions.

II

Haicéad — himself of 'Old English' landed gentry — was born north of Cashel, Co. Tipperary, in Butler territory, and had close links through marriage with a cadet branch of the Butlers, the Earls of Dunboyne.

The main Butler family, the Earls of Ormond, was one of the four pivotal Anglo-Norman families in Ireland in medieval times. Unlike the Earls of Desmond, Kildare and Clanrickarde, the Earls of Ormond were quite slow to take to Gaelic ways. It is rather ironic that it was precisely at the time when they were in the process of being gaelicised — to the extent, indeed of offering patronage to poetry in Irish — that the Tudor policy of cultural conquest began. One of the consequences of this policy was that the various Earls of Ormond were now brought up in England, and, in fact, became related through marriage with British monarchs. The eleventh Earl of Ormond, a contemporary of Haicéad's, had been educated in England and was a Protestant.

Other branches of the Butlers remained much more supportive of the Irish language and of Gaelic ways. In fact it appears that a major part of the new accentual poetry written at the end of the sixteenth century and at the beginning of the seventeenth century emerged under the aegis of the Butlers. Haicéad's cousin, the third Earl of Dunboyne, was particularly revered by poets: for instance, three of them (including Haicéad himself) wrote him poems of deeply-felt commiserations when he suffered a severe leg injury. The third Earl seems to have consciously resisted anglicisation; yet one should remember that his father too had been educated in England and had actively aided the Crown (and the Earl of Ormond) to quell the Catholic inspired Desmond rebellion [Chambers, 1986, 147]. While the Earls of Dunboyne remained Catholic and were in constant conflict with the Earls of Ormond about matters of family property, they were probably loyal in principle to the British crown. To judge from Haicéad's eulogies, even the third Earl did not think of offering opposition to British political hegemony in Ireland.

As an 'Old English' Catholic family the Dunboyne Butlers would

33

have supported Haicéad in his clerical education at home, and abroad in Louvain. Haicéad returned to Co. Tipperary, a Dominican priest imbued with a hatred of Protestant 'heresy' and intent on resisting the Elizabethan conquest on religious grounds. In his verse he becomes very much the truculent cleric, urging the people of Ireland to unite together in a holy war. The crunch came for him during the period of The Confederation of Kilkenny (1642-9) when a national and international effort was being made to bind 'Old English' and 'Old Irish' families in an alliance to protect the interests of the Catholic religion. The Marquis of Ormond was amongst those who finally undermined the alliance and the 'Old English' left the Confederation. Haicéad was deeply embittered by these events, in particular as the Fourth Earl of Dunboyne, son of his patron-cousin, was one of those who supported Ormond and was consequently excommunicated by the Pope. The poet's comments on all those who had jettisoned the Catholic cause are scathing:

> They are the evil progeny of their mother [Ireland],
> they are dishonourable sons in remote places,
> they are a heap of excrement from a leper-house,
> they are vipers in our breasts [trans.].

Haicéad never seems to have written a religious or didactic poem; indeed at no time does one feel that he wishes personally to urge the new Catholic reforms on Irish people. Nor does he seem to have had a basic aversion to a British political presence in Ireland: in that he would have been at one with his patron-friend, the third Earl of Dunboyne, who most likely valued cultural independence much higher than political independence. The difference which had now come about between himself and the fourth Earl of Dunboyne stems from the fact that for Haicéad the chief cultural mark of distinctiveness between Ireland and England had become that of religion, and special political arrangements had become necessary to protect that distinctiveness. These political arrangements having failed, Haicéad spent his last sad years back in Louvain meditating savagely on the heretics who had undermined the old Irish order, and seeking to have the Pope lift his excommunication on the fourth Earl, his former patron's son.

Literary patronage in the Butler areas receded rapidly after the collapse of the Confederation of Kilkenny and the subsequent Cromwellian wars and plantations. Many of the more Gaelicised Butlers suffered dispersal all over the European continent; a small number of them in Ireland managed ultimately to regain possession of some of their ancestral lands. But even in the case of those Butlers who somehow survived at home in the second half of the seventeenth century there is no record of any substantial patronage being offered

34

by them to Irish poets or literary figures. It is interesting to note, however, that one of the most haunting of Irish folk poems, 'Cill Chais/Kilcash' (*An Duanaire*, no. 90), composed sometime in the eighteenth century, laments the fall of another Butler house where the Catholic brother of the eleventh Earl of Ormond lived in Haicéad's time. The author of 'Cill Chais', in a studied understatement, says of the house: 'Earls from abroad would visit there/and the sweet mass was celebrated'. The religious issues which divided the Butlers a century before that were still very much alive in the popular mind.

If the events following the collapse of The Confederation of Kilkenny led to a major disruption of literary patronage in the Butler territories, the events following the Battle of the Boyne, half a century later, led to a disruption of similar magnitude in the 'Old Irish' McCarthy territories in the south-west of Ireland. This is specially traceable in the record of the relationship between Ó Rathaille and those patrons who supported him.

Ó Rathaille grew up on a holding near Killarney, Co. Kerry, which was leased by his parents from Sir Nicholas Browne. His primary loyalty, however, was to the McCarthys who formerly owned the territories now legally held by the Brownes.

The Brownes had been gradually acquiring confiscated McCarthy and other territories — some 140,000 acres — during the seventeenth century. They had come as colonisers to Ireland in the late sixteenth century, and were, somewhat exceptionally, Catholics. They inter-married with various Irish aristocratic families, amongst them the family they had supplanted, the McCarthys, and had become, at least minimally, gaelicised. Their practice of allowing formerly privileged people (under the Gaelic order) to hold land at nominal rents allowed some of the remnants of the 'Old Irish' nobility (and possibly well-connected poets such as Ó Rathaille) to live in a certain luxury.

Historically the main branch of the McCarthys, the McCarthymore family, had managed by devious means to hold on to a moderately large estate in the Killarney region, independently of the Brownes. With these McCarthys in particular Ó Rathaille appears to have had ancestral ties — probably through his mother's family who may have been hereditary poets and scholars to the main branch of the McCarthys. So it was that Ó Rathaille, for a time, was basically maintained on Browne territory, and was casually patronised by various Catholic (and even Protestant) aristocrats, amongst them the Brownes and McCarthys, in the environs of Killarney. It is clear, however, that at this stage any major literary patronage on the part of the McCarthys was quite unlikely. Their estate was debt-ridden and they were rapidly being anglicised through intermarriage with Anglo-Irish gentry.

After the Battle of the Boyne (1690), The McCarthymore, by

changing his allegiance from the Catholic Stuart king to the Protestant King William, succeeded in holding on to his estate. Not so Sir
Nicholas Browne. He had opted wholeheartedly for the Stuart king in
the Jacobite war and, as a consequence of the defeat at the Boyne, his
vast estates were to be confiscated for his lifetime. Ó Rathaille and
some of the cadet McCarthy families were accordingly dispossessed
of their holdings on the Browne estate. One of the most memorable
poems in all Irish literature was composed by Ó Rathaille on the
occasion of his having to find shelter subsequently in a hovel by the
sea [An Duanaire, no. 45].

Around the years 1707-8 new efforts were made to re-launch the
Stuart cause from France. The Brownes, and their colonist friends,
were to the fore in preparing for a new invasion of the west of Ireland
by the Catholic king. In this movement Ó Rathaille — unlike many
of the more notable McCarthys — was quite emotionally involved,
and some of his vision-poems on the expected return of the Stuart king
are amongst the most vividly imagined and best-crafted of his works
[An Duanaire, nos. 44, 50, 51]. Hope of a Stuart invasion finally
petered out dismally about the years 1720-23. Worse was to follow
when the heir to the Browne properties, an English educated Catholic
called Sir Valentine, came into possession of his father's former estate
(c.1720). Ó Rathaille, after initial elation, discovered to his horror
that Sir Valentine would not or could not (legally) restore him to his
old family lands [An Duanaire, no.52]. In despair he proclaimed his
loyalty in his deathbed poem [An Duanaire, no.53], not to the
Brownes but to the discredited McCarthymore family 'the princes my
forebears served before the death of Christ'. One of the odd ironies of
Irish history is that not many years after Ó Rathaille's death the self-
styled 'last McCarthymore' ended up in England an officer in the
British army.

It is clear that the type of poetry written by Ó Rathaille in Co. Kerry
in the first half of the eighteenth century was dictated to a great
extent by the patronage that was available to him; so it was also with
Haicéad in Co. Tipperary in the first half of the seventeenth century.
As a result of this their cultural responses were different. In many
ways Ó Rathaille's reflect more centrally the medieval bardic
tradition. Unlike Haicéad, who was basically maintained by his
religious order, Ó Rathaille, having lost his property, had to depend
on casual patrons for whom he sometimes wrote formal eulogistic or
elegiac verse, which from the point of view of content, could as well
have been written in the sixteenth century. Despite the religious strife
and persecutions, despite the efforts to disseminate post-Tridentine
teachings, this kind of verse in particular shows very little evidence of
any new religious awareness. Ó Rathaille does rail in a few of his more
personal poems against anti-Catholic laws, but the ideals and virtues

he attributes to his patrons, live and dead, are those of the heroic non-Christian type which we associate with the great bulk of traditional bardic work. In one poem only, an elergy on the death of a priest, does he imagine the ordinary Christian virtues to be part of a gentleman's character.

Ó Rathaille is not strongly motivated by religious issues in his wish to extirpate the forces of the Protestant king; nor does it give him any pleasure on his deathbed that the old familiar territories are once again under the rule of Catholic nobility. His emotional stand is based firmly on his desire to repossess his status as poet (and thereby his property) and to live in a society which would fully appreciate the traditions he represented. He could contemplate with equanimity an Ireland ruled by a foreign king [An Duanaire, no. 50], or a former McCarthy stronghold inhabited by an English-speaking colonist [An Duanaire, no. 46] provided that the cultural life he and his people enjoyed could still flourish. In all this he is very much at one with the medieval Irish mind.

III

For want of patronage during the eighteenth century, poets increasingly became wandering teachers or musicians or labourers, and fell more frequently into poverty. Yet one cannot account the poetry of the eighteenth century to be in any way peasant poetry. All the major literary figures continue to compose with extraordinary virtuosity within the norms of the traditional aristocratic literary tradition. Mac Cruitín (c.1670-1755) berates the Irish uncultured classes for their boorishness and pretentiousness [An Duanaire, no. 54], Mac Dónaill (1691-1754) savages a colonial landlord for not behaving as an Irish chieftain would [An Duanaire, no. 56], Mac Cumhaigh (1738-73) laments the disappearance of the aristocratic O'Neills [An Duanaire, no. 57], Ó Súilleabháin (1748-84), hints at his own special status as poet and shows a certain reluctance to engage in lowly manual work [An Duanaire, no. 58]. Even a late poem such as the 'Lament for Art O'Leary' [An Duanaire, no. 62], composed in a popular keening tradition, bears all the marks of a mind nurtured in an aristocratic Gaelic milieu.

As one proceeds through the eighteenth century one feels that, while impositions such as unjust rents are resented (An Duanaire, no. 55] there is a reluctant acceptance of conquest, and a more general awareness that the English language and the Protestant religion go hand in hand with brutish oppression. At the same time one cannot say that the teachings of the Protestant religion always caused revulsion. It is a matter of record, at any rate, that at least three of the better-known poets of the period (Mac Craith, Mac Gearailt, Mac

Cumhaigh) flirted for a time with the alien religion, while some others did not show great interest in religious practices of any kind. Many of the eighteenth-century poets emerge as quite independent minded figures. There is a sense of gaiety and recklessness about some of them (Ó Súilleabháin, Mac Craith, Mac Cumhaigh, Mac Giolla Ghunna) that one does not associate at any rate with the scholarly priest-poet figure such as Haicéad and Céitinn in the early seventeenth century. The jocular, and sometimes challenging, rôle they assumed in relation to priests (a number of whom were poets themselves) can be seen in a whole series of lighter poems such as the well-known '*Barántaisí/Warrants*' [*An Duanaire*, no. 48], or in the more risqué verses addressed to some clerics by poets such as Mac Craith. It is undeniable at any rate that our poets do not always treat the sacerdotal figure with great reverence.

While it is true that the priest or priest-poet figure in the earlier period of the conquest carried great authority, and seemed for a time to be on the point of filling the hierarchical rôle in Irish society being vacated by the native aristocracy, from the second half of the seventeenth century on we see him lose dominance and status. As a result of penal measures against the Catholic religion ministering clergy became quite thin on the ground — in the five years after Haicéad's death, for instance, only one bishop had residence in Ireland — and clerical training became rudimentary. Priests on ordination had to promise on oath to complete their education abroad. Yet of 1,089 registered priests in 1704, less than a quarter of them had gone abroad. A report on the clergy in Ireland in 1733 declared that the details 'would make a good Catholic's hair stand on end', and that many of the daily scandals were 'caused by an exorbitant number of priests roving about without any function but to say Mass and to marry young couples' [Ó Dufaigh and Rainey, 1981, 13-17]. The situation of semi-literate priests with little Latin and less learning caused great dismay to the declining number of scholarly ecclesiastics. Towards the end of the seventeenth century the Ulster author of the prose and verse satire *Comhairle Mhic Clamha* ridicules a newly ordained priest:

> Brother Arsaigh, may you live to enjoy the state of your new priesthood, and I pray you do not be depressed because of the poverty of your Latin, as the amount of Latin necessary for saying Mass for the common congregation is slight.... However, on beginning the *Introibo* bless yourself with a loud full voice and give your vigorous prominent body a firm sturdy aspect and let your two eyes be sloping and nunnish in your head while looking at the lord.... Then raise your voice to a sort of melodious humming and wheezing and

coughing ... O blessed loud-voice priest, as you are a fine fellow, a splendid bumpkin, a sweet-sounding rascal, a merry tippler and a big-heeled rattler of a priest [Ó Dufaigh and Rainey, 1981, 67–69; trans.].

Given the situation of a semi-literate clergy, it is not at all surprising that the poets became the dominant community figures in the early eighteenth-century 'Hidden Ireland'. Of the many hundreds of poets whose work has been recorded, most were men of substantial traditional learning: they read or transcribed manuscripts which contained material going back to early Christian times; some knew Latin; some taught English, navigation, mathematics, at hedge-schools. When they assembled in Courts of Poetry during the year [Corkery, 1941, 90-125] they read their poems, exchanged views and manuscripts and engaged in extempore repartee in verse. On some occasions they fulfilled one of the most traditional rôles of the poet in Irish society by imposing sanctions on wrongdoers and acting as arbiters of social issues. For instance when four young men from the district of Croom joined the British Army, a number of the poets associated with the Court of Poetry there condemned their action in various verses; similarly many of the same poets lampooned a Dominican priest who became a Protestant minister.

In no other sphere did the poets influence people so powerfully as in that of the issue of the country's future freedom. From earliest times in Ireland the notion of the whole country (in the guise of a queen figure) being united with a redeemer king had always been a vague aspiration, and the king's coming had been prophetically and endlessly foretold. Now that the McCarthys, the Butlers and the various other 'Old Irish' and 'Old English' aristocrats — with their concentration on their own particular local territorial objectives — had departed the scene, the time became ripe for the popular development of the saviour-king theme which Ó Rathaille had handled so artistically in the *aisling* genre. Consequently scores of poets in the eighteenth century wrote vision-poems in which the exiled Stuart princes were imagined as the promised redeemers and rulers of the *whole Irish people*. Even though the return of a Stuart prince seemed most unlikely after the defeat at Culloden in 1745, no other redeemer-figure was at hand and the composition of the *aisling* genre continued unabated. It was after all 'a poetic dream, convenient for poetic purposes and for the unification of history' [Leersen, 1986, 286]. If one is to judge by what has been preserved in oral tradition, of all the high literary work of the seventeenth and eighteenth centuries it would seem that it was the *aisling* which made most impact on the popular mind. Much of this, one suspects, is due to the fact that many eighteenth-century poets began to reach a much wider audience by writing their lyrics to well-known musical airs. Consequently the *aisling* prepared a large section of the Irish people for a unique understanding of nineteenth-century nationalism, even though their sympathies seemed often to lie more with a monarchical nation-state than with a republican nation-state. Almost all the leaders of the revolutionary late nineteenth-century Fenian movement, for instance, 'at one time or another indicated that they were not wholly opposed in principle to monarchy' [De Paor, 1985, 175].

In the absence of necessary dated or detailed evidence, it is exceedingly difficult to speculate fruitfully on how the conquest affected the development of the more popular types of literature, how the 'Irish mind' in general responded. Vast areas of this literature await analysis.

Two special branches of literature which were enjoyed and shared widely since medieval times by all classes, both lowly and aristocratic, were those of Ossianic lore and love-song. The Ossianic tales and lays were afforded the type of reverential attention given to religious rituals in other cultures [Nagy, 1985, 13], and are quite significant for the light they cast on the hero-figure which Irish people mostly admired and identified with. In Nagy's fine structuralist study he emerges as one who is poet/sage and outsider [17–40]; who gives service to 'the kings of Ireland, who represent in medieval ideology the stability and prosperity of the entire island' [42]; who at the same time could be a rebellious employee threatening 'the very authority of kingship' [42]; who is 'righteous plunderer, avenger and agent of distraint' [46], 'reacquiring what one is legally entitled to within society' [48], and 'never attains full adulthood and the traditional sexual relationships that adulthood entails' [52]. One is tempted to ask whether it was such community expectation of a hero's attributes that threw up the rake-poet type such as Eoghan Rua Ó Súilleabháin who, in the late eighteenth century, was intent on making straight the way for the rightful king [*An Duanaire*, no. 59] or, on a quite different plane, the majestic rogue-sage type of public hero such as Daniel O'Connell in the nineteenth century, and many others since. If so, the 'Irish mind' far from being eroded by the conquest continued to develop and adapt.

As with Ossianic literature the great Irish love-songs [*An Duanaire*, xxxi, nos. 64-83] were highly esteemed at different levels of society as very special works of art. The values which they reflect regarding love and marriage emanate from the mores of medieval Irish aristocratic society and are very much at variance with orthodox Christianity. The attitude to sex which they reveal contradicts in practically every detail that preached by early seventeenth-century reformist clerics such as Archbishop Aodh Mac Aingil in his *Scáthán Shacramuinte na hAithridhe* [Ó Cuív, 1978, 533]. On the other hand it seems clear that the mass of people had traditionally been quite stringent in their views as to how day-to-day matters regarding love and marriage should be conducted amongst themselves [Connolly, 1985]; it was mostly, it appears, at the higher levels of society that 'unorthodox' behaviour was approved of and provided for by special economic arrangements [Cosgrove, 1985]. Could it be, one is tempted to ask, that the extraordinary prevalence of love-songs in eighteenth-century society indicates a growing identification of the part of ordinary people with the 'unorthodox' non-Christian aristocratic values? If so, deteriorating economic circumstances in the nineteenth century and the English universal education system put an end for some time to any such tendency. There is little doubt, however, that ambivalent attitudes to sex and marriage continued and continue to be a feature of Irish society.

There is at least one major question to be asked if not to be answered finally: is not eighteenth-century Gaelic Ireland, in many respects, a period of extraordinary cultural growth rather than of decay? Under the new colonial landlord class the mass of people may have existed in fairly miserable living conditions and may have been denied their traditional rights or advancement; on the other hand — economic conditions apart — they were left more to their own devices. In the absence of native authority figures, attitudes to political, social and moral matters seem to have taken on new dimensions. There were considerable new literary developments in the genres of vision-poems, confessional poems [An Duanaire, no. 60], comic warrants and occasional poems [An Duanaire, nos. 40, 41, 42, 43, 44, 63]. There is evidence for growing participation and interest in dancing, hurling, faction-fights and other entertainments. One feels that, as living conditions improved in the second half of the eighteenth century, both poets and people achieved a certain freedom to develop denied to them in previous centuries. And allied to this freedom, one often experiences a great sense of gaiety, the sort of gaiety associated with the behaviour and *obiter dicta* of the poet Eoghan Rua Ó Súilleabháin, the sort of gaiety portrayed as late as 1827-35 in the diary of Humphrey O'Sullivan [De Bhaldraithe, 1979]. The Hidden Ireland was in all probability a much merrier Ireland than we have been led to believe. The merriment may have been, of course, the sort of merriment which often emerges at a time of societal chaos.

————————

The main feature of Gaelic culture which had visibly declined in the eighteenth century was the Irish language itself. Yet it is still likely that two out of every three people in the country habitually spoke Irish at the end of the eighteenth century, so that literature in Irish continued to be the predominant literature down to the middle of the nineteenth century. As one commentator points out, however [M. Wall, 1969, 82], the determining factor in favour of major language change at this stage was that all those people who wielded power in Ireland, who had formal education or professional careers, now spoke English as their preferred language. The training of priests — who now began to oust the poets as authority figures — came under the control of English-speaking authorities, and as a result the Church gradually helped to impose both Victorian religious values and the English language on Irish people. More significantly, perhaps, the universal educational system which had been established in 1831 with the objective of educating Irish children through English, and in English, was an overwhelming success. While the numbers of English speakers increased rapidly, so ironically, due to unusual population growth, did the numbers of Irish speakers for some time. In fact at the time of the Famine (1845-7) there were probably more Irish speakers — as well as more English speakers — in Ireland than ever before in recorded history. When the Famine struck, vast numbers of the poorer Irish-speaking population, in particular, died or emigrated. From then on until the end of the century speaking and writing in the Irish language declined disastrously.

And so it happened that the wishes of Sir John Davies were finally fulfilled, to the extent that the majority of Irish people now adopted the English language. On the other hand Tudor policy regarding religion in Ireland failed completely. For in the same period that the Irish language came close to extinction the Catholic Church was able to re-organise itself in a highly efficient manner and become a power in the land.

FURTHER READING

It is envisaged that this essay be read in conjunction with Ó Tuama and Kinsella, *An Duanaire, Poems of the Dispossessed*, Dublin 1981. Other works to which reference is made are:

A. Bliss, 'The English Language in Early Modern Ireland', *A New History of Ireland* III, ed. Moody et. al., Oxford 1976, 546-60.

A. Chambers, *Eleanor, Countess of Desmond*, Dublin 1986.

S.J. Connolly, 'Marriage in pre-famine Ireland', *Marriage in Ireland*, ed. A. Cosgrove, Dublin 1985, 78-98.

P.J. Corish, *The Catholic Community in the Seventeenth and Eighteenth Centuries*, Dublin 1981.

D. Corkery, *The Hidden Ireland*, Dublin 1941.

A. Cosgrove, 'Marriage in Medieval Ireland', *Marriage in Ireland*, ed. Cosgrove, Dublin 1985, 25-50.

T. de Bhaldraithe, *The Diary of Humphrey O'Sullivan*, Cork 1979.

L. de Paor, 'The Rebel Mind: Republican and Loyalist', *The Irish Mind*, ed. R. Kearney, Dublin 1985, 157287.

J.T. Leersen, *Mere Irish and Fíor-Ghael*, Amsterdam 1986.

J.F. Nagy, *The Wisdom of the Outlaw*, London/San Francisco 1985.

B. Ó Cuív, 'The Irish Language in the Early Modern Period', *NHI* III, Oxford 1976, 509-45.

S. Ó Dufaigh and B. Rainey, *Comhairle Mhic Clamha*, Lille 1981.

T. Ó Fiaich, 'The Language and Political History', *A View of the Irish Language*, ed. Ó Cuív, Dublin, 1969.

S. Ó Tuama, 'Stability and Ambivalence: Aspects of the sense of Place and Religion in Irish Literature', *Ireland, towards a sense of place*, ed. J. Lee, Cork 1985.

J.J. Silke, 'The Irish abroad, 1534-1691,' *NHI* III, Oxford 1976, 587-633.

M. Wall, 'The Decline of the Irish Language', *A View of the Irish Language*, ed. Ó Cuív, Dublin 1969.

4
'WHAT ISH MY NATION?':*
THEMES IN IRISH HISTORY
1550-1850

Thomas Bartlett

I

IT has been frequently claimed, most often admittedly by those who know their history through inspiration rather than through study, that there is only one theme in Irish history, whether the period under review is the Middle Ages or more recent times or, as here, the Early Modern period. The central theme of all Irish history, we are informed, has been the struggle of Ireland against England. There are at least two aspects to this theme, and I will look briefly at each.

In its most politically charged form, this theme argues that the struggle for national independence has provided the dynamic of Irish history. To break the connection with England, to get the English out of Ireland, by persuasion or by force of arms, and to set up an independent nation-state — such objectives and aspirations, it is claimed, constitute the very stuff of Irish history, at least from the arrival of the English (or Norman) adventurers in the late twelfth century, right down to our own day. Viewed in this light, the United Irishmen's rebellion of 1798 can be portrayed as a forerunner of the Young Ireland *émeute* of 1848 which in turn connects with the more significant rising of the Fenians in 1867: ultimately all are perceived as precursors of the Easter rebellion of 1916. Moreover, not only have the 'Boys of Wexford' in 1798 been seen as cousins of the 'Men of 1916' but the rebellion of 1798 itself has been cast as a successor to the Jacobite war of 1689-91, the rebellion of 1641, and further back to the wars of 1590s in the reign of Elizabeth I, and even beyond. In short, in the period under review, almost every generation has had its 'national uprising', its war for independence. Some were moderately successful for a time, others were instant and abject failures but, no matter, the struggle continued, if not decade after decade, then on a generation-to-generation basis. Stated thus, this theme will not take us very far in our attempt to find out what the period 1550 to 1850 is about.

*Macmorris in Shakespeare's *Henry V* (Act 3, Scene 2, lines 116-17). Macmorris answered his own question: 'Ish a villain and a bastard and a knave and a rascal.'

44

If we look first at the 1641 Rising, we are immediately confronted by the fact that the Ulster rebels claimed that they were fighting on behalf of Charles I, King of England. Not only did they assert this but they took the trouble to forge a commission from the king apparently authorising them to rebel, to become, as it were, king's rebels. Moreover, there is no evidence that the Confederate Catholics — to give the rebels of 1641 the title which they later adopted — were fighting for an independent Ireland. Indeed their whole frame of reference was English rather than Irish (it was never Gaelic) and they frequently appealed to the common law of England and to Magna Carta. And it is a similar story with the Jacobite war of 1689-91: if by some lucky chance James had won the Battle of the Boyne in 1690 and if by some miracle (the word is not too strong) he had managed to cross the Irish Sea and battle his way down to London and depose William, Ireland would have remained just as English dominated as before: James II, after all, was an English king. Finally, it is difficult to see the 1798 rebellion as a national uprising. Its localised and episodic nature, its sectarian manifestations, and perhaps more than anything the fact that it was crushed by Irish troops to a very large extent — all tend to suggest that so far from being a rebellion against English rule, it appears to bear more the character of a civil war between Irishmen.

Is the theme of Ireland versus England then totally inappropriate in this period? In this highly coloured form, it undoubtedly is but yet if we narrow our focus considerably and concentrate our attention on the 1790s then there is something in it, for this was Tone's decade. Theobald Wolfe Tone was the first person to argue that Ireland's ills were owing totally to the English connection and that the only remedy was for Ireland to break away and set up for herself as an independent nation. In the 1790s when, under the influence of events in France, Tone first formulated this doctrine it was not all that widely accepted — Tone himself appears to have had doubts on occasion about its validity. None the less, in the years after Tone's death in 1798 (he committed suicide after capture), and especially with the publication in America of his voluminous writings and diaries in the mid-1820s, his influence grew rapidly and he can be regarded as the father of Irish republicanism and of militant Irish separatism. After Tone, for good or ill, the benchmark of an Irish patriot was one's contribution towards his goals.

There is, however, another dimension to the theme of Ireland against England; and this one may on examination be found to be more useful in explaining what happened in Ireland in the period under review. This theme maintains that during these years Ireland can best be regarded as a colony of England; that the Anglo-Irish governing elite who dominated Ireland, at least from 1650 to 1850 if not beyond, should be seen as the colonisers; that in short the relationship between Ireland and England was essentially and fundamentally a colonial one. This is an attractive theme: it lifts Irish history to some extent out of a rigid Anglo-Irish framework and sets it in a wider imperial one; it invites contrasts and comparisons with other colonies (French Algeria is currently much favoured); but more important it casts light on the gritty realities of the Anglo-Irish nexus for it exposes the perennial complexities of assimilation/alienation and integration/rejection involved in all colonial relationships.

There can be no doubt that Ireland bears most, if not all, of the hallmarks of a colony during this period. A serious attempt was made to regulate (and restrict) Irish trade and manufacturing in the interests of the imperial power in the period 1650 to 1778, and the Irish parliament, despite its antiquity, was subject to humiliating restraints by the English parliament — in fact the Irish parliament had fewer powers than most of the avowedly colonial assemblies in the New World. Moreover, the Anglo-Irish Ascendancy which governed Ireland for most of this period seems to be the very model of a colonial elite: aping in an exaggerated way the manners of the metropolitan governing class, yet viewed by the latter with undisguised contempt; allegedly engaged on *une mission civilatrice* yet frequently distinguished by the degenerate qualities of the 'natives' around them i.e. excessive drinking, lavish (and ruinous) hospitality, a propensity for violence, a love of gambling, and excessive (and unjustified) pride.

As we move further into the eighteenth century the colonial aspect of Irish history becomes ever more prominent. Perhaps as many as 70,000 Irishmen, mostly Presbyterians from Ulster but with a significant number of Catholics too, left Ireland to settle in the North American colonies, and it was to be their descendants who took such an active rôle in the struggle for American independence. And the American War (1776-83) had an enormous impact on political affairs in Ireland for the American example and American ideas, indeed the very vocabulary of 'representation', 'democracy', 'consent' and 'freedom' in which these ideas were expressed, proved inspirational to those groups in Ireland dissatisfied with the existing 'colonial' relationship between Ireland and England. Moreover, the calamitous course of the war from the British point of view made Lord North's government (1771-82) uniquely vulnerable to Irish pressure. The result was that at the very time that the American colonies declared themselves independent, 'patriot' members of the Irish parliament aided by the extra-parliamentary paramilitary force, the Irish Volunteers, succeeded in adjusting the constitutional relationship between Ireland and England and in giving Ireland for the first time something that looked like an independent parliament. This experiment did not last beyond 1800, for mounting popular unrest in Ireland in the 1790s culminating in the 1798 rebellion made change desirable, necessary and, above all, practicable. Accordingly, the Act of Union of 1800 abolished the Irish parliament and provided that one hundred Irish MPs would henceforth attend the Westminster parliament. In short, within thirty years Ireland went from being a dependent colony, to a self-governing (but still dependent) colony, and finally after 1801, to being a province of metropolitan Britain: an internal colony of Britain. The colonial nexus in its various forms could scarcely be made more explicit. And yet, before the theme of Ireland-as-a-colony is elevated to a new orthodoxy, some important caveats need to be entered.

Perhaps the most important reservation is that few Irishmen — Protestant or Catholic — accepted that Ireland was a colony with the attendant attributes of inferiority and subordination. To them, the true relationship between Ireland and England was that of 'sister' or 'brother' kingdoms and while they would concede 'elder sister' or 'elder brother' status to England (and hence a slight degree of deference) they could rarely be brought to admit the validity of the mother-child metaphor which dominated English perceptions of the relationship between Ireland, the child-colony, and England, the mother-country. Both Irish lawyers and politicians argued vehemently that Ireland was a separate kingdom (though sharing the same king with England) and they pointed out that Ireland had her own parliament and that laws were made in Ireland by the King, Lords and Commons in parliament assembled. What other 'colony', they asked, could boast as much? Where was the King of Virginia or the parliament of Massachusetts? What 'colony' had a genuine aristocracy?

Moreover, if we maintain that Ireland can best be understood as a colony in the period 1550 to 1850, or even later (or earlier) then we encounter massive problems of definition. Unlike other colonies Ireland was not located in some distant continent, nor did she supply the mother country with otherwise unobtainable raw materials or exotic products. And those theorists who have countered this objection by declaring that Ireland was an 'internal colony' within the British state have signally failed to demonstrate why this concept cannot be applied to any area beyond the boundaries of the British seats of government and administration, Westminster and Whitehall. Viewed in these lights, it is not surprising that when the author of an extremely able short study of the typology of colonies came to consider Ireland, he could only conclude lamely: 'I hesitate and waver' [Finley, 1976, 188]. Moreover, if we move back from theory to history and consider the many hundreds of thousands who departed these shores between 1700 and 1850 to seek opportunity in Canada, Australia, Britain and especially America, then surely Ireland, so far from being a colony, should be considered as a mother country in her own right?

47

If then the theme of Ireland vs. England, whether in a nationalist or colonial sense, seems to obscure as much as it illuminates perhaps we should leave this external aspect of Irish history and look to the internal: a perennial struggle between Ireland and England may not fit the bill but what about Protestants vs. Catholics?

At first glance this theme seems all too appropriate. Contemporaries certainly saw matters in this light. To them, the rise of Protestant power, indeed the emergence of a Protestant nation in eighteenth-century Ireland was necessarily founded on the destruction of Catholic power, the confiscation of Catholic land and the eclipse of that religion. 'There was no medium' wrote William King, the Protestant Bishop of Derry in 1691, 'but that either we or they must be undone' [King, 1691, 292]. And in general the writing of historians have confirmed this theme as being of central importance.

Between 1550 and 1650 a struggle was waged in Ireland between the forces of the Protestant Reformation and the Catholic Counter-Reformation. It was, however, an unequal contest in two ways. First, given that Protestantism was to be imposed in Ireland (and by all accounts in England) through the agency of the Tudor state, it is of the utmost importance to understand that in the mid sixteenth century Tudor power in Ireland was far more notional than real. Ireland may have been England's and the King of England may have rejoiced in the title of King of Ireland but these claims signified little outside of the 'Pale', a strip of territory on the eastern seaboard of Ireland and centring on Dublin. The stark fact was that Tudor government in Ireland was not at all equipped to implement major changes. The result was that it was not until after the Tudor conquest of Ireland in the late sixteenth century that a determined effort (though one bedevilled by shortages of cash and by theological disputes) was got underway to Protestantise the Irish. Long before then, perhaps as early as the 1560s, the Catholic Counter-Reformation had begun to establish a secure hold in Ireland. That the Counter-Reformation *preceded* the Reformation in Ireland may explain why the Reformation so signally failed in Ireland.

None the less the Tudor conquest of Ireland was a reality: and from this reality stemmed a second incongruity. By 1603 full English control had been achieved throughout Ireland, but political unification had not been accompanied by religious unity and the resulting tension between a Protestant state, the achievement of the Tudors, and a Catholic people, the achievement of the Counter-Reformation, would dominate, where it did not determine, the ebb and flow of events in the next three hundred years. From an early date in the seventeenth century it was clear that so far as the English government was concerned the future control of Ireland would lie with those

English Protestants and their descendants who resided in Ireland. The loyalty of all others, whether Catholics of Gaelic Irish stock or Catholics of English descent (sometimes called the Old English), was vitiated by the very fact of their stubborn, and it seemed perverse, adherence to Catholicism. By the 1660s, largely as a result of the punitive policies of the Cromwellians, Catholic political power had gone. Fifty years before they had constituted a majority in the Irish parliament but in 1661 only one Catholic was elected and it is doubtful if he ever took his seat. For the next 140 years the Irish parliament would be a Protestant parliament for a Protestant people. Moreover, by the end of the Cromwellian regime (1650-60), Catholic control of the more important Irish towns and boroughs had been broken and Catholic economic power crippled as a result. Perhaps more startling than anything was the collapse of Catholic land ownership: by 1660 Catholics owned barely 12 per cent of Irish land; thirty years earlier they had owned nearly 60 per cent (see Map 2). The Cromwellians had regarded their work as necessary for security reasons but equally they saw it as a just punishment on Irish Catholics for their participation in the bloody massacres of the 1641 rebellion and in the ensuing war. Irish Protestants applauded this retribution, and their descendants in the eighteenth and nineteenth centuries were well aware that their ascendancy was based on the destruction of Catholic power and, especially, on the confiscation of Catholic land. Admittedly, the 1660s and 1670s had witnessed a partial Catholic recovery, and the policies of James II and his Irish Lord Deputy, Richard Talbot, in the late 1680s seemed certain to bring about a complete Catholic resurgence. But it was not to be, and Catholic hopes of a successful counter-revolution rolling back the Protestant gains of the previous hundred years ended in defeat and disaster at the Boyne (1690) and, especially, at Aughrim (1691). No one could now doubt that the Protestants of Ireland were under God's special protection, that they were His chosen people in Ireland, and that the future lay with them.

Viewed in this light, the long eighteenth century from 1690 (if not 1660) to 1829, can best be regarded as the era of the Protestant nation. This was the period when the Protestants of Ireland constituted, as Swift put it, 'the whole people of Ireland' and when, self-assured and confident, they even developed a nationalism (as valid as any that came after) to bolster their self-esteem and legitimise their position in Ireland. This 'Protestant Ascendancy' (the term itself was only coined in the 1790s) was not to last, but its memory as a period when loyalty to the English connection *and* a developed sense of an Irish nationality went hand in hand, was to endure into the late nineteenth century and beyond.

In the 1760s, however, changes within the Irish political structure, within the Catholic community and within English politics and society allowed something called the Catholic Question i.e. the issue of equal civil and religious rights for Catholics, to emerge. By the late 1770s there was considerable pressure for the Penal Laws which had been passed in the early eighteenth century and before to be repealed. These laws had been designed (according to one school of thought) to keep Catholics poor and (according to another) to make them Protestants. The Penal Laws in fact did neither, and the pressure for change came largely from the English government which saw the Catholic church in a European context as a force for stability. It may also be that successive English governments were alert to the possibility of using the threat of Catholic relief as a disciplinary device against the increasingly recalcitrant Protestants. It was well known that full civil and religious rights for Catholics held fearful consequences for Protestants: put bluntly, the brute facts of sectarian arithmetic determined that Catholic equality with Protestant meant Catholic superiority *over* Protestant. By the late eighteenth century the Catholic Question was the Irish Question. It was strongly argued, for example, that only in a united parliament could Catholic demands for equal rights be conceded and this argument played a part in ensuring Catholic neutrality or support in the struggle to pass the Irish Act of Union in 1800. But Catholic emancipation when it came eventually in 1829 was not conceded with grace but was rather extorted by mass pressure in a campaign led by Daniel O'Connell. From this point on may be dated the declension of Protestant power, and the rise of Catholic Ireland.

Overall then, the theme of Catholic vs. Protestant seems to encompass the major developments within Irish history in the period under review. Moreover it unquestionably conveys what many observers considered to be — for want of a better term — the true flavour of Irish life. The struggle between Catholic and Protestant was never just a legal or a political abstraction and the history of the period since 1550 is punctuated with appalling sectarian murders, massacres, and mutilations. Protestant vs. Catholic, then, regrettably perhaps, but none the less accurately appears to be the major theme of Irish history.

But is this so? Before we close the book some caveats once again need to be entered against this theme as being all-embracing.

First, the word 'Protestant' is deeply misleading. In Irish history 'Protestant' has generally referred to any Christian who is not a member of the Catholic Church and the assumption has been that there was throughout this period a 'Protestant' community in which all sects — Anglican, Presbyterian, German Palatines, Methodists, Congregationalists and Independents — merged their theological differences in the face of the common enemy, Catholicism. There is, of course, some evidence for this assumption: in 1688, for example, in the face of the Catholic resurgence under James II, Anglicans and Presbyterians drew together to such an extent that it was reported that 'they scrupled not (nor wee) to hear one anothers' way of worship and sermons' [Stewart, 1977, 65]. But it would be a dangerous simplification of Irish history to see 'Protestant' Ireland as constituting a monolith. For much of the period under review Protestant division was as remarkable as Protestant union: and the rivalry between church and kirk, Anglican and Presbyterian, was at times as intense as the more general Protestant/Catholic hostility. It should not be forgotten that the Protestant nation of the eighteenth century was confined by and large to Anglicans, and that the Dissenters were, like Catholics, subject to Penal Laws, though the laws against them were more irksome than onerous. Second, the word 'Catholic' is equally problematic, and here too division is as common as union. In the first half of the seventeenth century the religious customs and practices of the Old English Catholics differed so much from those favoured by the native Irish Catholics that neither was prepared to accept the other as 'true' Catholics. And throughout the late eighteenth and early nineteenth centuries rivalries *within* the Catholic camp — clerical/lay, urban/rural, merchant/nobleman — were at such a level as to obstruct Catholic efforts to obtain redress of their grievances. Finally — and more generally — the apparent inevitability of Catholic/Protestant rivalry (however defined) can induce a certain blindness to the possibilities that offered at various junctures in the period 1550 to 1850 for a fundamental realignment of the Irish political scene. Thus, in the early 1640s some Catholics and Protestants acted together to bring about the downfall of the Irish Lord Deputy, the Earl of Strafford, because he was 'a most cursed man to all Ireland' [Beckett, 1966, 65]: in the period 1690 to 1720 Anglican/Presbyterian hostility was such that a new religious struggle seemed certain to break out in Ireland; in the 1790s Presbyterian/Catholic relations were sufficiently harmonious to allow a well-known effort at political co-operation in the Society of United Irishmen to take place; and O'Connell's campaign to achieve Catholic emancipation was supported by a very large number of 'liberal' Protestants — for example, from as early as 1815 a majority of Irish MPs at Westminster supported Catholic relief. In short, Protestant vs. Catholic seems, on examination, to gloss over as many problems as it resolves.

III

Let us leave Protestant-Catholic rivalry for the moment and examine instead a more secular conflict — the struggle for the land. There can be no doubt that this theme, dealing as it does with the plantations of the sixteenth and seventeenth centuries, with landlord-tenant relations in the pre-Famine period, and with the Land War of the late nineteenth century, is central to the course of Irish history over these years. Not for nothing did Michael Davitt, the architect of the downfall of landlordism, aver that Irish history was about the land.

The traditional view of the Irish land question can be quickly sketched in. As noted above, the confiscation of the seventeenth century and, moreover, the slow drip-drip of adverse court decisions, had caused the amount of land owned by Catholics to plummet from around 60 per cent in 1630 to about 12 per cent in 1700. But though ownership changed, occupancy did not, and this fundamental social disequilibrium — that those who worked the land did not own it, and *vice versa* — was at the root of that perennial tension, even smothered war, between the new, English-speaking, Protestant landlord and his Gaelic-speaking, Catholic tenant. Given that the great estates of the eighteenth century owed their origins to confiscation (to the Irish, confiscation was a polite name for theft) it is scarcely surprising that a malignant social and economic structure should have evolved on the land; and contemporaries and later commentators have been quick to pass judgment.

Accordingly, Irish landlords have been vilified as greedy, grasping and profligate, uninterested in their tenants' welfare or in estate improvement. But while landlords generally have been denounced, absentee landlords have been singled out for special condemnation. Living it up in the flesh pots of London or fluttering, butterfly-like, around the ancient ruins of Italy and Greece, these 'blood suckers of the Irish economy' simultaneously deprived Ireland of much-needed capital and the Irish peasantry of an essential model of civilised living. Moreover, in so far as they appeared to be responsible for introducing 'middlemen' to the Irish rural scene, their culpability for Ireland's depressed and lawless state grew proportionately. Middlemen, i.e. those who leased a large area from a landlord and then sub-leased that land in small lots, had an unenviable reputation for rapacity and out-rageous behaviour. And in perfect counterpoint to this lurid picture of the oppressor-landlord there was the image of the oppressed tenant clothed in rags and sheltering in a crude one-roomed mud cabin, eking a living on a miserable potato-patch from which he was liable to be evicted at a whim, and for which he paid an extortionate rent. Further-more, as if to emphasise the deplorable state of social relationships in rural Ireland in the eighteenth and nineteenth centuries, there came in succession a large number of peasant secret societies which waged intermittent war on landlords and their agents.

These secret societies — the Houghers of the early eighteenth century, the Whiteboys of the 1760s, and Hearts of Steel of the

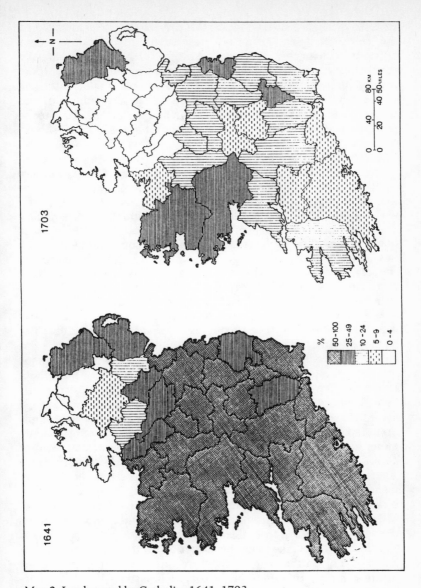

Map 2: Land owned by Catholics 1641-1703

Source: J.G. Simms, 'The Restoration and the Jacobite War,' in T.W. Moody and F.X. Martin eds, *The Course of Irish History*, Dublin 1967, 204-16.

1770s, the Rightboys of the 1780s, the Defenders of the 1790s, the Terry Alts, Shanavests and Rockites of the early nineteenth century — constituted a type of rural trades' union which protected the tenantry against landlord depredations and helped keep him in check. The final act in this historic drama was played out in the late nineteenth century when through mass agitation landlordism was destroyed, the landlords were bought out and the land returned to the people. By 1910 Ireland was by and large a nation of small owner-occupiers.

This unfolding of the land question from its origins in seventeenth-century confiscation through landlord oppression and tenant misery until the period of mass agitation, had a dramatic quality to it that made it emotionally satisfying. Moreover the land war was, after all, *won:* no such verdict could be pronounced either on the language question or, more damaging to Irish self-esteem, on the national question: and this fact has tended to make the outcome all the more heroic. Unfortunately for those who were gratified by the success of the struggle for the land the comforting simplicities of the traditional story have not withstood the rigours of academic enquiry.

In particular, landlords, absentee or resident have to a large extent been rescued from the opprobrium which contemporaries and later generations had heaped on them. Research has shown that absentee landlords had frequently good reasons for being absent (and some were undoubtedly a good riddance). Some absentees wished to pursue military or diplomatic careers abroad; some had estates in both Ireland *and* England and necessarily they could not reside constantly in both; some had estates in widely separated parts of Ireland and the same held true for them; some were 'internal' absentees who simply preferred to live in Dublin rather than exist in the country. More important, the casual correlation that has been made between absenteeism and neglect has been shown to be unfounded. Some 'absentee' estates were poorly managed but most were no different from the estates of resident landlords: it may even be the case that the estates of absentees were rather better managed than those of resident landlords for absentees sought to appoint competent agents to run their estates in their absence. Moreover it has been shown that Irish landlords did take an interest in agricultural improvement, and it has been argued that Irish agriculture was quite productive in the nineteenth century. Again, it has been demonstrated that the land-lords' capacity to influence, much less determine, the shape of Irish agriculture was severely circumscribed by custom, climate, soil-type and the state of the market. The phenomenon of middlemen, too, has been scrutinised and it has been shown that they were neither as numerous or as long-lived — they were on the way out by the 1820s because landlords began to bypass them by leasing directly to the tenantry — nor as widespread as many had imagined. In fact it has even been argued that middlemen served a useful function in backward areas of the country as primitive suppliers of capital or capital goods: and social historians have noted their rôle as cultural intermediaries or agents of social control between landlord and undertenant and some have traced the rise in Irish rural violence to the disappearance of this rural middle group. In short, what appears to be emerging out of the studies of individual estates is that Irish landlords, whether absentee or resident, and perhaps even Irish middlemen, were essentially peripheral to the main course of agrarian development in the eighteenth and nineteenth centuries. From being a centre-stage villain in the epic of Irish history, the Irish landlord, in particular, may turn out to be no more than a supporting player. Arguably, this would be the most devastating criticism yet levelled against him.

The rôle of the Irish tenant — generally thought of as oppressed and downtrodden — has likewise been carefully reassessed. In particular, the importance of the lease, a binding contract between landlord and tenant, has been stressed. Previous accounts of landlord-tenant relations ignored its existence. Leases were in fact common throughout Ireland in the eighteenth century and, among other things, they described the area to be leased, stated the rent to be paid and indicated the date of expiry of the lease. In so far as leases were legally enforceable contracts they gave a real security to tenants and those historians who have examined landlord-tenant relations in the eighteenth century have concluded on the basis of a study of leases that rents were generally low, leases long (at least in comparison to English or Scottish practice) and eviction rare and difficult to achieve. Moreover the sharp rise in land values in the period 1760 to 1815 is now held to have benefited, not so much the landlord, but his tenants, secure with their long leases (during which rents could not be raised). Nor has the presence of rural secret societies controverted these findings, for recent research into them has stressed their traditionalist assumptions, their defensive character and their limited ends. They were not really anti-landlord, much less 'nationalist' in inspiration. Rather they were protests against the introduction into certain areas of rural Ireland of demands and practices that were held to be noncustomary or excessive, or both. Moreover they appear to have been the product of a sustained improvement in the Irish economy, and not at all the result of rural wretchedness. Admittedly when we turn the corner into the nineteenth century the picture changes considerably, for the massive population growth concentrated in the lower areas of society in the period before 1845 overwhelmed the existing social structure and led to a significant deterioration in landlord/tenant relations. Leases were not now so favourable to tenants and the number of farmers who were lease-less (tenants-at-will) grew alarmingly.

The appalling tragedy of the Famine with its countless deaths, numerous evictions and mass exodus has tended to give to the later stages of the land question an almost miraculous quality, but even here the certainties of earlier generations have been challenged. In fact it could be said that no area of modern Irish history has been so re-written and re-thought as the fall of landlordism from 1870 to 1910. Cumulatively the result has been to undermine the heroic nature of that contest: indeed it could plausibly be argued that an unloved but not oppressive landlord class was overwhelmed by a rapacious tenantry. It has been pointed out, for example, that the slogan of the Land War, 'the Land for the People' did not refer at all to the rural poor, nor to the urban population, nor indeed to the millions who had fled Ireland since 1850. The 'people' here were the strong farmers, hard-faced men who had done well out of the Famine: it was they who won the Land War. In sum, the traditional view of the Irish land question is in ruins but no new synthesis has as yet emerged. This is *not* to say, however, that the Land Question was marginal to the course of Irish history during the period under review. It was in fact the motor of Irish history, the dynamo of change and the repository of the hopes and fears of successive generations from the sixteenth century to our own day: but it operated in ways that defy simplistic — or moralistic — analysis.

IV

So far the themes we have examined — Ireland/England, Protestant/Catholic, landlord/tenant — have all had to do with conflict and, as we have seen, while each has something to be said on its behalf none is entirely satisfactory. Perhaps it is the general theme of confrontation that is at fault? Is struggle at the heart of Irish history? Specifically, is violence normal and peace abnormal in Ireland? Let us conclude this essay by considering a theme that stresses peaceful rather than tumultuous change: the economic development of Ireland 1550 to 1850.

At one time this theme aroused little scholarly debate for the few writers who addressed themselves to it merely elaborated what appeared to be an unchallengeable orthodoxy. Their central thesis was, in essence, a simple one: over the centuries, England's selfish commercial policies and vindictive legislation had systematically beggared Ireland. Ireland's poverty, in short, was a product of English rapacity. They instanced the devastating wars of the 1590s, 1640s, and 1689-91 which caused severe economic dislocation: but especially they pointed to the Cattle Acts of the 1660s, which killed

56

off at a stroke the flourishing Irish livestock trade, the Woollen Act of 1699 which destroyed the Irish woollen industry, and the numerous English restrictions on Irish exports for most of the eighteenth century and they took it as self-evident that these wars and selfish policies combined ultimately to deny Ireland the possibility of modest economic advance, much less the chance of an industrial or agricultural revolution. The tragedy of the Great Famine (1845-7) and the mass emigration of the nineteenth century were only the culmination of a centuries-old policy designed to keep Ireland poor.

Hardly any of these arguments will pass muster today. The devastation caused by the seventeenth-century wars may have been exaggerated: certainly the Irish economy showed considerable resilience in recovering when the wars had ended and this suggests that the destruction wrought may not have been as extensive as claimed. Moreover, it is now clear that the legislative restrictions of the English parliament on Irish trade were not as damaging as contemporaries and later historians have made out. The Irish cattle trade was already in the doldrums as a result of low prices in England when the Cattle Acts of the 1660s put an end to it. Indeed in so far as the Cattle Acts spurred Irish merchants to concentrate on the export of 'dead' stock (salted beef, tallow and leather) rather than livestock, the acts may be regarded as a useful boost to the Irish economy rather than a crippling blow. Similarly, the Woollen Act of 1699, and the commercial restrictions of the eighteenth century, have had their importance downplayed. The first is now regarded as mainly significant for its constitutional implications, and the second is likewise seen as important politically rather than economically. Irish economic historians are, in general, hostile to the thesis that depression (or prosperity) can be brought about by act of parliament and they stress instead such economic factors as market size, demand and communications. Finally, the pessimistic view of earlier economic historians concerning Ireland's economic progress (or rather, lack of it) has been convincingly demonstrated to be altogether erroneous. In particular, it has been shown that during the period 1660 to 1815 Ireland enjoyed an increasing prosperity. Population rose rapidly from around two million in 1690 to about six million in 1815; land values over the same period recorded as much as a six-fold increase; the value of Irish exports — linen dominant among them — rose dramatically; and there was a noticeable commercialisation of Irish agriculture. Moreover, the evidence suggests that this rising prosperity benefited all sections of the population (there was an absence of famine between 1740 and 1820, and there was a disproportionate increase in such consumer 'luxuries' as tea, sugar and tobacco). But these findings, exciting though they are, raise in their turn a further problem, one which lies at the heart of modern Irish economic history. If, as now seems certain, there was substantial economic development and a modest prosperity over the period 1660 to 1815 why then did that economic advance stall in the nineteenth century and why did that Irish prosperity prove so brittle and so precarious? Early modern Ireland ended in famine and flight, deindustrialisation and underdevelopment — why was this?

In seeking answers to these questions Irish economic historians have begun to compare Ireland's economic development with that of Scotland. Both countries have a similar topography and climate and historically both have stood in roughly the same relationship to England and there were, as well, other similarities to do with population size, language change and religious division. But there the similarities ended for each country's economic development was quite different. In 1700 it has been plausibly argued that 'Ireland seemed to hold more promise of a bright economic future that Scotland' [Cullen and Smout, 4] for in terms of exports, and perhaps even agriculture, Ireland appeared to have the advantage. Furthermore the tens of thousands of Scots who came to Ireland in the late seventeenth century were clearly voting with their feet in favour of the economic future of their new home. But by 1800 Scotland had clearly pulled away from Ireland and by 1850, while Ireland suffered famine and the Irish economy remained firmly based on agriculture, Scotland had begun to modernise, urbanise and above all industrialise. By 1900 there were three industrial jobs in Scotland to every one in Ireland. When and why did the Irish and Scotish economies diverge to Ireland's disadvantage?

No clear answer has, as yet, emerged to either of these questions but on balance it seems certain that the divergence began in the eighteenth century; equally, it is clear that there is no simple explanation for it. Some have argued that Ireland's exclusion, for most of the eighteenth century, from the colonial trade of North America was the decisive factor, for undoubtedly Scotland, and particularly Glasgow, benefited much from this lucrative trade. Others have pointed to the deleterious effects of the Irish penal code on Irish investment and agriculture. (There was a Scottish penal code but it was relatively unimportant.) Again, the behaviour of Irish landlords has been considered of fundamental importance; ironically, they are now faulted for being too easy-going compared to their Scottish counterparts. Divergent rates of population growth have also been canvassed as an explanation for divergent economic paths; and cultural factors such as literacy and attitudes towards work have likewise been brought in. Clearly, this debate is by no means over but it has already served to re-open the search for the key determinants of Irish economic development. It has also brought forward the question of Ulster's economic divergence from the rest of Ireland. From being the poorest province in Ireland in the seventeenth century, by the end of the eighteenth century she was well on her way to being the most productive. By 1850, Ulster, or at least the north-eastern region with its factories, mills and urban development, was more akin to Clydeside in Scotland that to the rest of Ireland. It is tempting to conclude that the roots of 'Ulster's' separateness are to be found in its divergent economic development from the rest of Ireland.

The question of Ulster's separateness, however, takes us away from peaceful change and brings us back to our general theme of conflict. This is of course appropriate, for the two are intimately linked: violent confrontation and peaceful encounter walk hand in hand in Irish history, and assimilation and rejection are no strangers to one another. This is the subject's fascination and, in the end, it may be that the attempt to reconcile opposites is the central theme of Irish history.

REFERENCES

J.C. Beckett, *The Making of Modern Ireland 1603-1923*, London 1966.

M.I. Finley, 'Colonies — an attempt at a typology', *Transactions of the Royal Historical Society*, 5th Ser. 1976, 167-87.

W. King, *The State of the Protestants of Ireland under the late King James's Government*, Dublin 1691.

A.T.Q. Stewart, *The Narrow Ground: Aspects of Ulster 1609-1969*, London 1977.

L.M. Cullen and T.C. Smout eds, *Comparative Aspects of Scottish and Irish Economic and Social History 1600-1900*, Edinburgh 1978.

FURTHER READING

There are extensive bibliographies covering the period 1534 to 1800 in:

T.W. Moody, F.X. Martin and F.J. Byrne eds, *A New History of Ireland, vol. iii: Early Modern Ireland 1534*-1691, Oxford 1976.

T.W. Moody and W.E. Vaughan eds, *A New History of Ireland vol. iv: Eighteenth-Century Ireland 1691-1800*, Oxford 1986.

More specialised reading may be found in:

T. Bartlett and D. Hayton eds, *Penal Era and Golden Age: essays in Irish History 1690-1800*, Belfast 1979.

C. Brady and R. Gillespie, *Natives and Newcomers: The Making of Irish Colonial Society 1534-1641*, Dublin 1986.

N.P. Canny, *From Reformation to Restoration: Ireland 1534-1660*, Dublin 1987.

S.J. Connolly, *Religion and Society in Nineteenth-Century Ireland*, Dublin 1985.

D. Dickson, *New Foundations: Ireland 1660-1800*, Dublin 1987.

S.G. Ellis, *Tudor Ireland*, London 1986.

A.P.W. Malcomson, *John Foster: The Politics of the Anglo-Irish Ascendancy*, Oxford 1978.

W.E. Vaughan, *Landlord and Tenant in Ireland 1848-1904*, Dublin 1985.

Irish Historical Studies and *Irish Economic and Social History* are the two specialist journals for all serious students of Irish history.

5
EMIGRATION AND
EXILE

Chris Curtin, Riana O'Dwyer, Gearóid Ó Tuathaigh

AT various times during the past century and a half the flood of emigration out of Ireland has been so strong that commentators have speculated that Irish society was, in effect, in danger of haemorrhaging to death. Thus, Engels in the later 1860s reflected that 'if this [emigration] goes on for another thirty years, there will be Irishmen only in America.' The emigration did indeed 'go on', though the pace slackened for a time in the later nineteenth century. Moreover, the dominant emigrant routes also changed in the course of time. By the later 1930s the main route was no longer across the Atlantic, but across the narrow waters to neighbouring Britain. After the establishment of an Irish Free State in 1922, as before, the rate and volume of emigration fluctuated from decade to decade. But by the 1950s the rate of emigration to Britain had become so high that again the chorus of despair was bewailing the fate of 'the vanishing Irish' and asking, in panic, 'Is the Irish race dying?' The temporary halting of emigration during the 1960s and early 1970s gave hope that the days of 'involuntary exile', at least, were now very much in the past. But such hopes were premature; and the several economic crises which have shaken the Irish economy since 1973 (the oil crises of 1973 and 1979, exacerbated by inappropriate domestic responses in Ireland) have also seen emigration figures rise significantly since the late 1970s, with an accompanying rise in public concern (expressed by social commentators, politicians and disappointed parents) at the loss being suffered by Irish society as a result of the resumption of heavy emigration. Those who have spoken positively of emigration, as an opportunity for the now well-educated youth of Ireland to take full advantage of their country's membership of the EEC, remain a minority. Emigration is still widely perceived in Ireland as a vote of no confidence in the capacity of the Irish state — and Irish society — to provide a decent living for its own people at home. This deeply-ingrained attitude can only be understood in the context of Ireland's historical experience of emigration. For, even if we choose to remain calm in the face of the more strident responses to the crisis decades, we cannot ignore the fact that emigration has been a central part of the Irish experience (arguably the single most important and constant fact of

Irish social history) from, at the latest, the 1830s through to the present generation. It may not explain fully every development or every facet of social change in Ireland throughout this long period, but no satisfactory explanation of anything can be undertaken without reference to it. Not surprisingly, it is also a major theme of Irish literature, not only in the works of the major writers but also in the vast repertoire of songs, ballads and stories which comprise the rich store of Irish popular literature and folklore.

Of course, the Irish did not wait until the nineteenth century to begin emigrating. The navigational legends of Brendan may at least remind us of the tradition of Irish seafaring which extends back to our earliest history. Patterns of economic and cultural exchange between Ireland and Britain and continental Europe in the early and medieval centuries indicate quite clearly that Irish travellers and settlers in other lands were quite common. The more notable of the early emigrants were the missionaries who brought Christianity to many parts of Europe during the early middle ages. The fact that for some, at least, of these missionaries, leaving Ireland was perceived as a sad exile, a white martyrdom, a *deoraíocht*, may have established a deep-seated sense of loss in leaving Ireland which was to be shared by countless emigrants in later times. This, indeed, is the view advanced by Kerby Miller in the most comprehensive account so far written of the great Irish diaspora of the nineteenth and early twentieth centuries.

If the departing monks of ancient Ireland saw emigration largely in terms of exile, then we might expect sadness or regret to be the dominant note, also, in the attitudes of those Irishmen (mainly soldiers) who left Ireland at various times between the Flight of the Earls (1607) and the early eighteenth century as a result of the military defeat (and the forfeiture of land and status) of the old Gaelic order, and later of the Catholic aristocracy as a whole, in the course of the seventeenth century wars. These soldiers — and a significant non-military group drawn from landed and wealthy Catholic families — who were granted safe passage or who simply fled the country in the aftermath of the various military campaigns of the seventeenth century, were to become romanticised as the Wild Geese. They and their descendants were later to serve in the armies of France or Austria or other European powers in the wars of the eighteenth century, or else become involved in trade and commerce in continental Europe and in the various colonies of the European powers.

Others who left after defeat were not so lucky in their destination or their professional opportunities. In the mid seventeenth century, after the Cromwellian campaign in Ireland, large numbers of papists were banished to the West Indies, from whence many of them later made their way to the American colonies. For other groups, such as the Quakers in the early eighteenth century and the Presbyterians (overwhelmingly from Ulster and of Scots planter stock), a desire to enjoy full religious liberty was probably an important additional spur to the primary economic motivation which sent them across the Atlantic during the eighteenth and early nineteenth centuries. Indeed, for many of the Scots-Irish Presbyterians of the eighteenth century the journey across the Atlantic to Pennsylvania or the Carolinas was the 'second stage' (even if not originally intended as such) of their migration, since they had moved into Ulster as part of a planter society in successive waves during the preceding hundred years. When this first frontier did not meet their expectations many simply resolved to try again in the new world across the Atlantic. Nor was the Scots' emigration into Ulster the only example of migration and emigration within Britain and Ireland in the early modern period. The several plantations (e.g. in south-east Leinster and in Munster) which, either as planned experiments in colonisation or simply as the result of land forfeiture and redistribution after military conquest, had taken place in Ireland from the mid sixteenth to the late seventeenth century, had brought English Protestant settlers, largely though not exclusively of a landowning class, into Ireland. Again, some of these early planters were to move in time to the second frontier in colonial America.

Traffic between Britain and Ireland was not all one way. Throughout the late medieval and early modern period there were growing numbers of immigrant Irish settling in Britain. By the late eighteenth century there were already sizeable Irish settlements in, for example, London and parts of Lancashire. In sum, what needs to be emphasised is the fact that Irish emigration did not begin with the Famine exodus, or indeed even with the opening of the nineteenth century. The best available evidence indicates this quite clearly. Between 1720 and 1820 it is probable that some 600,000 or so Irish-born emigrants came to the North American colonies and the young Republic. Perhaps 100,000 or more of these were Catholic. Of the 500,000 or so Protestants in this emigrant wave, the majority were Presbyterians, but there was also a sizeable Episcopalian element. Many of these Presbyterians or their descendants — for reasons which had to do with the patterns of church development in colonial society — became Baptist or Methodist in the new world. A portion of the 100,000 or so Catholics also, as it seems, lacking a church structure of their own to absorb them effectively, became part of various Protestant congregations in pre-revolutionary America.

These early waves of Irish immigrants were to be found well dispersed in colonial society, from southern New York state to the Georgia border, with particularly strong settlement in Pennsylvania, the Carolinas, Delaware and Maryland. The past twenty years or so — and especially since the American bicentenary celebrations in 1976 focused attention on pre-revolutionary America — have seen a significant revival of interest in this largely Protestant (and especially Scots-Irish) aspect of Irish emigration to colonial and early republican America. The causes which prompted the emigration (economic difficulties related to crises in textile manufacture or in agricultural conditions among the planter smallholders in Ulster, exacerbated by religious discrimination imposed by the Episcopalian Protestant Ascendancy in Ireland); the predominantly family-group character of the migration (in contrast to later patterns of migration); the areas of settlement and the rate of assimilation; all of these aspects are now reasonably well-documented. So also is the fact that the term Scots-Irish as a description of this largely Ulster and north-midlands Presbyterian immigrant community become increasingly common in the early nineteenth century, as the influx of poorer Irish Catholic emigrants began to gather momentum, and as the earlier settlers sought (by describing themselves as Scots-Irish) in Lawrence McCaffrey's phrase 'to avoid the penalties of anti-Irish American prejudice'.

It was, of course, the deteriorating economic condition of a growing number of the Irish rural poor — labourers, cottiers and small farmers — in the decades after Waterloo which provided the impetus for the rising tide of Catholic Irish emigration, not only across the Atlantic but also across the Irish Sea to Britain and, at a much lower rate, to Australia). The fact that by the mid 1840s perhaps a third of the population of over $8\frac{1}{2}$ million were locked into a subsistence economy, depending for their diet almost exclusively on a vulnerable potato crop, and that off-land employment (apart from an industrialising enclave in the north-east) was unable to absorb the population increase, all pointed towards a gathering crisis. That crisis came with the Great Famine of 1845-51. Where pre-Famine emigration had been a rising tide, the Famine exodus was a tidal wave, with (it is estimated) perhaps as many as $2\frac{1}{2}$ million emigrating in the decade 1846-56. Moreover, while the one million or so Irish emigrants who left between 1815 and 1845 included an increasing proportion of the poorer, unskilled rural labourers and cottiers, there was still some measure of calculation and prudential planning involved for most of those who went on the longer journey (to America or Canada) before the Famine. But the trauma of the Great Famine seems to have broken, for a time, the bonds of calculation and reason, and produced a mood of panic which drove the destitute and the most ill-prepared into precipitate flight from the stricken land in the crisis years of 1846-52. The harrowing journey of the destitute of these years left an indelible mark not only on the minds of those who endured it, but on the collective memory of their descendants wherever they settled: the notorious coffin-ships on which thousands died en route to Quebec or, after 1848 as the Canadians raised port taxes to stem the inflow of vessels carrying the poor and disease-stricken Famine Irish, to the American ports; the hostile reception which often greeted the gaunt survivors who made it (as countless thousands did) to the further shore, in the St Lawrence ports, in Boston, New York or Philadelphia.

Emigration in the post-Famine decades, though not as heavy in absolute numbers as the great haemorrhage of the Famine and immediate post-Famine years, continued high as a proportion of a steadily declining Irish population. In all, probably as many as four million emigrated from Ireland between the late 1850s and 1914, bringing to over eight million the total number of emigrants estimated for the period 1800-1921. The population of Ireland fell from c.6.6 million in 1851 to 4.4 million in 1911, the loss being attributable overwhelmingly to emigration. Moreover, in periods of heavy emigration (as during the early 1880s) the increase in the rate of emigration was bound to have severe consequences for the ever-declining population at home. In fact, no other European nation saw as high a percentage of its population leave to emigrate overseas during the nineteenth century as Ireland did.

Several salient aspects of this huge emigration deserve notice. Firstly, Irish emigration was unusual in European terms for the high percentage of single women included in the emigrant stream: as high as 40 per cent in the pre-Famine decades, at no time thereafter far from 50 per cent, and by the end of the nineteenth century higher than 50 per cent. Secondly, the Irish who emigrated over long distances, to North America, Australia or New Zealand, tended to stay there; there is a lower rate of 'return' for the Irish immigrants than for most other European ethnic communities. In terms of religion, the large majority of the post-Famine Irish emigrants — perhaps around 85 per cent — were Catholic. Again, the Irish emigrants, from the 1830s at the latest, were overwhelmingly young (18-35 years) and single. The majority — probably as many as three out of four during the period 1860-1920 — were of rural background, with a relatively low level of skills or with no skills at all other than their willingness to work hard. That is to say, most of the men were unskilled labourers when they arrived in their new country, while the occupation to which the majority of the single Irish females aspired or gravitated was that of domestic servant. These generalisations, of course, need to be qualified. For example, the emigrants from rural Connacht and Munster were more likely to be unskilled labourers than those of Leinster or Ulster, from which areas a lighter share of the post-Famine emigrant stream included a higher quota of farmers or townsmen with some artisan skills. Again, emigrants to Australia, probably due to more careful screening of prospective emigrants and more careful consideration of the decision to go, seem to have been better equipped (whether in skills or simply in general attitudes and habits of industry) than the poorer elements who headed for the cities of Britain and America. It must be remembered, of course, that, unlike the emigration to Britain or America, a large proportion of the Irish going south to Australia (and New Zealand) were sponsored emigrants, their passage being paid by some agency, whether private or public. As for motivation in general, the dominant motivation for most emigrants was undoubtedly economic; the desire 'to do better', to improve one's prospects and one's standard of living. A secondary factor, in many cases, was a frustration with and ultimately a rejection of the monotonous torpor of Irish social life, which emigrants contrasted with their perceptions (fuelled by immigrant letters) of the good life in America or elsewhere.

During the period 1800-1921 probably as many as 60 per cent of all Irish emigrants went to the United States. Canada probably took between 10 and 12 per cent during the same period, while Australia accounted for less than 5 per cent of total Irish emigration during the nineteenth century. Emigration to Britain is notoriously difficult to estimate. In the first instance, since Ireland and Britain were, in fact, joined together as the United Kingdom after 1800, movement between the two countries wasn't, in one sense, emigration at all. Furthermore, up to the 1860s there was a sizable traffic in seasonal migration between Ireland and the agricultural districts of England and Scotland. But the figures suggest that in 1861, when the number of Irish-born residents reached its peak, there were around 800,000 Irish immigrants in Britain, and as late as 1901 it was still as high as 632,000.

Now, while these figures are important they only tell us part of the story. We must also look at the relative 'weight' of the immigrant Irish in their new societies if we wish to assess their influence with any degree of precision. Thus, for example, when considering the heavy Irish emigration to America we must remember that, over the nineteenth century as a whole, the Irish constituted just over 10 per cent of the total inflow of emigrants to the United States. From the late 1850s the Irish emigration to America was outpaced by German emigration; by the 1880s it was still about 14 per cent of total American emigration, but by the early years of the twentieth century it had fallen to below 4 per cent. On the other hand, the much smaller number of Irish who emigrated to the southern dominions were, in relative numbers, a highly significant element in their new society. The Irish, for example, accounted for almost a quarter of all emigrants to Australia during the nineteenth century.

Of course, these figures, which only concern Irish-born

immigrants, considerably underestimate the 'effective' Irish immigrant communities, comprising more than one generation and, in the early stages of settlement, often heavily concentrated in particular areas or localities. On this latter point it is worth remembering that, contrary to what is widely accepted, there were interesting variations in the patterns of Irish immigrant settlement overseas. Thus, for example, whereas the Irish emigrants to nineteenth and twentieth century Britain became overwhelmingly urban immigrants, the evidence from nineteenth-century Canada suggests that a sizable portion of them (among the one-third Catholics as well as among the two-third Protestants who comprised the Irish emigration stream to western Canada) became well-adjusted and successful rural dwellers. Again, the Australian evidence suggests that, allowing for some regional variations, a reasonably even spread of settlement took place across the country, and between city and country. So far as the United States is concerned there were undoubtedly very heavy settlements of immigrant Irish in the cities of the industrial heartland of America (from the north-east to the Great Lakes cities); and the story of these emigrants is perhaps the most richly documented of all aspects of the Irish emigrant experience. But the Irish were also in the van of the great drives southwestward and westward to the cities of the Pacific coast, especially California. The Irish were mobile and responsive to the regional changes in the growth-path of American economic development. Moreover, it has been suggested that a larger number of Irish immigrants settled in smaller towns or in rural areas across the country than historians have hitherto suspected. Finally, there were smaller communities of Irish immigrants in, for example, Argentina and other parts of South America. Their story is of considerable intrinsic interest, but their numbers make them rather marginal to the main narrative of the Irish diaspora of the past century and a half.

In geographical terms there are aspects of the Irish emigrant routes which merit closer attention. Up to the 1830s, at least, Ulster and the north midlands provided a disproportionately high share of the Irish emigrants. The Famine exodus was widely drawn, but Ulster was below average in its contribution. In the post-Famine decades emigration was lighter from the north-east and south-east than from other regions, though it seems that the western periphery was mainly sending its emigrants to Britain from the 1850s to the 1870s. However, by the final decades of the century the province of Connacht and the other counties of the Atlantic seaboard were providing a disproportionately large part even of the trans-Atlantic emigration. Again it has been noted by several commentators that while emigrants from Connacht and the Atlantic counties were more likely to be heading for the American ports by the late nineteenth century, Ulster and the north midlands emigrants (though of smaller volume than the Connacht outflow) were still strongly inclined towards Canada. More local links have also been observed, such as, for example, between Clare and Australia, Waterford and Newfoundland, and between several Irish counties and various American cities.

Given the 'chain' migration of young emigrants from Ireland, the concentrations of Irish from particular areas at home in particular localities in their 'new world' are not surprising. The letter home, containing vital information and often, even more vital, the fare; the inclination of newly-arrived emigrants to seek out relatives and friends in 'familiar' surroundings (the church, the club or pub where fellow-countrymen congregated); the networking through which employment could be secured: all of these features of Irish immigrant settlement in the cities tended to produce such 'clustering' of immigrants in particular neighbourhoods in their new society. The fact that in the Famine and immediate post-Famine flood, the poor and unhealthy formed a considerable part of these 'clusters' led to the establishment of Irish ghettos which became bywords for slum living in some of the major cities of Britain and America, with all the major social and health problems characteristic of the urban slum. Some of these Irish ghettos lasted several generations. But by the late nineteenth and early twentieth century a combination of urban renewal schemes, upward social mobility among the children and grandchildren of immigrants (generally leading to a movement out from the ghetto to more 'desirable' neighbourhoods), and the arrival of later waves of new immigrants to take the place of the Irish at the bottom of the social and occupational ladder, inexorably began to disperse the main urban ghettos of the Irish on both sides of the Atlantic.

So far as upward social mobility is concerned, it seems that while such mobility did indeed occur among Irish-born immigrants in America (who showed a strong desire, for example, to become home-owners), the Irish-born were less impressive in this regard than some other immigrant groups, notably the Germans or the Jews. But the children and grandchildren of immigrants undoubtedly moved upward on the social ladder, especially those who availed of the growing network of educational facilities (both public and church-run) from the 1850s onwards. In Britain, also, there is clear evidence of some upward social mobility among the descendants of Irish immigrants in the later nineteenth and early twentieth century, though it is difficult to assess whether the immigrants did better or worse in this regard than those of the host population drawn from within the same social class.

Whatever about social mobility there is no denying the real, physical mobility which was a feature of the Irish immigrant experience in the dynamic, developing economies to which they emigrated. For example, it has been estimated that about a third of the

Irish immigrants in working-class neighbourhoods of American cities in the mid nineteenth century moved house at least once in the ten year inter-censal period. More often than not those who moved out from the east coast urban ghettos of America to the mid and far west were among the more ambitious, resourceful and enterprising; while the more recently-arrived poorer Irish immigrants of the later nineteenth century were more likely to cling to the familiar surroundings of the ghetto, thereby prolonging its life. A further consequence of the high mobility of Irish labour — following a railroad or in search of new frontiers of economic opportunity — was the high incidence of female heads-of-household, many of whom took in lodgers or did washing or piece-work, sewing or knitting at home, in order to raise their families while their menfolk were absent for long intervals or indeed permanently. Yet, despite these various kinds of mobility — social as well as physical — the Irish immigrants were an exceptionally endogamous group right into the early twentieth century. This is as true of the immigrants in Britain as of those in America.

Undoubtedly one of the main factors which caused the Irish immigrant poor to cling together was the intense hostility which they encountered — especially in the desperate middle decades of the century — from many of the respectable 'natives' (first colonists, that is) of the host society. At various times, in various places, and with varying degrees of intensity, anti-Irish or anti-Catholic prejudices (with, frequently, the one re-enforcing the other) forced the immigrant Catholic Irish back on their own resources. Notwithstanding their poverty and the multiple problems of ill-health and social deprivation that derive from poverty, these resources were not negligible; the profile of the newly-arrived Irish immigrant poor is not exclusively a black chronicle of handicaps. They were, compared to other immigrant peoples, already highly literate in the English language; by 1850 over 70 per cent claimed literacy and by 1910 this figure had gone up to over 95 per cent. Making due allowance for exaggeration and error, this high level of literacy gave the Irish a clear advantage over later waves of European emigrants to America. Literacy in English was less a comparative advantage than a prerequisite in Britain and in Australia-New Zealand, where non English-speaking immigrants were not a major part of the colonial settlements of the nineteenth century.

Literacy in English in itself, of course, was no shield against those who, very often, enlisted peculiarities of dialect and accent as part of the armoury of anti-Irish prejudice. These prejudices (expressed in cartoons, in discriminatory practices in work and lodgings, and occasionally in more overtly violent ways) were probably at their most intense in the middle decades of the nineteenth century. By the end of

68

the century they had clearly begun to weaken on both sides of the Atlantic, as the descendants of Irish immigrants became more successful and more assimilated into the new societies (and as new groups of immigrants replaced the Irish at the bottom of the pile and took the brunt of anti-immigrant prejudice). That anti-Irish prejudices lasted so long was due to two main aspects of Irish culture which the emigrants took with them, and which many of them sought to transplant — not without some mutations — in their new country. These were their religion and their politics.

Religious and political convictions (notably opposition to Anglican privilege) had, of course, already been an important aspect of the contribution made by Ulster Presbyterians and their descendants to colonial and early republican America. But religious tensions became especially acute as the dominant Protestantism of the American republic and of mid-Victorian Britain felt increasingly threatened by the huge influx of Catholic Irish (followed by other immigrant European Catholics) from the 1840s onwards. Throughout the middle and late Victorian decades a strong strain of popular anti-Catholicism was current in both American and British society, sustained in both cases by the dominant foundation myths of Protestant liberty strongly entrenched in the national story of both societies. This current of anti-Catholicism was easily stirred into something more turbulent at times of particular excitement. The heavy influx of poor Catholic Irish; the more insistent claims to authority of a besieged Papacy under Pius IX; the irregular but excited response of Protestant evangelicalism; these were some of the factors which triggered public displays of virulent anti-Catholicism among sections of society in America and Britain. The Irish were the first major wave of Catholic immigrants in both societies, and the first wave usually takes the brunt of the enemy fire and suffers casualties. In time this anti-Catholicism abated, though the experience of Al Smith in America in the 1920s should remind us how slowly this occurred. But the Irish could scarcely escape such anti-Catholic prejudices as were current throughout English-speaking countries. Whether in numbers or power (or both) the Irish dominated the Catholic Church in these countries. As late as 1900 (notwithstanding the heavy influx of German, Polish, Italian and other immigrant Catholics) the Irish still accounted for more than 60 per cent of the American hierarchy and for a disproportionately high percentage of the clergy. Likewise in Australia, the Catholic Church of the later nineteenth century was largely an Irish immigrant creation. In Britain also, the Catholic numbers of the later nineteenth century were heavily Irish, though here the Irish-born clergy never succeeded in taking the commanding heights of the hierarchies of England and Wales and Scotland, and Irish names only appear among the British hierarchy in later generations and then only after a considerable measure of cultural assimilation had taken place.

In the case of Irish Catholic immigrants their Catholicism was not only inextricably bound up with their ethnicity, but from the second quarter of the nineteenth century their sense of 'peoplehood' was also highly politicised. That is to say, from O'Connell's popular politics the Irish masses had learnt to see themselves as being capable of formulating a political demand and of mobilising themselves politically to achieve it. The 'cause' which the more politically active Irish immigrants espoused was the Irish nationalist cause at home; that is to say, the demand for an Irish national state enjoying some measure or form of political sovereignty. Immigrant support meant, in the first instance, setting up branches or support organisations for whatever nationalist movements happened to be current in Ireland from time to time (Fenian republicanism, Home Rule, and later Sinn Féin). But inevitably these Irish nationalists 'in absentia', as it were, as well as maintaining their commitment and loyalty to 'the old country', had to relate their political activity to their circumstances in the new society. The Irish nationalism of the immigrants in America or Britain or even Australia could never be simply a direct transplant of what was currently flourishing at home. Indeed, it has been persuasively argued by Thomas N. Brown that the intensity of Irish-American commitment to the Irish nationalist cause (and its partiality to the more extreme versions) was as much a defiant gesture of solidarity among the suspicious immigrants towards the natives who despised them in their new country as an unquenchable thirst for freedom for their fellow-countrymen at home.

But the two concerns were related in numerous and subtle ways. In particular, Irish immigrants throughout the English-speaking world, where the older dominant culture was rooted in British Protestant traditions, felt that the creation of an independent Irish state would greatly enhance their own standing, lift their pride, and bring an accretion of respect and dignity to them in their new country. They were clearly the children of a European mother-country; they would feel better (and be better regarded) if that mother-country were also a free and independent state. Thus, their commitment to the cause of Irish freedom had, in part at least, a life of its own, independent of circumstances in Ireland. This led to regular misunderstandings, recriminations and splits between Irish nationalist leaders at home and various Irish nationalist organisations among immigrants, especially but by no means exclusively in the United States. While ultimate objectives might be shared, there was ample scope for disagreement on strategies and methods, timing and tactics, resources and responsibilities. Distances — increasingly cultural as well as physical — between the Irish at home and those abroad, plus

70

the play of strong personalities on this complex machinery of trans-oceanic political agitation, all combined to place considerable strains on the cohesiveness of 'home' Irish and 'hyphenated' Irish nationalism in the decades between the Famine and 1922.

The involvement of Irish immigrants in Irish nationalist 'agitation' in America or Britain or elsewhere was inevitably a matter of controversy, and caused many difficulties for the immigrants themselves. In America the attempts of the Irish to make their presence (and their numbers) felt in domestic American politics, and to make 'the Irish question' an issue in American foreign as well as domestic politics, caused resentment among many Americans. As late as 1919 Woodrow Wilson (who had, admittedly, been under severe Irish pressure in the fateful years after 1914) spoke highly of the 'Irishman whose heart crossed the Atlantic with him, unlike some Americans, who needed hyphens in their names, because only part of them had come over.' But the Irish could and did reply that they were fully committed to the American ideals of liberty and freedom (freedom from colonial rule, freedom of conscience); that they had been ardent democrats since the early Jacksonian days; and that, in stating the case for their homeland, they were only exercising their democratic rights in lobbying American political leaders. Moreover, the American Civil War gave thousands of Catholic immigrant Irish a chance to demonstrate their full commitment to the Republic by joining the army. Again, during the 1914-18 war thousands of Irish immigrants and their descendants joined the armed forces, notwithstanding the activities of Irish nationalist lobby groups in America — whether calling on America to avoid entanglement in the war as Britain's ally or later protesting at the British response to the 1916 Rising in Ireland.

In Britain and Australia and the other dominions, Irish immigrant political activity in the cause of 'Irish freedom' also caused controversy and resentment in the seventy or so years before 1922. Here, however, within an imperial/dominion context, Gladstone's conversion to the cause of Irish Home Rule in 1886 was a vital event. It made 'respectable' in British domestic and dominion politics at least a version of Irish nationalism; it enabled the Irish immigrants in the dominions to claim that they only sought for their homeland that which the dominions had very properly sought for themselves. This, of course, is not to suggest that hostility to the insertion of 'Irish issues' into the domestic politics of other dominion countries had altogether disappeared by the early twentieth century. The more hard-line advocates of Irish republican separatism continued to arouse suspicion and hostility both for the substance of their demands and, perhaps more importantly, for the methods which they adopted (frequently resorting to violence) in making these demands. But the political settlements of 1920-22 not only brought to an end a chapter in Anglo-Irish relations, they also saw the end of a chapter in Irish 'nationalist' political agitation among Irish expatriates in other lands. The immigrants and their descendants now concentrated exclusively on the political life of their land of residence, leaving the new post-1922 Ireland to get on with her own life. Apart from sporadic activity among Irish expatriates in Britain (relating to the partition of Ireland) the 'Irish question' ceased to be a major concern in the political life of Irish immigrants and their descendants until the outbreak of the conflict in Northern Ireland after 1969 revived interest, and led to the renewed involvement of expatriate Irish in events in the old country.

Apart from their political objectives, it is worth recording that some of the political methods — call it the political style, if you will — of the immigrant Irish also attracted hostility, especially in America. The O'Connellite legacy — the solidarity of a barely literate peasantry behind a strong 'community' leader, and the ruthless use of weight of numbers — was deemed responsible for the development of a number of highly successful Irish political 'machines' (presided over by Irish political 'bosses') in urban America. These machines — based on a tight and responsive network of communications and control from the precinct level to city hall — gave the Irish political control of several American cities in the later decades of the nineteenth century. This Irish political power in urban America (symbolised in popular legend by Tammany Hall) was undoubtedly based on careful attention to patronage, contracts and the use of political power to favour those whose support had helped in the winning of that power. There was undoubtedly more than a whiff of venality and corruption in some of the smoke-filled backrooms. But at no stage was this the whole story of Irish-American urban politics. The Irish, largely as Democrats in American party politics, proved remarkably adept at building coalitions of interest among different ethnic and social groups in urban society. They produced their political rebels as well as their machine bosses; they supplied urban reformers as well as shrewd fixers. What David Doyle has written of ethno-religious politics in America also holds good for urban 'boss' politics: namely, that while the American-Irish neither 'instigated nor created [it].... their presence intensified it, and they in turn welcomed it as a natural and traditional way of seeing and doing things.'

Finally, in considering the significance of emigration in the decades before the establishment of an Irish State in 1922, let us turn to the vexed question of the economic and social *compte rendu* of emigration for both the donor and receiving societies. So far as the host societies are concerned it is clear that, whatever the social problems the poorer Irish of the mid century brought with them, the Irish immigrants as a whole were a dynamic part of a labour force (highly mobile at crucial times and in vital occupations) essential to the rapid economic development of the expanding 'new' countries of America and Australia and also for the intense industrialisation of nineteenth-century Britain. Given the class to which most of the immigrants belonged, it is not surprising to find that they contributed more than their share of leaders to the labour and trade union movement in America, Australia and Britain. But, over time, the Irish immigrants also added an impressive share of names to the roll-call of entre-preneurs and successful businessmen in the 'new world'.

So far as the impact of emigration on nineteenth-century Irish society is concerned, there are differing views among commentators. The loss of a disproportionate part of the 18-35 age group is often cited as a big factor in explaining the increasing social conservatism of Ireland in the decades after 1850; the argument, in effect, is that the more ambitious people, the potential constituency of challenge and dissent within the society, simply left it in their thousands. To this is usually added the further claim that emigration of the young was the principal cause of that monotony and torpor in Irish social life which most commentators, foreign visitors as well as priests and social activists at home, noted in the later nineteenth century, and which the several new voluntary organisations (such as the GAA and the Gaelic League) sought to dispel. Whatever about such qualitative assess-ments, it is incontestable that the class structure of rural Ireland was changed significantly by the Famine and post-Famine emigration. As Oliver MacDonagh has reminded us, whereas in pre-Famine Ireland the landless (or near landless) classes of cottier and labourer out-numbered the independent farmers by about four to one, by the year 1900 the cottiers had virtually disappeared, there were more farmers than labourers, and the number of labourers was still in decline.

In more strictly economic terms, it is argued that the loss of a large segment of the more productive 18-35 age-group was potentially a significant economic loss; that it left an excessively high 'dependent' population of the old and the very young in Ireland; that it reduced the aggregate pool of enterprise available to Irish society; and that it cer-tainly reduced the size of the domestic market for goods and services. On the other hand the inflow of emigrants' remittances (perhaps as high as one to two per cent of Irish national income in the 1880s) undoubtedly contributed to maintaining or raising the living standards of those who remained at home (perhaps enabling many families to continue living on holdings too small or too poor to provide an acceptable living for a family). By reducing the labour pool emigration probably contributed to the improvement in wages for those who remained behind. But whatever one's views on the balance of these arguments, it is hard not to agree with Cormac Ó Gráda's verdict that nineteenth-century Irish emigration 'must be seen as

73

inevitable . . . a by-product of the Industrial Revolution', related to the location of the raw materials of early industrialisation. For Ó Gráda, as for others, the emigration option was a fortunate one for labour surplus economies such as Ireland in the last century, facilitating the adjustment of labour supply to demand in ways which many labour surplus economies of the Third World in the later twentieth century must surely envy. This view may now seem sensible, with the benefit of hindsight. But for generations of Irish nationalists (and indeed social reformers such as Horace Plunkett who were not nationalists at all), emigration on the scale experienced by Ireland in the period 1845-1922 was a sign of failure and a matter for indignation or shame. For nationalist writers, in particular, it was a function of Ireland's general subjugation and exploitation 'under British rule'. An independent Irish state, it was claimed, would not tolerate such a haemorrhage out of the country. Its primary social task would be the ending of emigration. With the political settlements of 1920-22, the partition of the island in 1920 and the creation of the Irish Free State in 1922, it now remained to be seen whether these nationalist claims had substance in them.

EMIGRATION SINCE THE FOUNDATION OF THE IRISH STATES

Although at a much reduced rate, emigration continued to exact its toll on Ireland's population after partition. Its impact on the twenty-six counties was particularly striking. Each year between 1926 and 1936 close to 17,000 persons emigrated and the numbers rose to 19,000 in 1936-46, 24,000 in 1946-51 and 42,000 in 1956-61. The level of emigration reduced considerably in the 1960s and for the first time in the state's history, in the intercensal period 1971-9, a net inflow of over 100,000 persons was recorded. This positive development was of short duration, however, and net outflow population increased from 1,000 persons in 1981-2 to 31,000 persons in 1985-6 (see Table 2).

Emigration from Northern Ireland was considerably less than that from the twenty-six counties until the 1960s when the rates in the two states converged. In the 1970s emigration rates from Northern Ireland were actually higher than those from the twenty-six counties. Indeed at a time when the latter was experiencing a net inflow of population, Northern Ireland's population was falling for the first time, as a result of high emigration. It should be noted that these figures do not take into account the full impact of seasonal migration which continued to be numerically, socially and economically important in a number of northern and western counties, particularly Mayo and Donegal, until the 1960s.

Table 2. Estimated Net Migration, 1926–1986, Twenty-Six Counties.

Intercensal Period	Net Migration	Per 1,000 population
1926–1936	166,751	5.6
1936–1946	187,111	6.3
1946–1951	119,568	8.2
1951–1956	212,003	14.8
1961–1966	80,605	5.7
1966–1971	53,906	3.7
1971–1979	+108,934	+4.3
1979–1981	5,045	0.7
1981–1986	75,000	4.3

Source: Census of Population

If the Irish emigration rate has fluctuated so also has the popularity of the emigrant's destination. In the period 1926–36 overseas destinations (countries outside Europe; mainly the United States but also Canada, Australia and New Zealand) comprised 55 per cent of total net emigration. Between 1936 and 1946 overseas emigration was practically non-existent while between 1946 and 1951 it accounted for only 16 per cent of total emigration. By the 1950s practically all emigration was to Great Britain and this contrasted with the earlier experience when the vast majority of emigrants went to the United States. As a consequence of this change the numbers of Irish-born persons living in the United States decreased from 1,037,000 in 1921 to 678,000 in 1951. In this same period the numbers of Irish-born in Great Britain increased from 524,000 to 720,000. Thus by the 1950s there were more Irish-born persons in Great Britain than in the United States, whereas sixty years previously the number in Great Britain had been only about one-third of those in the United States. The numbers of Irish-born in Australia and to a lesser extent in Canada also declined between the 1920s and the 1950s. Most of the inflow of population to the twenty-six counties in the 1970s was from Great Britain. While we lack firm information on the current wave of emigration there is little doubt that the United States has resumed its former popularity. There were for example over 200,000 Irish applications for the so-called Donnelly visas in 1986 and estimates of illegal Irish workers in the United States vary between 100,000 and 200,000.

While Irish emigrants were mainly from rural areas, they tended to seek out and settle in larger urban centres in the host country. The 1940 United States census revealed that 90 per cent of emigrants born in the twenty-six counties were living in urban areas and that over half of these were living in the cities of New York, Chicago,

Boston, Philadelphia and San Francisco. A similar picture emerges from the 1951 British census which showed that over one-third of Irish emigrants in England and Wales were living in the Greater London area and that in Scotland two-fifths of Irish emigrants were living in Glasgow. While many Irish in the United States and Great Britain climbed up the social hierarchy, most new emigrants' first experience of work was in low skill occupations. In the absence of hard occupational data, travel permits issued in the twenty-six counties between 1939 and 1952 provide some clues, if only to the aspirations of future emigrants. These show that 37 per cent of males gave unskilled labourer as their intended occupation while 54 per cent of females intended to go into domestic service or housework. Although the most recent group of Irish emigrants have an abundance of skills and educational credentials, some find employment in jobs which do not demand much in the way of formal qualifications and many find it very difficult to find any work at all. Indeed, recent surveys of young Irish people in London suggest that as many as four out of every five were unemployed. Many of the new-wave emigrants to the United States also leave themselves open to exploitation because of their illegal status, but some have been quite resourceful in acquiring the coveted social security number. While the Irish were gradually assimilated into the mainstream culture of their host country, many who congregated into such places as Camden Town and Cricklewood in London or Queens and the Bronx in New York lived out their lives in an almost totally Irish environment. They were in the new society but not of it.

Residual anti-Irish prejudices, though greatly diminished from their nineteenth-century virulence, remained a problem for the immigrant Irish in Britain. Elsewhere they had almost entirely disappeared, and the election of John F. Kennedy as President of the United States may be considered the final laying to rest of anti-Irish prejudice in America. In Britain, however, the continuing impact of partition on Anglo-Irish relations, and especially the anti-partitionist activities of several Irish immigrant groups, were sources of potential friction between Irish immigrants and many of the host population. When such anti-partitionist activity took violent form — as with the IRA bombing campaigns in Britain during the Second World War and again since the outbreak of the latest phase of violence in Northern Ireland in 1969 — anti-Irish attitudes, often rooted in old prejudices, can and have become a major problem for Irish immigrants in Britain. However, such prejudices and friction encountered by the immigrant Irish in recent decades may be deemed of little consequence when compared to the tensions and prejudices based on colour which have been encountered by later waves of immigrants in Britain.

From the 1920s to the 1950s the majority of Irish emigrants continued to be from rural areas; children of agricultural labourers and small farmers being particularly numerous in the outflow. Three out of every four males who received travel permits between 1939 and 1952 gave their last occupation as that of unskilled labourer, builder's labourer or agricultural worker while more than half the females were described as domestic servants. This pattern had changed considerably by the 1980s and the new wave of Irish emigrants includes a high proportion of skilled persons. While there is little difference in the overall emigration figures for males and females, significant gender differences do emerge between intercensal periods. Males exceed females in the emigration figures between 1936 and 1946, mainly because during the Second World War the British government placed legal restraints on the number of women it was prepared to accept. The end of the war brought the removal of restrictions and the resulting increase in the level of female emigration was such as to cancel the effect of the decline in the number of male emigrants. A majority of the 1981-6 emigrants were male. A remarkable characteristic of twentieth-century Irish emigration is its youthful composition. Information from the travel permit records shows that for the years 1943 to 1951 over half the males and over two-thirds of the females were under twenty-five years. Indeed two out of every five females were aged between sixteen and nineteen years. These records also show that the average age of the applicants continued to decline. This youthful pattern continues to be evident in the present generation of emigrants. Before the 1980s the highest rates of net emigration were from the poorer western counties such as Kerry, Mayo, Donegal, Leitrim, Galway and Clare. This pattern has changed somewhat in recent times and the new emigrants are drawn from all parts of the country with the largest single group coming from Dublin.

Irish emigration since partition cannot be explained by reference to one single cause. Rather a set of interrelated factors, economic, social cultural and political are involved. Again emigration cannot be explained by reference to internal 'push' factors alone; external 'pull' factors such as the level of industrial activity or demand for labour, war or restrictions on entry are also of great importance.

Irish emigrants continued to be strongly motivated both by a desire to find employment and to improve their standard of living. Up to 1960 most emigration was from rural areas where there was little local industry or prospect of off-farm employment. In these areas men and women were forced to leave in search of employment. By so doing they improved the conditions of those who remained at home by reducing pressure on resources and thereby maintaining or even increasing income per head. In addition many of the families of those who emigrated had their incomes increased by emigrant remittances.

77

In farming households emigration was also part of the process of generational renewal, the dispersal of non-inheriting children being a necessary precursor to the marriage of the nominated heir. Indeed one of the most common uses of the 'dowry' was to assist the process of emigration. Higher emigration rates among small farmers in the 1950s were in no small measure due to the widening gap in their way of life, as they persisted with traditional techniques, compared to that of larger farmers who adopted new ones. Because they could not adopt the new farming methods without acquiring additional land, and because there was none available, giving up agriculture altogether was the only way open to them to improve their standard of living. Moreover, the successful adoption of labour-saving techniques on the larger farms reduced the need for farm labourers who now found that they could only maintain or improve their standard of living through emigration. As opportunities for employment improved dramatically in the twenty-six counties during the 1960s and 1970s, emigration gave way to an inflow of people principally from Great Britain, many of whom had made their money and now had the skills and resources to establish their own businesses. Many were attracted by the prospect of bringing up their families in Ireland. Unlike the typical emigrant many of those who returned did so in family groups. The upsurge in emigration in the 1980s has coincided with record unemployment levels at home and the conviction that employment opportunities exist abroad, particularly in the United States.

Emigration from rural areas in the past was certainly encouraged by the absence of such basic social amenities as water or electricity and by what was for many young people a dull, monotonous and conservative life style. Measured against these criteria urban life with its organised entertainment and the ready availability of a range of recreational facilities appeared all the more attractive. Many males left to avoid a lifetime of subservience to their father while emigration for females represented both the prospect of improved personal status and marriage opportunities. Emigration had also generated a momentum of its own, having become a path to be followed as a matter of course, facilitated by kinship and friendship connections. Emigrants were not venturing so much into the unknown but rather going to places where their friends and relations awaited them. Many households in the West of Ireland had more affinity with and knowledge of New York, Boston, London or Glasgow than Dublin. The existence of opportunities was continuously confirmed by 'successful' returned emigrants, glowing accounts in letters and more recently by television programmes.

Religious differences have both affected and are reflected in emigration patterns in post-partition Ireland. The population of the twenty-six counties would actually have increased between 1926 and

1946 had it not been for a 24 per cent decrease in the Protestant population. In this period emigration of entire families was more common among Protestants than Catholics. Protestant emigration was also unusual in that it came equally from urban and rural areas. By contrast, in Northern Ireland Catholics have a much greater tendency to emigrate than Protestants. For example between 1951 and 1961 Catholic males were twice as likely and Catholic females three times as likely to emigrate as their Protestant counterparts. High rates of emigration from Northern Ireland in the early 1970s reflect both severe economic problems and heightening sectarian tensions. One of the implications of these higher emigration rates is that Catholics, despite their greater fertility, are unlikely to alter their minority status in Northern Ireland.

While the consequences of emigration over the past sixty-five years are explored in some detail in Chapters 10 and 12 a few general points can be made here. It has been the dominant factor in Irish demography affecting most aspects of population structure and composition. Its economic implications are both numerous and complex. For example, it has siphoned off labour which the Irish economy could not absorb but at the same time it has removed many of the brightest and most enterprising young people who might have developed Irish resources to a level where more people could be employed. Officially the 'curse' of emigration was condemned again and again; unofficially it may have been welcomed by many of those who remained behind in so far as it supported their standard of living. This is not to understate the emotional tragedy it represented for all involved. Emigration has also played an important rôle in ensuring that Ireland remained a conservative and backward looking society. It acted as a safety valve for the social tensions that might have proved a basis for social change. It was in many ways the Irish solution to a universal problem.

IRISH WRITERS AND THE THEME OF EMIGRATION

A distinction must be drawn at the outset between the biographical and the literary relationship of writers to the theme of emigration. Many writers have found it necessary to leave Ireland, some from economic and some from intellectual necessity. The difficulty of making a living from writing in Ireland is alleviated by spending time teaching and lecturing abroad. This frequently allows writers, especially in recent years, to alternate periods of earning away from home with periods of writing in Ireland. For other writers, however, the restrictions on freedom of expression, especially when censorship was very strict from the 1920s to the 1950s, created an atmosphere in which they could neither live nor write. Many of these, most notably

Joyce, O'Casey and Beckett, made their homes permanently abroad, in a state of self-imposed exile, which has for many people become synonymous with the courageous exploration in literature of the reality of Irish society.

The thematic expression of exile, however, reveals a more complex relationship between writers and Ireland than the simple one of stay and conform or leave and be free. It is possible to discern four phases of relationship to Ireland, within the context of the exile theme. First, there is the exploration of Irish identity, the search for a sense of community and continuity frequently expressed as a celebration of the place-names and landscape of Ireland, what Seamus Heaney has called the 'Sense of Place'. Second, there emerges in other writers a contrary theme of alienation and separation, a breakdown of the relationship between the community and those who do not subscribe to its values or who reject them. In this group the writing focuses on the factors that force individuals into positions of isolation, from which, in the absence of concessions on the part of the community, there is no escape but departure. Third, there is the writing done from the vantage point of distance by writers who have consciously exiled themselves from Ireland in an effort to achieve objectivity and artistic integrity. In this category also are novels, plays and poems which deal with the experience of exile, studying the effects of separation on those who have had to leave. Last, there is the increasingly significant topic of return, reflected both in the biographies and the themes of writers who complete the circle by making a new start in the Ireland which they rejected or which rejected them. In all of these phases the departure and return may sometimes occur in the context of internal exile, as for example that of Patrick Kavanagh from Monaghan to Dublin.

During the Irish Literary Revival the development of a sense of intrinsic Irishness was frequently associated with the exploration of the local, of the customs, folklore and linguistic idiosyncracies of the townlands and villages of rural Ireland. A value was restored to a way of life which had tended to be scorned and associated with poverty and ignorance during the nineteenth century. At the very point when local traditions and the Irish language were dying, Douglas Hyde, W.B. Yeats, Lady Gregory and others began the work of retrieval and restoration by a process of mediation which aimed to create appreciation of this lifestyle among the educated people who had never been interested in or aware of its significance. In this context, those who were impoverished were the middle-class town or city-dwellers who had become separated from the sources of their Irishness. These began, like Miss Ivors in 'The Dead', to visit the Aran Islands, Connemara and the West of Ireland, to experience at first hand the vitality of the culture expressed by Synge in *The Playboy of the Western World*.

Sean O'Casey, in his early plays, revealed the existence of a similar vitality among the tenement dwellers of Dublin. The Abbey Theatre provided a forum for peasant plays which soon came to dominate the repertoire of the national theatre. This writing was not always celebratory, failings as well as virtues were revealed, but the identification of the sources of Irish identity with the lives of working people in the countryside enabled writers like Liam O'Flaherty, Peadar O'Donnell, Frank O'Connor and Sean O'Faolain to explore the reality of lives lived within the boundaries of tradition and custom. This process is continued to the present day in the north Galway plays of M.J. Molloy. The poet Richard Murphy uses history as an adjunct to place in the exploration of identity in *The Battle of Aughrim*, and reverses the process in the anthropomorphic sonnets in *The Price of Stone*. Brian Friel, in *Translations*, delicately disentangles the linkages of place-names, association, memory, language and history to expose the undergrowth of minutiae which contribute to the primal connection so many Irish people feel to their place of origin. It is a theme which has become central to the poetry of Patrick Kavanagh, John Montague, and Heaney himself, who expresses it as follows in his essay, 'A Sense of Place': 'Yet those primary laws of our nature are still operative. We are dwellers, we are namers, we are lovers, we make homes and search for our histories' [Heaney, 1980, 131-49].

This vision of the positive and supportive qualities of the local environment and history emerged from the attempt to repossess and reactivate a sense of Irishness. It is oriented towards an ideal, even a romantic image of tradition, which validates the lifestyle of the poor and deprived in opposition to the values of the middle classes and the educated.

The alternative experience of alienation, however, is much more prevalent in Irish literature. It expresses itself in an emphasis on realism rather than mythology, on social reality rather than history, on a view of community which is critical, rather than accepting. The exile here is internalised: the hero of the fiction or drama finds himself marginalised by a community whose values he cannot accept. In his story 'Home Sickness', George Moore investigates the situation of a man who returns to his native place having made some money in America. He is in a position to be very successful by the standards of the townland, yet becomes so oppressed by the servility of the people and the social rather than moral power of the local priest that he abandons it all and returns to the Bowery. His escape involves the betrayal of the innocent girl who loves him, and initiates the association of freedom with betrayal which is central to so much later Irish fiction.

A *Portrait of the Artist as a Young Man* is Joyce's enunciation of this theme, where religion, family and country become the nets which

81

seek to trap the escaping writer and prevent him from achieving artistic freedom through exile. In order to be able to write, Stephen Dedalus has to reject the expectations of his mother and of the church. In the Journal which forms the conclusion of *Portrait* Stephen records the process of separation: 'Then she said I would come back to faith because I had a restless mind. This means to leave church by backdoor of sin and reenter through the skylight of repentance. Cannot repent' (*Portrait*, 248). This process takes precedence over the separation from the myth of Ireland, represented by the old man from the west, with red eyes and short pipe, but Stephen acknowledges: 'It is with him I must struggle all through this night till day come, till he or I lie dead' (*Portrait*, 252). Stephen is leaving physically, and separating himself emotionally, in order to return fictionally to Ireland: 'the shortest way to Tara was *via* Holyhead' (*Portrait*, 250).

A similar sense of oppression and alienation from the values of traditional communities is frequently expressed by other writers through the exploration of internal exile, for example by a move from the countryside to the city. Patrick Kavanagh graphically depicts the sexual and social stagnation of rural Ireland in *The Great Hunger*. Maguire, the central figure, does not escape, and becomes no better than the animals he tends, bound like them to an unending cycle of seasons and drudgery. Tarry Flynn, the hero of his novel of the same name, is infantilised by the necessities of rural economics. He cannot marry until his sisters are provided for; his dreaming interferes with success as a farmer; he is deceived by his best friend in a deal over land and chooses to leave rather than continue the struggle. In doing so he abandons his mother, and takes the knowledge of her inarticulate grief with him, as well as the lyrical memory of the countryside he loves, and will continue to celebrate through his songs. John McGahern's novel *The Dark* expresses a similar struggle. The unnamed boy who is the protagonist is engaged in a struggle for his freedom from the outset. A lone boy in a houseful of girls he battles for his education against his father, who opposes the process which will inevitably rob him of a helper on the land and a successor. The freedom at stake here is not even creative freedom, simply the right to follow a different path, and leave the farm for an alternative future in the city. Gar O'Donnell, Brian Friel's emigrant in *Philadelphia Here I Come*, undergoes the same process in a small town setting, with the further implication that his destiny abroad will not be very different from what he can expect if he stays at home: low-paying jobs in an American city, punctuated by holidays in Ireland, still encumbered by family responsibilities.

In these texts, the act of leaving one's birthplace is not merely a geographical move. It is also a realignment of relationships, a refusal to fulfil the economic and family rôles imposed by a traditionalist and conservative society. The escape is frequently presented as a break with parents as well as adverse social conditions, and the abandonment of the home place also involves abandonment of the very traditions and beliefs which elsewhere are perceived as sustaining mythologies. Religious inflexibility and sexual frustration are recurring themes which occur together in Edna O'Brien's *A Pagan Place*. The heroine, again unnamed, tried to fulfil the demands of church and family, sustained by an adolescent crush on a local priest, who attempts to seduce her and causes her rejection, rather than support, by her parents. The girl makes her escape to a convent, rather than to the city which was the destination of Cait and Baba in O'Brien's earlier novel *The Country Girls*. None of these girls really escape, they change their location only to enter new versions of bondage which are the inevitable consequences, in O'Brien's world, of their insufficient girlhoods. In *Mary Lavelle*, by Kate O'Brien, the heroine does escape, in the sense that she undergoes a significant reassessment of herself and takes control of her life as a consequence of a passionate affair with a married man. In order to begin her new life she too must painfully separate from her staid Irish fiancé, in a more mature version of the process we have been tracing.

Censorship in Ireland ensured that *Mary Lavelle*, published in 1936, did not exert any great influence and that Edna O'Brien's novels of the sixties seemed to be the first explicit exploration of Irish women's sexuality. The theme of alienation had, however, been significant in Irish fiction and drama since the 1880s, and involved the central realisation that traditional communities tend to marginalise those who do not conform to their values. Departure as a solution to this situation has many shortcomings: it may not lead to anything better, in economic or emotional terms, and even when it does it involves betrayal and abandonment of the family and traditions left behind.

Many writers took the route they ascribe to their characters and left Ireland in order to achieve the freedom to write as they wished. For many of them Ireland remained the subject of their creativity, most notably Joyce who retained Dublin as his setting in *Portrait, Ulysses* and *Finnegans Wake* even as his experiments with language and novel techniques made him a formidable exponent of modernism in fiction and an influence on the world development of the novel. The later plays of Sean O'Casey retain an Irish setting while they employ a range of techniques for the expression of his criticism of the narrowness of Irish institutions and the construction of human values. Samuel Beckett absorbed his Dublin youth into a vision of existence which does not depend on realism for its expression, nor is he concerned to analyse or expose society, but to explore the act of living itself. Francis Stuart found exile the paradigm for his personal sense of isolation, and in his novels the situation of the scapegoat, who must carry the burden of guilt for others, focuses the aspect of betrayal which is touched on by many of the plays and novels of departure.

Some writers who left began to write about life outside Ireland, for example Edna O'Brien in *Casualties of Peace*, and Brian Moore in *Fergus*. For many emigrants Ireland is left behind, and with it the guilt that its memory evokes. Their effort becomes directed towards adaptation to the new country and the assumption of a new identity which will replace the discarded Irish one. This forms the subject of Thomas Kilroy's play *Double Cross*. Brendan Bracken and William Joyce (Lord Haw Haw) expiate their sense of separation by becoming the British Minister of Information and an instrument of German propaganda, respectively, during the Second World War. Bracken sought to become accepted as a member of the British upper class. Joyce claimed, at various stages, British, German and American citizenship. Kilroy comments, in his introduction, that 'this play attempts to deal with one kind of mobility, one kind of action across the barriers, the restrictive codes which separate countries from one another. It is the kind of action which is usually called treason' [*Double Cross*, 6]. Since departure, as analysed in Irish literature, frequently involves personal betrayals, treason would seem to be the state of existence natural to exile. It may express itself in perpetual, schizophrenic rôle-playing, as in *Double Cross*, or in a dissolution of the sense of reality, as in Brian Moore's *Fergus*. The cause, as analysed by Thomas Kilroy, arises from the close Irish association of personal identity with the place of origin: 'To base one's identity, exclusively, upon a mystical sense of place rather than in personal character where it properly resides seems to me a dangerous absurdity' [*Double Cross*, 6-7]. The act of departure may be a step towards personal freedom and creativity, but only when the conflicts associated with leaving have been resolved.

Finally there is the phase of reassessment of the myth of exile, the assumption that local life is insufficient and that real life is elsewhere. For many writers the exile is unproductive; separated from the original sources of stress, tension and discovery it may prove impossible to engage with the issues of another culture. The flight to freedom may turn out to have been a flight from the real battle field, or the entire conflict may have accompanied them unabated into exile in the suitcase of memory. The conditions and terms of return or of remaining have therefore become more frequent themes in Irish writing since the 1950s. John Montague, in *The Rough Field*, literally takes us on the journey of return, along the road from Belfast to Garvaghey, reassessing the implications of the places that we pass.

Back in his own place he is enabled to re-explore the territory; educated by his own experience it can now yield up some of its meaning to him. The return may not always be fulfilling, however. In Tom Murphy's play, *Conversations on a Homecoming*, the returned exile has retained his illusions while those who remained have had to come to terms with reality. In this case they re-introduce him to life as they are forced to live it. In 'The Gold Watch' by John McGahern, the son who has left the small farm to work in Dublin retains the illusion of continuity by returning annually to help with the hay. The reality of the break he has made is symbolised by the exchange he makes with his father of a broken gold watch for an efficient new one, which his father destroys in a barrel of acid potato spray. Yet in 'Bank Holiday' also by McGahern, a successful but lonely middle-aged civil servant discovers that his city life has, after all, something to offer him, when he unexpectedly finds somebody to love, and who loves him. This discovery, significantly, takes place when the death of his parents releases him from his ties to the place where he was born.

There is a price to be paid for return, as there was for departure. The restrictions which oppressed the intending exile will still be there to greet him on his return. Literature has not charted any great upheavals or tension lines of readjustment which could have transformed a restrictive situation into a supportive one. There is no specific text one can point to as a watershed for writers coming to terms with Ireland sufficiently to live here and devote their creativity to the expression of its reality. Writers such as Des Hogan, Bernard McLaverty, Derek Mahon, live and work outside the country. Yet poetry and drama, in particular, are at present in a phase of intense productivity. It now seems possible to many writers to find both material and a public within Ireland, which will not restrict their creativity. Thematically, departure is no longer the conventional conclusion it once was to Irish novels and plays. Increasingly, the conflicts set up in literature are allowed to develop to a conclusion of breakdown or resolution without the outlet of departure, while for many writers exile has become a matter of choice, and a temporary affair.

FURTHER READING

T. Brown, *Ireland: A Social and Cultural History 1922-1979*, Glasgow 1981.
A. Carpenter ed., *Place, Personality and the Irish writer*, Gerrard's Cross and New York 1977.
Commission on Emigration and Other Population Problems, Dublin 1956.
D. Fitzpatrick, *Irish Emigration, 1801-1921*, Dublin 1985.
J.W. Foster, 'The Geography of Irish Fiction', *The Irish Novel in Our Time*, Lille 1975.
S. Heaney, *Preoccupations: Selected Prose 1968-1978*, London 1980.

James Joyce, *A Portrait of the Artist as a Young Man*, New York 1964.

R. Kennedy, *The Irish, Emigration, Marriage and Fertility*, Los Angeles 1973.

T. Kilroy, *Double Cross*, London and Boston 1986.

K. Miller, *Emigrants and Exiles: Ireland and the Irish Exodus to North America*, Oxford 1985.

C. Ó Gráda, 'Across the Briny Ocean: some thoughts on pre-Famine emigration to America, in T. Devine and D. Dickson eds, *Ireland and Scotland 1660-1900*, Edinburgh 1985.

G. Ó Tuathaigh, 'The Irish in Nineteenth Century Britain: Problems of Integration', *Transactions of the Royal Historical Society*, vol. 31, 1981.

6
THE IRISH TRADITION AND NINETEENTH-CENTURY FICTION: A REVIEW

Patrick Sheeran

I
THE IRISH TRADITION

THE question of tradition in Ireland is extremely fraught, in large part because it borders on the related problem of identity. Rather like those cosmologies which divided early Celtic Ireland into two, five or seven parts, the modern Irish tradition has been charted in terms of various typologies. In one version Gaelic Ireland is pitted against Anglo-Irish Ireland in the rôles of colonised and coloniser. In another both together enter an uneasy alliance to face a third, menacing English presence. More recently, events have taught us to recognise and to add to our conceptual map a Presbyterian culture in the north of the island. The most comprehensive — and therefore controversial — delineation of the multiple strains within our culture has been that of F.S.L. Lyons in a study with a revealing title: *Culture and Anarchy in Ireland 1890-1939*. Here it is claimed that 'the key to the Irish problem in its modern form was the competitive co-existence within Ireland, not just of a simple dualism between native and settler, but of a complex of Irish and Anglo-Irish cultures operating within, and powerfully affected by, the dominant English culture' [Lyons, 1979, 26]. To complicate matters even further, disillusion with the present state of affairs — economic, political, social — has led others to claim that the Irish today have inherited neither the Gaelic, Anglo-Irish nor English cultural traditions but a barren residue of all three. Indeed, there is a comprehensive emotional definition of Irish culture, partly stemming from James Joyce, which sees it as a repository of speech, gesture and ritual characterised by a sense of dispossession, grievance and paralysis. An extreme view would hold that the Irish tradition hardly exists: 'Ireland is a nothing — a no-thing — an interesting nothing, to be sure, composed of colourful parts, a nothing-mosaic'.[1] This point of view is worth pursuing if only because it is in line with a number of recent assertions that the Irish tradition is something we have yet to create.

If we insist on comparing ourselves with such long established and powerful nation states as France, England and Germany then it becomes abundantly clear that we can claim little of their unity and coherence over many centuries. The continuity of the Gaelic tradition was broken by the near extinction of the Irish language, the elimination of native elites, religious persecution and a general condition of deprivation. From the seventeenth century onwards the vernacular culture gradually went underground and was replaced by that of an alien ruling minority. Here lies the nub of the problem. During this time a complex, hybrid tradition composed of elements drawn from both English and Irish culture was fabricated. As a consequence we face today a two-fold embarrassment. First, the foundations of our culture were laid, in large part, by members of the Anglo-Irish Ascendancy class. Second, the privileged position enjoyed by the Anglo-Irish observers frequently led them to idealise and distort their vision of Ireland. Hence the 'Irish Mystique', so often a target of radical critics in our own day. The inquisitors of Yeats, Gregory, Synge and Russell turn for sustenance to another tradition, more rooted in everyday reality and less tainted by the colonial enterprise. This tradition, associated in particular with the names of Joyce and Kavanagh, is believed to show a way out of the vicious circle of myth and stereotype in which so much Anglo-Irish experience was caught. Here the unheroic individual, vulnerable to the pressure of modern life, is at the centre.

The opposition Yeats *versus* Joyce leads us to consider two corresponding intellectual currents in modern Irish culture. One is associated with values derived from Romanticism and stresses the past, the mythical, the rural, the national and the transcendent. The other endorses the values of the Enlightenment. It is urban, secular, cosmopolitan and is orientated towards the future. This hasty notation is of necessity simplistic and it cannot take into account all the nuances of attitude and allegiance we find in the work of individual writers (especially Yeats and Joyce). However, it points to the fact that, rather than being heirs to a simple system or coherent cultural whole, we are surrounded by the detritus of past and recent ideologies. Yeats, we recall, fabricated an Anglo-Irish heritage out of Swift, Burke, Berkeley and Goldsmith. Pearse conjured a revolutionary succession out of Tone, Emmet, Mitchel, and Lalor. And Dr Paisley mimics the rhetorical gestures and great coat of Sir Edward Carson. The existence of near-continuous crisis in Ireland over the last 300 years has created a constant demand for traditions which would legitimise various institutions and actions and symbolise the social coherence of a variety of communities. Given this, it does not make a great deal of sense to decry *invented* traditions. There is no such thing as an uninvented one, with the exception of those divinely revealed. What seems indisputable is that Irish culture today is a *mélange* of traditions which borrow one another's clothes, clash or merge or cancel one another out. This predicament is not all loss. Out of the continuous struggle and interpenetration come the great innovators in European literature: Yeats, Joyce and Beckett.

There is a final paradox. However problematic and confused the modern Irish tradition may be, it is found by a number of observers to embody distinct and recognisable signs. It is enough to look at Vivian Mercier's *The Irish Comic Tradition*, David Krause's *The Profane Book of Irish Comedy* or the collections of essays edited by Heinz Kosok and Wolfgang Zack to discover that Irish literature, despite everything, reveals certain recurring patterns that account for its continuity. Very crudely, we may distinguish four indices of Irishness: generic, linguistic, thematic and ideological.

With regard to genre we encounter the predominance of the comic mode in drama, the elegiac in poetry and romance forms in fiction. The two studies by Mercier and Krause demonstrate the pervasiveness of the comic in Irish dramaturgy. It is extremely varied in its manifestations spanning as it does the comedy of manners, Boucicault's stage-Irishry, Behan's carnivalesque comedy and the grotesque of Beckett. The elegiac mood in poetry responds to a sense of loss and dispossession. Its roots lie in the tradition of Gaelic lament, one of which in particular, *Caoineadh Airt Ui Laoghaire* (Lament for Art Ó Laoghaire) continues to haunt contemporary poets. Much of the best work of Heaney, Montague, Murphy and Mahon is cast in this mould. Conversations with the dead, encounters with revenants, autopsies and nostalgic reminiscence are central to the genre as practised in Ireland. Finally the presence of a great oral, folk tradition accounts, in part, for the prevalence of romance forms in fiction, particularly nineteenth-century fiction. As we shall see in our survey of the novel during this period, the proclivity for romance was reinforced by the pressures of a deeply divided, often violent society.

It is already something of a critical convention to quote a passage from James Joyce's *A Portrait of the Artist as a Young Man* to illustrate the unease the Irish are reputed to feel in relation to the English language. Stephen Dedalus and the dean of studies, an English Jesuit, come to a misunderstanding over the words 'funnel' and 'tundish'.

> The little word seemed to have turned a rapier point of sensitiveness against the courteous and vigilant foe. He felt with a smart of dejection that the man to whom he was speaking was a countryman of Ben Jonson. He thought: 'The language in which we are speaking is his before it is mine. How different are the words *home, Christ, ale, master,* on his lips and on mine! I

cannot speak or write these words without unrest of spirit. His language, so familiar and so foreign, will always be for me an acquired speech. I have not made or accepted its words. My voice holds them at bay. My soul frets in the shadow of his language.[2]

This declaration seems almost a piece of coquetry if we consider the fact that it occurs in such a linguistic masterpiece as *A Portrait*. In literature written by Irishmen in English, rather than unease, we encounter a fascination with the word. Swift, Carleton, Wilde, Shaw, Joyce, Yeats, Beckett, O'Brien, Heaney all share a highly verbal tradition which constantly breaks conventional barriers in language and discovers new potentialities within the word.

When we turn to consider the thematic preoccupations of Irish literature, two in particular call for attention: the concern with death and with place. Ireland, it may be argued, is a funerary culture, one where the signs associated with death and funeral carry a large semantic freight. These signs are constantly reactivated in a literature which dwells obsessively on the subject of death, paralysis and decay. We have come to consciousness, as Seamus Heaney puts it, by leaping in graves. The related preoccupation with place is especially powerfully voiced in poetry where the ancient Gaelic affiliation to a particular location has been taken up by contemporary poets. This topomania is conspicuous in the work of Northern writers in whom the sense of place is deeply implicated with the sense of identity.

Finally, one of the distinctive characteristics of Irish literature (especially the Anglo-Irish contribution) is a particular outlook marked by divided loyalties. A number of scholars have unearthed a connection between the ambivalence of the Anglo-Irish mind and the ironic tone that so often enters the work of such writers as Swift, Synge and Yeats. The classic statement of the dilemma is found in the 'General Introduction for my Work' which Yeats wrote in 1937. Meditating on the relationship between England and Ireland, English literature and his own achievement, he exclaims: '... my hatred tortures me with love, my love with hate.'[3] This ambivalence of attitude, the mutual presence of acceptance and rejection, is not confined to writers from the Anglo-Irish tradition. We find it deeply inscribed for example in the work of all the leading novelists of the nineteenth century, to whom we now turn.

II

NINETEENTH-CENTURY FICTION

Prose fiction in Ireland during the nineteenth century differs markedly from that being written in England and France during the

90

same period. As we have indicated above, it is probably best to consider it as belonging to the romance genre rather than to the novel proper. However, in our brief survey, for the sake of convenience, we will follow conventional terminology.

Some of the reasons for the dominance of romance forms are to be found in the continuing crises and drastic transformations of Irish society that occurred between 1798 and 1890. The major writers all remarked on the ways in which their art had to engage with forces which were utterly destroying society and which made not only concern with the personal life seem a luxury but the practice of fiction itself an irrelevance. Typical of the sense that life in Ireland had repeatedly overwhelmed art is the preface which William Carleton appended to *The Black Prophet*. Writing in the first year of the Great Famine he defended himself against the expected charge that he had exaggerated the horror of his description of the earlier famine of 1817-22:

> But why talk of exaggeration or contradiction? Alas! do not the workings of death and desolation among us in the present time give them fearful corroboration, and prove how far the strongest imagery of Fiction is frequently transcended by the terrible realities of Truth?[4]

Maria Edgeworth wrote in a similar vein when she explained that 'realities are too strong, party passions too violent'[5] to continue with her fictional exploration of Irish life. Lady Morgan too was silenced by that 'great melodramatic tragedy now performing on the shores of Ireland — the Celtic Exodus.' It exceeded 'all the poetical tragedy that has ever been presented on the stage, or national novelists have ever depicted in their volumes.'[6] In short, the circumstances in which Edgeworth, Morgan and Carleton wrote impelled them to move far beyond the traditional subject matter of the novel — private experience, manners, the relation of men to society, the growth and development of the individual — to encompass more public, ideological concerns. They were, in Lady Morgan's words, 'national novelists'. Such themes as the relationship between Irish and Anglo-Irish, Catholic and Protestant, tenant and landlord were found to be best articulated in terms of political allegory, philosophical fable, pastoral idyll, gothic horror and melodrama. All of these can be subsumed under the larger category of romance. The latter is less devoted to exact depiction of the nuances of social relationships and more hospitable to a high-pitched, often grotesque, perception of the world.

This perception made special demands on the reader. Much Irish fiction during the nineteenth century was addressed to a foreign, often incredulous, audience. Local circumstances need to be explained, the historical and social context filled in, an image of life elaborated which would be both exotic enough to be alluring and recognisable enough to be understood. For an English audience, as a writer in the *Edinburgh Review* pointed out, Connemara was as much *terra incognita* as Timbucktoo. The Irish novels of the period are part and parcel of the whole, century-long effort to translate Irish experience into a new language, and to find forms adequate to depict an unstable and often violent society. Not only was the material itself recalcitrant but the discourse in which it might be transcribed was itself marked by a collision of different idioms. Again it is in Carleton, with his often incongruous mixture of English, Irish and Latin, that the linguistic instability and strife is most evident.

Several strategies were evolved to cope with these difficulties. For purposes of exploration and elucidation a number of novels — Maria Edgeworth's *Ennui* and *The Absentee*, Lady Morgan's *Wild Irish Girl*, Griffin's *The Collegians* among them — bring over to Ireland an affable, educated young man and gradually initiate him into the realities of Irish life. This pattern is not merely a narrative convenience. The young man can always be manipulated into meeting and marrying a suitably sanitised daughter of a Gaelic Chieftan or Anglo-Irish landowner. Maria Edgeworth's *Ormond* is the most ambitious undertaking of this kind. While not a returned absentee like so many of his confreres, Harry Ormond is left orphaned and propertyless and thus does not have a prescribed direction in life. He is free to choose the Ireland to which he will give his allegiance. His rôle models are provided by a Gaelic chieftain (Corny O'Shane, King of the Black Islands), his uncle, a venal government official called Sir Ulick O'Shane and thirdly Sir Herbert Annaly, an English gentleman resident in Ireland. Ormond, in the most wildly optimistic solution to the Irish problem in nineteenth-century fiction, marries Annaly's daughter, inherits King Corny's feudal lordship and settles down to being an enlightened landlord.

Edgeworth's novel draws our attention to a central opposition which structures much, if not all, of the fiction of nineteenth-century Ireland, that between native and foreigner. Thence derive many others: colonised and coloniser, the natural and the civil, anarchy and order, cabin and Big House, Connacht and Dublin, tribe and state, passion and reason. The action of many novels aspires to reconcile these oppositions by means of a racial marriage. Marriage is clearly a metaphor for the project of unifying the nation by bringing together Ascendancy good sense and Gaelic passion.

The nuptial myth engendered a whole gallery of stock characters; improving landlords, incorrigible rakes, rapacious agents, feckless peasants, noble patriots, wild Irish girls and wild Irish boys. A larger stereotype emerged which portrayed the Irish, however charming and imaginative in their better moments, as irresponsible and disorderly in contrast to a solid, disciplined England. The very questionable notion of an Irish national character was put to many uses. On the one hand, by emphasising the more appealing aspects, it could be employed to seduce an indifferent audience. Again and again our novelists resorted to it in an effort to make the English reader understand the innate nobility of the Irish people. On the other hand it offered a ready, all too convenient explanation for those who wished to ascribe Irish ills to temperamental weakness rather than to the effects, for example, of bad government.

The relationship between coloniser and colonised, as it emerges in our fiction, is not simplistic or diagrammatic. The very first novel to take up the theme, Maria Edgeworth's *Castle Rackrent* (1800), reveals the complex interpenetration of native and settler. The Rackrent family are themselves of Gaelic descent. Thady is both servile and subversive, collaborating in the destruction of a feudal myth which he half creates. While the tale is his, the authoritative footnotes, preface and afterword are those of the Ascendancy author in the guise of editor. Already the first Irish novel, so called, is marked by that dialogic imagination which will reach its fullest intensity in Joyce. Nor is the urge to conclude a story with an unlikely marriage, to achieve in fiction what could not be realised in fact, always yielded to. Murrough O'Brien, the central character of Lady Morgan's *The O'Briens and the O'Flahertys*, tests all the opportunities for creative public action available to him in his day from the liberalism of Grattan to the radicalism of Lord Edward Fitzgerald. He finds them all unavailing and goes into exile in France where he becomes one of Bonaparte's generals. The choice of exile as a way out of the Irish dilemma will gain its own mythical elaboration in the next century in the work of Moore and Joyce.

Dominating the fiction of those writers who came from an Ascendancy background, however distantly, is the emblem of the Big House. We see it in various stages of disrepair, renovation and ruin from *Castle Rackrent* through Charles Lever's *The Martins of Cro'Martin*, Anthony Trollope's *Castle Richmond*, George Moore's *A Drama in Muslin* and Somerville and Ross's *The Real Charlotte*. While it is true that images of sweetness and light tend to cluster around the walled demesne and those of darkness and sullen anger gather about the mud-walled cabins, their most interesting elaborations show the interplay of light and shade within the Big House itself. The haunted ruins portrayed by the Irish Gothic writers, Charles Robert Maturin and Joseph Sheridan le Fanu, are the most telling — and terrifying — image for the growing isolation and impotence of the Ascendancy class. The former masters are threatened both by an external enemy and inwardly debilitated by the guilt that has accumulated over centuries. The nuptial dream of Edgeworth and Morgan ends in nightmare.

Not all the novelists of the century, of course, were of Anglo-Irish stock or viewed Ireland from the perspective of the Big House. In the work of Gerald Griffin, the Banim brothers and William Carleton the emergent Catholic middle class and the peasantry find their voice in fiction. No less than the Ascendancy novelists these writers found that the forms they borrowed from the English tradition buckled and broke as they tried to impose them on refractory material. To carry the violence and anarchy of rural life into fiction they resorted to melodramatic forms, often verging on the shilling shocker. *Crohoore of the Bill-Hook*, the first of the *Tales of the O'Hara Family* by John and Michael Banim is exemplary in this regard. It is a story of great savagery dealing with the atrocities perpetrated by the Whiteboys. At the climax of the novel a tithe proctor is buried up to his neck and has his ears removed to the accompaniment of fiddler, piper and attendant hedge poet. The Banims write of a society where justice is meted out by hanging judges on one side and mutilators on the other. It is not one that is very amenable to the fictional conventions of, say, Jane Austin's *Emma*. We can catch a glimpse of the collision of the two worlds represented by the English novel and the Irish romance in *The Nowlans*, an unusually realistic portrait of Irish life. It is yet one more effort to mediate between the old contraries of Orange and Green and attempts to do so in the manner established by the Ascendancy novelists. Father John Nowlan, himself the son of a mixed marriage, falls in love with a Protestant girl. They flee to London but Father John cannot forget the judgment of the Church on his state; once a priest, always a priest. He has broken his vows and is living in mortal sin. For him, heaven, hell and judgment are all compelling realities. The polite social world in London and Dublin to which his wife introduces him takes on the lineaments of Hell. He is isolated and tormented by his own metaphysical concerns. The situation is emblematic. For the Banims and many others who followed them, the figure of the priest (unlike the parson of English fiction) is charged with energies difficult to accommodate within a purely realistic, empirical framework. The final descent of Fr John into poverty and mental illness makes him yet another victim, mutilated by the conflicting codes of Irish society.

History and fiction collide, with history gaining the upper hand, in *The Boyne Water*, an important novel written by John Banim alone. Frequently compared to Sir Walter Scott (Banim was 'The Scott of Ireland') this historical novel is more instructive for the way in which it differs from the work of the Scottish master. The rapprochement between Highlands and Lowlands offered Scott the possibility of reconciliation in his novels. Since, however, the division between

Orange and Green remained obdurate in Ireland, no such harmonious ending, except by rhetorical contrivance, was possible for Banim.

In alluding to the work of the Banims we have made glancing references, by way of highlighting contrasts, to English literature. Perhaps a more illuminating comparison is to be found in the American tradition. Richard Chase, in proposing a native American tradition of the novel, remarks: '. . . there are some literatures which take their form and tone from polarities, opposites and irreconcilables, but are content to rest in and sustain them or to resolve them into unities, if at all, only by special and limited means. The American novel tends to rest in contradictions and among extreme ranges of experience. When it attempts to resolve contradictions it does so either in melodramatic actions or pastoral idylls . . .'.[7] The terms of this description could be applied not only to the Banims' novels but to the whole Irish tradition, where we note similar unresolved tensions.

Perhaps the most forceful novel to combine dramatic action and pastoral idyll was Gerald Griffin's *The Collegians*. The central opposition of Irish and Anglo-Irish is here cut across by a further confrontation, that between the natural and the civil in the persons of Hardress Cregan and Kyrle Daly. Hardress is a romantic figure, an embodiment of turbulent power like Emily Brontë's Heathcliff. Kyrle is more pallid, an embodiment of restraint and civilized urbanity. The plot in which the two are embroiled is perhaps better known from the adaptations that have been made of *The Collegians* by Boucicault (*The Colleen Bawn*) and Benedict (*The Lily of Killarney*) than from the novel itself. Hardress at first falls in love with, and later murders, the young peasant girl Eily O'Connor. He has fallen in love with a woman from his own class and creed, Ann Chute — who is also loved by Daly. Griffin manipulates his plot so as to kill off Hardress and have Kyrle and Ann marry one another. The marriage has the usual emblematic significance but here the nuptial ending is bought at the price of emasculating the Catholic tradition and enfeebling the Ascendancy. Our sympathies, inevitably, go with the anarchic, energetic Hardress.

It is in the *Traits and Stories of the Irish Peasantry* by William Carleton that the submerged world of rural Ireland comes most vividly to life. While his many novels are led astray by didactic purpose or polemical intent, the Tales, at their best, have a wonderful immediacy. The source of Carleton's intimacy with the life to which he gave such abundant expression is described in his unfinished autobiography:

> My native place was a spot rife with old legends, tales, traditions, customs and superstitions, so that in my early youth, even beyond the walls of my own humble roof, they met me in every direction. It was at home, however, and from my father's

lips in particular that they were perpetually sounding in my ears. In fact, his memory was a perfect storehouse, and a rich one, of all that the social antiquary, the man of letters, the poet, or the musician would consider valuable. As a narrator of old tales, legends, and historical anecdotes he was unrivalled, and his stock of them inexhaustible. He spoke the Irish and English languages with equal fluency.[8]

Traits and Stories gives to this material what Carleton called 'a linked embodiment'. It is an astonishing performance, an unrivalled portrait in depth and intensity of the traditional culture which was slowly passing from the land. Its antipodes are marked by two stories. The first of these follows Denis O'Shaughnessy on his riotous way to Maynooth. Here the verbal comedy is carried off with complete success because the pedantry, so often obtrusive elsewhere in Carleton, is intrinsic to the character of the poor scholar. The other pole is represented by the fearsome Wildgoose Lodge where agrarian violence and its consequences are relentlessly depicted.

Carleton, like Edgeworth, Lady Morgan, the Banims and Griffin is the celebrant and anatomist of a vanishing world. He described himself as *ultimus Romanorum* — the last of the Romans — and predicted that following his death there would come 'a lull, an obscurity of perhaps half a century'.[9] Although that obscurity was to be broken by novels such as Charles Kickham's *Knocknagow* and Charles Lever's *Lord Kilgobbin*, it is difficult to deny Carleton's acute sense of the times.

REFERENCES

1. Vincent Buckley, *Memory Ireland: Insights into the contemporary Irish condition*, Harmondsworth 1985, ix.
2. Harmondsworth 1960, 189.
3. *Essays and Introductions*, London 1961, 518-19.
4. William Carleton, *The Black Prophet*, London 1899, viii.
5. Augustus Hare, ed., *The Life and Letters of Maria Edgeworth*, London 1894, vol. ii, 202.
6. W. Hepworth Dixon, ed., *Lady Morgan's Memoirs: autobiography, diaries and correspondence*, London 1862, vol. i, 262.
7. Richard Chase, *The American Novel and Its Traditions*, London 1958, 2.
8. David J. O'Donoghue, *The Life of William Carleton*, London 1896, vol. i, 5-7
9. Ibid., vol. ii, 144.

FURTHER READING
Tradition

J.C. Beckett, *The Anglo-Irish Tradition*, London 1976.
T. Brown, *Ireland: a Social and Cultural History 1922-79*, London 1981.
S. Deane, ed. *The Crane Bag: The Idea of Tradition*, vol. 3, no. 1, Dublin 1979.

S. Deane, *Civilians and Barbarians*, Field Day pamphlets 3, Derry 1983.

S. Deane, *Heroic Styles: the tradition of an idea*, Field Day pamphlets 4, Derry 1984.

R. Kearney, *The Irish Mind: Exploring Intellectual Traditions*, Dublin 1985.

T. Kinsella, 'The Divided Mind' in *Irish Poets in English*, ed. S. Lucy, Cork 1975.

H. Kosok, *Studies in Anglo-Irish Literature*, Bonn 1982.

D. Krause, *The Profane Book of Irish Comedy*, Cornell 1982.

F.S.L. Lyons, *Culture and Anarchy in Ireland 1890-1939*, Oxford 1979.

W.J. McCormack, *Ascendancy and Tradition in Anglo-Irish Literary History from 1789 to 1939*, Oxford 1985.

V. Mercier, *The Irish Comic Tradition*, Oxford 1962.

W. Zack, *Literary Interrelations: Ireland, England and the World*, 3 vols, Tübingen 1987.

Nineteenth-Century Fiction
J. Cahalan, *Great Hatred, Little Room: The Irish Historical Novel*, Dublin 1983.

J. Cronin, *The Anglo-Irish Novel; the Nineteenth Century*, Belfast 1980.

T. Dunne, *Maria Edgeworth and the Colonial Mind*, The 26th O'Donnell lecture, Cork 1984.

T. Flanagan, *The Irish Novelists, 1800-1850*, New York 1958.

W.J. McCormack, *Sheridan le Fanu and Victorian Ireland*, Oxford 1980.

P.F. Sheeran, 'Colonists and Colonised: Some aspects of Anglo-Irish literature from Swift to Joyce', *Yearbook of English Studies*, Vol. 13, 1983, 97-115.

7
WRITING IN GAELIC SINCE 1880

Noel McGonagle

TWENTIETH-CENTURY Ireland is rather unusual in having two languages viz. English and Gaelic. The former is by far the more widely spoken and understood, the more officially promoted and ably practised. The Gaelic language is predominantly located on the western seaboard, in Connacht, Munster and Ulster. It is the preserve of a minority who use it mainly as a means of oral communication among themselves. Both languages enshrine a literature, the greater corpus by far in the English language. Both, to a certain extent, reflect the history, traditions, actualities and preoccupations of their own particular environment and experience. Irish literature written in the English language is of a relatively high literary standard and has a universal profile. That written in Gaelic is confined to Ireland and, even there, not widely publicised or appreciated.

A proper analysis of the formative years of modern Gaelic literature requires some general background information concerning the history of the Gaelic language and its literature. Ireland was last totally Gaelic speaking in the twelfth century. From that period onwards, the whole Gaelic way of life and, with it, the Gaelic language and its literature, began to be eroded, gradually and virtually imperceptibly at first but gathering momentum with the passage of centuries. This occurred initially as a result of external influences but later was due to a process of almost internal combustion.

Such was the strength of the Gaelic world in earlier centuries that it survived waves of different invasions, religious, political and cultural. The new languages and cultures (Christian, Norse and Norman) were readily assimilated into the existing native mould and posed no threat to the indigenous culture. By the beginning of the sixteenth century Ireland was still Gaelic speaking with the exception perhaps of some small pockets in Leinster and certain urban areas. However, the sixteenth and seventeenth centuries can be regarded as a watershed in the history of Gaelic Ireland. In that period the Gaelic order met its demise and with that came the dismantling of its political, social and legal system. The flight of native chieftains to the continent or their disenfranchisement at home meant that the Gaelic *literati* were without their patrons. Increasingly, therefore, the Gaelic tradition was consigned to the ordinary illiterate people of Ireland. The Gaelic language which for centuries had been expertly sieved, nurtured and cultivated, was released from official, centralised restraint to develop unimpeded into regional dialects, a situation which has resulted in the present century in virtual linguistic anarchy.

As a result of plantations and wars from the seventeenth century onwards, the relative positions of the Gaelic and English languages as the everyday language of the people of Ireland changed. The anglicisation of Ireland was well under way. By the nineteenth century, English was the official everyday language of all Irish administrative, political, economic and social life. Before the Great Famine, Ireland boasted some four million Gaelic speakers, the greatest number ever recorded. However this was the result of the unprecedented growth in population which was concentrated in the lower income groups which were comprised almost entirely of Gaelic speakers. The decimation of the Irish populace due to starvation and emigration as a result of the Great Famine was keenly felt in the Gaelic speaking regions.

From that period onwards emerged an awesome statistical record of the virtual disappearance of the Gaelic language from its natural habitat. According to the 1851 census there were over 1½ million native Gaelic speakers, in 1891 700,000, in 1922 when the Irish Free State was founded 300,000 and, at present, a paltry 25,000 to 30,000 in seven out of a total of thirty-two counties. The seeds of this catastrophe were germinating for many centuries, the rot only visibly and devastatingly manifesting itself in the last two centuries. The reasons for this outcome are legion. English was the language of all necessary, practical, official aspects of Irish life. It was the language of government, administration, economics, politics, education, literature, religion, trade, commerce, travel — even of emigration. The English-speaking world of Ireland and elsewhere encroached upon traditional Gaelic-speaking areas and eventually overran them. The people themselves actively aided the process. Flann O'Brien overstates their rôle somewhat when he says:

> The present extremity of the Irish language is due mainly to the fact that the Gaels deliberately flung that instrument of beauty and precision from them, thrashed it out of their children and sneered in outlandish boor's English at those who were a few days slower than themselves in getting rid of it.

In the space of a few generations, the Gaelic language had disappeared from most of Ireland 'like snow from the ditches'.

Gaelic literature fared even worse than the Gaelic language during the seventeenth and eighteenth centuries. Divorced from the benefits gained from the printing press, from the attention of a learned populace, from inclusion in the education system until 1878, it languished and was overtaken by Anglo-Irish literature. With a few notable exceptions, the small corpus of literature from that period was mainly of folk origin and existed by folk sufferance.

Salvation — or its seed — for the Gaelic language and consequently for the literature, did not emanate from the ordinary native Irish at first but from the Anglo-Irish Ascendancy. From the end of the eighteenth century onwards they developed a great interest, academic but antiquarian, in the Gaelic language of former times and in its literature. Charlotte Brooke's *Reliques of Irish Poetry* (1789) was to be the first public manifestation of this awakening of interest. As a result of this and other such expositions of early Gaelic literature in printed form, and prompted to some degree by the Romantic movement in Europe generally, several learned societies were founded in Ireland in the first half of the nineteenth century: the Gaelic Society of Dublin in 1807, the Iberno-Celtic Society in 1818, the Ulster Gaelic Society in 1830, the Irish Archaeological Society in 1840, the Celtic Society in 1845, the Ossianic Society in 1853. These societies reflected the views of their founders and membership — that Gaelic was not relevant in the modern world but had a romantic and heroic literature in former times. However, it must be said that they had a very salutary effect in that they developed interest in matters Gaelic which brought important results in later years. They informed and stimulated groups at home and abroad to investigate various aspects of Ireland's Gaelic heritage. Amongst these were linguists (Zeuss, Windisch, Zimmer, Thurneysen, de Jubainville, Dottin), folklorists (Wilde, Kennedy, Curtin, Hyde), poets and writers (O'Grady, Moore, Mangan, Ferguson). These diverse groups, however, did not envisage the Gaelic language as the everyday vernacular of the country, of the educational system, or of a creative literature.

Only in the second half of the nineteenth century was there concern for the preservation and even the restoration of the Gaelic language on a national scale. In 1876 the Society for the Preservation of the Irish Language was founded, and in 1880 The Gaelic Union, which had more radical aspirations. It was the latter group who founded *The Gaelic Journal/Irisleabhar na Gaedhilge* in 1882 which was the first publication in Ireland to attempt to fashion the Gaelic language as a contemporary linguistic and literary medium.

The Gaelic League/*Conradh na Gaeilge*, the most important and lasting of all Gaelic societies, was founded in 1893 by Douglas Hyde, David Comyn, Eoin Mac Néill, Fr O'Growney and others. Its aim was first and foremost to revive the Gaelic language as the vernacular of the people of Ireland and secondly to create a new literature in that language. Upon closer examination, it was a Gargantuan task given the insurmountable difficulties which existed at that time. Firstly, native speakers of Gaelic were in the minority nationwide and were predominantly living in *Gaeltacht* (= Gaelic-speaking) rural areas. Only a very small number of people were highly literate in Gaelic and these mostly hailed from and lived in English-speaking urban areas. The ordinary native speakers were barely literate in English, let alone Gaelic. (One can cite the example of Seán Ó Conaill [1853-1931) one of Ireland's most renowned Gaelic storytellers who could read neither English nor Gaelic.) Hence the Gaelic populace in Ireland was not one cohesive body, literate and centrally located. This heterogeneity has hindered the progress of the Gaelic restoration until the present day.

Further difficulties in the path of the Gaelic revival lay in the fact that at the time of the foundation of the Gaelic League, a mere twenty books were in print in the Gaelic language and these were mostly of a devotional, grammatical or folkloristic nature. There was nothing of a contemporary literary nature in existence. In addition, the Gaelic language had not been officially employed as a linguistic or literary medium for several centuries with the result that the language was chained to an antiquarian orthography which bore no relation to the actual spoken language — the situation can be compared to imposing the language of Chaucer on our contemporary speech.

However, fired with enthusiasm, the Gaelic League set to work, concentrating on their first priority — the restoration of the language. Books and booklets were written on Gaelic grammar (O'Growney's *Simple Lessons in Irish* in 1897, for instance). Branches of the League were established throughout the country, teachers were quickly and rudimentally trained and dispatched enthusiastically on their missionary task. The movement was under way.

The literary side of the Revival was faced with great practical problems from the onset. There was the question of the form of language to be employed in the formulation of this new Gaelic literature. There were those, among them the most literate and influential of the Gaelic movement itself, who believed that the antiquated language of former centuries should be employed. This was not practical, however. Few were *au fait* with this form of Gaelic and there was little material publicly available in this language. The bulk of the revivalists opted for a form of language based on the everyday speech of the people. Fr O'Leary, an eloquent exponent of this school, showed the way when he began to write his novel *Séadna* seriatim in *The Gaelic Journal* using the contemporary speech of West Muskerry, Co. Cork. With a few notable exceptions, his example was followed by the up and coming writers of the day. Writers of Gaelic ever since have tended to promote their own regional dialects in their works. This has given rise to a great amount of tribalism in the movement, rising at times to fever pitch, and has caused further splintering. It is to be regretted that Irish academics did not devise a standard form of the Gaelic language for the whole country until the 1950s. Even then, it was only tardily and half-heartedly implemented.

Once this problem was temporarily resolved by adopting the speech of the people, there remained the question of subject matter for this new literature. What themes would exercise the pens of the new writers? Two strong but diametrically opposed schools emerged — they could be termed traditional and innovative. The former believed that the oral tradition of the *Gaeltacht* — enshrining a wealth of folktales and songs — was the only unbroken literary tradition Gaelic Ireland possessed and that any modern literature should be based on that oral tradition. Fr O'Leary's would-be novel *Séadna* is basically a folktale, the story of a man selling his soul to the devil in return for material rewards and is a good example of the type of work envisaged.

There were other reasons also why such a literary doctrine should find widespread acceptance amongst certain elements of the Gaelic movement. From an ideological point of view, the members of the movement tended intrinsically to be fiercely national and insular in their outlook. The Gaelic oral tradition was native and Irish *in extremis;* hence it was to be promoted rather than adopting the pattern of foreign modern literatures current in other countries, particularly England.

From a more practical point of view, it must be remembered that by far the greatest part of the Gaelic-speaking world was concentrated in the *Gaeltacht*, the natural habitat of the oral tradition which was the staple literary diet of the people there. When these people and others who had acquired their knowledge of the Gaelic language and culture in the *Gaeltacht*, progressed from an oral to a written tradition, they naturally and readily wrote in the vein most familiar to them viz. the oral tradition. Also, many of these writers, because of their background, had no appreciation or experience of literary matters save what they experienced in their own households. It is interesting to note that up until the Second World War and even afterwards, but not to the same extent, those writers who wrote in a traditional vein were those who were native speakers of Gaelic, hailing from the *Gaeltacht* and imbued in the traditional Gaelic way of life.

The innovative school on the other hand had no desire for any such 'Gothic revival'. Folk literature belonged to a former period of time, to a defunct way of life, to a sterile frame of mind. They argued that a new Gaelic literature would have to be modern in diction, content and form. It would have to reflect the actualities of contemporary life — there was no room for an oral substratum in such a scheme. It would have to reflect the preoccupations of modern man. It is pertinent to remark that the main exponents of this new doctrine were mostly of the younger generation who were more widely read,

102

educated, travelled, literate and, for whom the Gaelic language was very often an acquired speech.

Closely related to these opposing doctrines was the question of *genres* in the modern literature. Before the founding of the Gaelic League there were no novels, no short stories, no dramas, no biographies or autobiographies in the Gaelic language. The only prose model existing in the oral tradition was the folktale. Hence the traditionalists have ever since cultivated the short story — a story which is short in length rather than one which adheres to the criteria of the short story genre. There are other practical reasons for the proliferation of the 'short' story in modern Gaelic literature. Firstly, it does not take long to write and does not require much literary expertise. This is fine as long as one does not impose any literary rating on the finished product. It is easy to publish in any of the Gaelic magazines or newspapers and gains financial remuneration. Furthermore, in the fullness of time, a collection of such stories can be published without extra effort but with further financial reward. It has never been possible in modern Gaelic literature to be a full-time writer and remain sane and/or solvent in the process as is testified by the case-histories of Pádraic Ó Conaire and Seosamh Mac Grianna.

It must be stressed that the preoccupation of the Gaelic League from the outset was the promotion of the Gaelic language. They looked upon the formation of a literature initially as a way to provide reading and learning material for a populace starved of reading matter. The material which would be published most readily and in greatest quantities was folk material. This policy was also endorsed by foreign and native academics like Dr Richard Henebry who had not a very modern perspective on Gaelic matters. Hence all the initial efforts towards the formulation of a new Gaelic literature were forced and contrived to a certain extent, dictated by exigencies other than purely literary ones. Many of the people who became involved initially in the formation of this literature did so out of an excess of zeal for the cause rather than because of any literary talents of their own. They were not equal to the task as is clearly evident from their efforts. People like Fr Pádraig Ó Duinnín, renowned for his unsurpassed Gaelic-English dictionary and scholarly editions of seventeenth- and eighteenth-century anthologies of poetry, wrote dramas and a novel. Other prominent members of the Gaelic League movement like Douglas Hyde and Peadar Mac Fhionnlaoich did likewise. The latter had a play, *An Táilliúr Cleasach*, published in 1902, which consisted of only seven pages but incorporated two acts and five scenes. Characters were scarcely on-stage before the scene was changed. Another of his plays, *Eilís agus an Bhean Déirce*, was just over three pages in length. Drama is a highly sophisticated art form which is not normally dreamed of by the uninitiated. However, these early plays were written mostly for educational reasons — mainly to be read, discussed, analysed from a linguistic point of view and used as a conversational aid. The dramas were published — sometimes even before they were staged — complete with vocabularies and sometimes with an English translation. Their *raison d'être* is obvious.

All the problems and difficulties inherent in the formation of a new Gaelic literature from essentially nothing have been cited. On the positive side, however, literacy in the language was spreading increasingly, streams of books, pamphlets, etc. were being published and circulated, more branches of the League were being formed nationwide, schools of thought were evolving, literary criteria and schools of criticism were developing. All of this was very salutary. Definite progress was being made. In literary terms, the founding of the Oireachtas in 1897 provided a great impetus. It was instituted to promote the cultural aims of the League on a more public level. It had various literary competitions — short story, drama, poetry etc. These increased and diversified over the years in order to strengthen and encourage different aspects of Gaelic literature. For young writers, the Oireachtas gave stimulus, incentive, financial reward, expert criticism of their works and publishing outlets in its own prize-winners' collections or in Gaelic or other newspapers of the day.

Two of the most important writers to enter the literary scene in the first decade of this century were Pádraig Mac Piarais and Pádraic Ó Conaire, both promoting the innovative school but independently and from different directions. The name of Pádraig Mac Piarais is inseparable from the whole history of the nation and cultural resurgence in Ireland at the turn of the century. He was one of the executed leaders of the 1916 Rising. In literary terms, his importance lies in the fact that he was a very erudite and scholarly person who coherently and repeatedly articulated a modernist, literary philosophy particularly from 1903 to 1909 when he was editor of *An Claíomh Solais*, the official organ of the Gaelic League. He was young, personable and attracted a substantial following. He discussed and formulated his literary principles and, more importantly, endeavoured to add example to precept. He wrote two collections of short stories, *Íosagán agus Scéalta Eile* (1907) and *An Mháthair agus Scéalta Eile* (1916). The first of these collections he referred to as a standard of revolt — a revolt against the folk form in favour of the adoption of a definite, modern, art form. As such they are an embodiment of his literary philosophy. The stories are all located in the *Gaeltacht*. The first collection deals with the innocence and naïvety of children. There is a strong lyrical quality about the stories and they are often referred to as prose poems. However, as a writer generally, he had a limited imagination and insight. His later collection of stories deals mostly with adults and shows significant development. There is not the same sentimentality in these later stories. On the whole he does not concern himself in his writing with the intricate psychological, social, political problems he himself espoused. However, with his practical example of story writing, he provided a tangible model for others to follow.

An important contemporary of Mac Piarais was Pádraic Ó Conaire (1882-1928) who arrived on the Gaelic literary scene — albeit in London where the Gaelic League was also strong — when he won an Oireachtas short story prize in 1904. Unlike Pádraig Mac Piarais, he was no literary doctrinaire but an important practitioner. Born in Galway in the west of Ireland of middle-class background, he spent his formative years in the Ros Muc *Gaeltacht*. He received his secondary education in Dublin and later went to London to work as a clerical officer in the Civil Service. He was actively involved in the Gaelic League there and it was there that he began his creative work. Ó Conaire was more *au fait* with mainstream literary matters than most members of the Gaelic League and in the first decade of this century, he wrote from London the type of contemporary literature that Mac Piarais was advocating from Dublin. Time has established him as one of Ireland's major Gaelic writers. Very prolific, he specialised in the short story but also wrote plays and an important novel, *Deoraíocht* (1910). The location of his works roams from the *Gaeltacht* to London and to an imaginative no man's land. His language is direct, unadorned, arresting. His themes are all-embracing — love, hate, revenge, lunacy, the artist's dilemma — in short, contemporary, relevant and searching. It is to be regretted that several years after Pádraic Ó Conaire's return to Ireland, he endeavoured to live by his pen with disastrous results for his creative talents. The writings of his later years are but a shade of his earlier works since they were prompted by financial necessity rather than literary inspiration. Unfortunately, it was only quite recently that a representative selection of his stories was translated into English. Until then, the outside world had to rely on early translations of two collections of his stories from this later period which did little justice to his true literary talents.

In spite of numerous difficulties, noticeable progress was made in the development of Gaelic literature in the first twenty years of this century due mainly to the efforts of modern-minded people like Mac Piarais and Ó Conaire. There were strong indications that their precepts would be followed in following years. However, 1916 came and went taking with it some very enlightened people like Mac Piarais. Subsequently came the fight for Irish independence, its attainment and the resulting civil war.

When the Free State was set up in 1922, the country had a native government for the first time in centuries. There was in existence no longer a government which was basically hostile towards the Gaelic language and its culture. The new government enshrined and espoused all the aspirations of the Gaelic cause. It actively promoted them as best it saw fit. In reality this resulted in a period of strong nationalist, insular, puritanical, ideological government which had a far-reaching effect on Gaelic literature. The depiction of the traditional Gaelic way of life was actively encouraged and promoted. No unseemly topics could be explicitly treated. The Gaelic language and its literature were compulsory in the educational system in primary and secondary schools. Most Gaelic books written would appear as text books for these schools and hence would have to be suitable from a moral and ideological point of view. The Gaelic academics in the universities belonged to the antiquarian school — mostly folklorists or dialectologists. Their only interest in a modern literary work was from the point of view of the folkloristic or dialect content. Folklore studies came very much to the fore in 1927 with the founding of *An Cumann le Béaloideas Éireann*/The Folklore of Ireland Society by Séamas Ó Duilearga who promoted the view that any literature written in Gaelic would have to be based on the oral tradition.

To give some tangible proof of its commitment to matters Gaelic, the government established its own publishing house — *An Gúm* — in 1926. *An Gúm* had a virtual monopoly over the publication of Gaelic writing for several decades and operated a strict pre-publication censorship. It must be remembered that when a writer of English in Ireland incurred the displeasure of the official state censors — as any serious writer inevitably did — he could leave the country and have his works published elsewhere. Gaelic writers had no such escape route. They succumbed to the demands of *An Gúm* or did not publish at all. The censorship on Gaelic literature was therefore particularly harsh. One writer, Seosamh Mac Grianna, claimed that even the dedication to one of his books was censored.

An Gúm devised a scheme of translation from other literatures, mostly English, into Gaelic as a means of aiding Gaelic writers in a practical way. The idea was that the financial reward for this translation would be very welcome to Gaelic writers. At £1 per thousand words, the money was hard earned and usually dissipated on drink afterwards to restore the literary sensibility of the writers. It was also thought that such work would help the writers to experience other literatures and thereby learn from them. The drawback here lay in the fact that most of the titles selected were fourth-rate English novels of the last century from which no modicum of literary sustenance could be extracted. The experiment was an expensive failure and many of the thousands of copies printed were subsequently reduced to pulp.

The new Irish government also had a commitment towards the

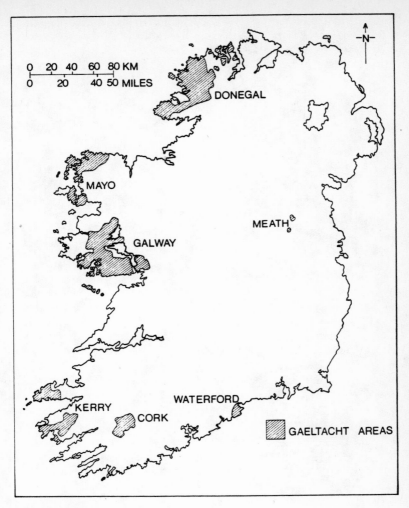

Map 3: Gaeltacht areas 1956

Source: *Atlas of Ireland*, Royal Irish Academy, Dublin 1979.

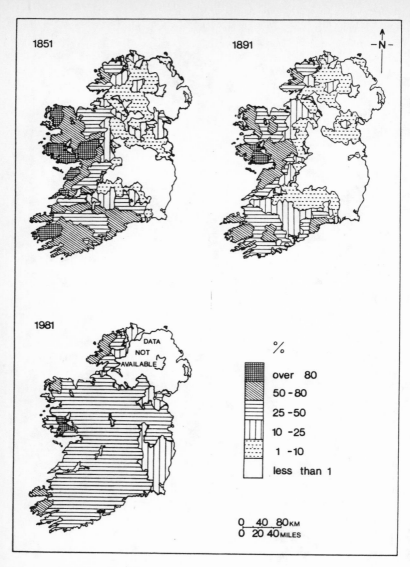

Map 4: Irish speakers 1851-1981

Source: *Atlas of Ireland*, Royal Irish Academy, Dublin 1979, 87; Census of Population of Ireland, vol. 6, 1981.

Gaelic language, particularly in relation to the *Gaeltacht*. A commission was established in 1925 to investigate and recommend how best the situation of the people of the *Gaeltacht*, long beset by poverty and emigration, could be ameliorated. Of the long list of recommendations only a handful were ever implemented. One successful one may be cited here. It was decided in the 1930s to transplant people from the various *Gaeltacht* areas throughout the country into an artificial *Gaeltacht* in Co. Meath. This colony has thrived until the present day despite all the odds.

Hence, a native Irish government was neither a salutary nor enriching experience as far as Gaelic matters were concerned. It had neither the zeal nor the unbounded enthusiasm of the earlier voluntary organisations. Bureaucracy has never been a great catalyst for language or literature.

The twenties and thirties are noted particularly for the emergence of two schools of writing hailing from the *Gaeltacht* — one in Donegal and the other in Kerry. Although emanating from the same cultural hinterland and having strong affinities with each other there are basic differences between the two schools. However, they combined to introduce a retrogressive step into Gaelic literature. All the inroads made by Mac Piarais and Ó Conaire were wiped out and Gaelic literature retreated into its oral past.

Of the Donegal school of writing, perhaps Séamas Ó Grianna (pseudonym *Máire*) was the most vehement, articulate and prolific. Born in north-west Donegal in 1889 in an area renowned for its wealth of oral literature, Ó Grianna enjoyed the traditional way of life of his forebears until he reached his early twenties. He then trained as a teacher, was involved in both wars in Ireland, was editor of several Gaelic journals in the twenties, wrote more than thirty books — short stories mostly, novels, autobiography, short biographies, poems and hundreds of articles. All his works reflect communal life in an idealised, defunct *Gaeltacht* society. There is no attempt at realistic exploration of actualities of *Gaeltacht* life. His language is that of the *seanchaí* (= storyteller): idiomatic, alliterative, stylized, clichéd. His work, however, was well received in the twenties and thirties because the climate was then ripe for such romantic, escapist work presented in flawless, idiomatic Gaelic. Many other Donegal writers wrote in a similar vein. Ó Grianna's younger brother, Seosamh, although starting his literary production in the twenties under the literary influence of his established writer brother, soon showed that he was of greater literary calibre and produced excellent works before his premature renouncing of the literary life in 1935. But he was the exception in the Donegal school of writing.

The second *Gaeltacht* school of writing emanated from the southwest coast of Ireland, from the Great Blasket Island off the coast of

Kerry. This particularly remote island produced three writers in the twenties and thirties who were to add an important new genre to modern Gaelic writing, the autobiography. Their work was subsequently to be used as a model for all would-be autobiographies in all *Gaeltacht* areas throughout the country. It was also to be translated and widely circulated thereby focusing universal attention on this area of modern Gaelic literature. It may be remarked here that of all the modern Gaelic prose written in this century, only about thirty titles or so have been translated into English, and as these are mostly in the realm of the autobiography, they present an erroneous and unbalanced picture of Gaelic literature to the outside world.

It is the normal practice in other literatures for autobiographies to be written by people of some eminence, be they politicians, writers or public personalities generally. Such people encroach upon our lives to some degree, hence our interest in their life stories. Not so in the case of the Gaelic autobiographies. The three pioneers in this field — Tomás Ó Criomhthain (1856-1937), Muiris Ó Súilleabháin (1904-1950) and Peig Sayers (1873-1958) — led very private lives compared to other people. Their autobiographies deal mostly with their life on the island and it is these accounts of communal island life which have so enthralled readers ever since. Right up to the evacuation of the island in the fifties, the Great Blasket was a world set apart from the rest of Ireland and Europe. It preserved a lifestyle which was primitive in manners, customs, beliefs, dress, speech, superstitions etc. It had not been tainted by the 'civilising' influences of the industrial and technological era. Hence its obvious attraction for those with 'the backward look', those interested in vestiges of an earlier civilisation, folklorists, linguists and those who sought an unheralded Gaelic Ireland. Scholars of that ilk regularly came to the Great Blasket and researched in their own particular fields of study, using the untutored islanders as mentors. Most notable among these was Robin Flower, an Anglo-Saxon scholar who was working on Gaelic manuscripts in the British Museum. He formed a close relationship with Tomás Ó Criomhthain. Another important name was that of George Thomson, a professor of Classics from England who persuaded Muiris Ó Súilleabháin to write *Fiche Bliain ag Fás*.

It was Brian Ó Ceallaigh, a native Irishman with an interest in literary matters, who persuaded Tomás Ó Criomhthain to write his autobiography. The genre of the autobiography was selected since these writers had very little formal education and even less experience of literary matters. Of all the genres, the autobiography was the least demanding on them. Ó Criomhthain was the first to write his autobiography, *An tOileánach* (1929) translated as *The Islandman* (1934) by Robin Flower. Next came Ó Súilleabháin's *Fiche Bliain ag Fás*

(1933) translated as *Twenty Years A-Growing* (1933) by George Thomson and Moya Llewelyn Davies. The third was Peig Sayers' book *Peig* (1936) which was translated as *Peig* (1974) by Bryan MacMahon. All three works, appearing in quick succession, gave a uniquely authentic account from the inside of a primitive lifestyle — referred to as Neolithic by one commentator — which was shortly to disappear. Their accounts preceded the scientific investigations in later years of such people as Arensberg, Kimball, Messenger, Fox etc. who, incidentally, were attracted to Ireland to some degree by reading the translations of these autobiographies.

The popularity of these works had far-reaching effects on Gaelic literature generally. Many people thought they could emulate these three writers since a high degree of formal education and literary skills was not a prerequisite. A stream of inferior autobiographies has been the legacy of this school right down to the present day from all *Gaeltacht* areas in Ireland.

Although the twenties and thirties were dominated by these two *Gaeltacht* schools, there were, however, some bright moments. Seosamh Mac Grianna was making considerable progress towards modernism in his work. Éamonn Mac Giolla Iasachta wrote a very respectable — in literary terms — novel *Cúrsaí Thomáis* (1927) which was translated as *The Small Fields of Carrig*. Gaelic drama enjoyed several splendid years. An all-Gaelic theatre — *An Taibhdhearc* — was founded in Galway in 1928 and exists to this day. It benefited considerably, as did Gaelic drama generally, from the active assistance and professionalism of Micheál Mac Liammóir who was wholly proficient in all aspects of the theatre.

These, however, were the exceptions. No major change came until the Second World War when Gaelic literature began to gravitate towards mainstream modern literature to which it has adhered ever since. One of the many reasons for this dramatic change was the publication in 1941 of *An Béal Bocht* (later translated as *The Poor Mouth*) by Myles na gCopaleen (1911-66), the pseudonym of the writer Brian Ó Nualláin who also wrote in English as Flann O'Brien (author of *The Hard Life, At Swim-Two Birds* etc.). Myles satirised both *Gaeltacht* schools of writing in this book and also ridiculed all the extravagant excesses of the Gaelic revival generally. He was to continue his crusade in his column in the *Irish Times* until his death. Aspiring literary fools were not as lightly suffered afterwards. The main thrust of Myles' philosophy was that literary standards could no longer be dictated by peasant usage.

A generation of new young writers arrived on the scene at this time and they introduced their modern views of literature. For the first time poetry blossomed in the works of Máirtín Ó Direáin (1910-88) and Seán Ó Ríordáin (1917-77). Ó Direáin, a native of the Aran Islands, has

111

had numerous volumes of poetry published since the forties. His early poems, written while living in Dublin, are personal lyrics full of nostalgia for his native Aran. His later works have progressed to trace the decline of values in modern urban life generally. Ó Ríordáin spent much of his life in Cork city and his poetry deals mostly with moral and philosophical problems. Of great importance was his treatise on the essence of poetry in the introduction to his first collection of poetry. These two poets by their poetry and discussions of their art have spawned many disciples down to the present day and helped to elevate the standard of Gaelic poetry generally.

A prose writer who has had considerable influence on our literature ever since emerged at this time in the person of Máirtín Ó Cadhain (1906-70). A native speaker of Gaelic from Conemara, a trained teacher, an enthusiast for folklore, a member of the IRA, he published a very pedestrian collection of stories, *Idir Shúgradh agus Dáiríre*, in 1939 which owed much of its inspiration to the sort of *Gaeltacht* literature in vogue at the time. While imprisoned for his Republican sympathies during the Second World War, Ó Cadhain experienced a literary conversion. He read widely of other literatures and his published writings — short stories and a novel — bear witness in later decades to his development as a writer. More than any other Gaelic writer he has experimented with linguistic diversity, variation, versatility, building on a Gaelic substratum which spans ages, provinces and even the Irish Sea. His themes range from traditional rural Irish ones — emigration, poverty, frustration — to Biblical ones reworked and revitalised, to modern, bureaucratic ones. In his private life, he led the life of the *écrivain engagé*, always fighting for the Gaelic Ireland in which he believed. In both literary and public spheres he exercised great influence during his lifetime and afterwards.

Coinciding with the emergence of this school of talented young writers, the forties also witnessed significant developments in the Gaelic publishing world. For example, the year 1942 saw the emergence of *Comhar*, a monthly magazine established by *An Comhchaidreamh*, an association of Gaelic-speaking university graduates. This has become the chief outlet for the publication of experimental Gaelic writing ever since. A new weekly newspaper, *Inniu*, was set up in 1943 and survived until 1984. In 1948 the Gaelic League established its own official magazine *Feasta* which is still in existence. In 1945 a new independent publishing house *Sáirséal agus Dill* emerged which helped to put the standard of published Gaelic works on a par with those being published in the English language in Ireland. In 1948 a Gaelic book club was formed which commanded a readership of some 3,000 which in turn encouraged other publishers to enter into Gaelic publishing and also encouraged Gaelic writers in their writing.

112

All of these developments aided the promotion of a new Gaelic literature by providing ample, unrestricted, rewarding and attractive outlets for the writers' talents. The writers responded in kind. Many new writers appeared in the following decades to introduce wider, more intricate and diversified areas of life. No longer would Gaelic literature be shackled to an oral tradition, constricted by a peasant speech, censored by a puritanical government. The climate was now right for expansion, diversification and experimentation. Séamas Ó Néill (1910-81) from Co. Down boldly tackled the problems faced by a newly-wed, middle-class couple in Dublin suburbia in his novel *Tonn Tuile* (1947). Máire Mhac an tSaoi (1922-) arrived as an exciting new poet with the publication of her *Margadh na Saoire* (1956) which contains some excellent lyrics. Liam Ó Flaithearta, better and more widely known for his writings in the English language, paid tribute to the new era of Gaelic literature when he had a collection of his short stories *Dúil* published in Gaelic in 1953 and this is arguably the best collection of Gaelic short stories in the history of modern Gaelic literature.

The effects of this rejuvenated literary climate were particularly felt in the realm of drama in the fifties and sixties. In 1955 Gael Linn, another newly-formed and very progressive Gaelic body, established a Gaelic drama club. They acquired a hall of their own which they transformed into a theatre. They gained the services of a professional producer and set about staging modern, professional drama regularly. For the first time in its history, Gaelic drama compared very favourably with English drama in Ireland. Young Gaelic writers took up the challenge. Plays were written which were new in content and form. Brendan Behan's famous play *An Giall* (translated as *The Hostage*) was premièred. Other dramatists like Máiréad Ní Ghráda, Eoghan Ó Tuairisc and Seán Ó Tuama came to the fore. Their work was expertly reviewed in the press and this in turn inspired them. The signs looked promising for the future.

Further developments occurred during this period which undoubtedly helped the cause of Gaelic literature generally. An official standard grammar and orthography for the Gaelic language was finally devised and adopted thereby lessening the debilitating effects of dialect partisanship. A modern English-Gaelic dictionary was published in 1959 which helped to keep the Gaelic language abreast of the modern world. Academics began to take a more constructive and informed interest in modern Gaelic literature and to publish their views on it. This led to a better appreciation of that literature among the populace generally.

From the sixties onwards, a new breed of writers emerged. By this stage the majority of Gaelic writers were not native speakers of Gaelic and this has been largely the situation ever since. Some of them like

113

poet, dramatist and novelist Eoghan Ó Tuairisc/Eugene Waters or poet Mícheál Ó hAirtnéide/Michael Hartnett have produced a considerable corpus of literature in both Gaelic and English. The latter eloquently sums up the linguistic dilemma of the modern Gaelic writer in the following:

... gan suim ionam ag criticí	critics ignore me
gan chuntas ó mo chairde,	friends neglect me
fear dearúdta ag an litríocht,	literature has forgotten me
im bhastard, im aonarán;	I'm a bastard, all alone.
tá na Gaeil amhrasach romham	the Gael distrusts me
'ceapann na Gaill gur	the Gall thinks me insane.
as mo mheabhair atáim.	
Siúlaim sléibhte iar-Luimní,	I walk the hills of west Limerick,
breac-Ghalltacht mo dhúchais:	my native half-English-speaking district;
do thréig mé an Béarla —	I have deserted the English tongue
ar dhein mé tuaiplis?	have I made a mistake?

Prose writers like Diarmaid Ó Súilleabháin, Dónall Mac Amhlaigh, Breandán Ó Doibhlin, Séamas Mac Annaidh and many others have left their distinctive seal on modern Gaelic literature. Most significant in recent years has been the emergence of a strong school of female poets like Nuala Ní Dhomhnaill, Áine Ní Ghlinn and Cáitlín Maude who have filled a traditional *lacuna* in our literature.

These writers have kept abreast of the changing face of modern Ireland, an Ireland which is shedding its past and all that it entails, an Ireland which has preserved very few of its native Gaelic-speaking environments, an Ireland which is becoming increasingly urbanised and cosmopolitan.

FURTHER READING
D. Corkery, *The Fortunes of the Irish Language*, Cork 1968.
A. De Blacam, *Gaelic Literature Surveyed*, Dublin 1929.
D. Greene, *The Irish Language*, Dublin 1966.
D. Greene, *Writing in Irish Today*, Cork 1972.
J. Jordan, ed., *The Pleasures of Gaelic Literature*, Cork 1977.
B. Ó Cuív ed., *A View of the Irish Language*, Dublin 1969.
M. Ó Murchú, *The Irish Language*, Dublin 1985.
S. Ó Tuama, ed., *The Gaelic League Idea*, Cork 1972.

8
TRANSLATION AND TRANSITION: WRITING IN ENGLISH 1700-1900

Riana O'Dwyer

THE process of separating English writing in Ireland from that in England began in the seventeenth century with the analysis in pamphlets and letters of the political and economic differences between the countries. This had as its original objective the attainment of similar treatment for the populations of the two jurisdictions. The Anglo-Irish class was charged with the administration of English government in Ireland, but was frequently denied the rewards which might have been expected for carrying out similar duties in England. From Richard Stanihurst's *Treatise Concerning a Plaine and Perfect Description of Ireland* (1577) to Wolfe Tone's *An Argument on behalf of the Catholics of Ireland* (1791) or Edmund Burke's *A Letter on the Affairs of Ireland* (1797), Ireland and its subordination to England absorbed the attention of the most thoughtful writers on Irish affairs. The audience addressed included the policy makers in England as well as the educated governing classes in Ireland. As Seamus Deane has pointed out, the analysis of the situation divided in Ireland on the same broad lines as the contemporary political debate in England: the clash between traditional and Enlightenment values. In the writings of Swift, Berkeley and Edmund Burke the traditional view 'insisted upon the limitations of human reason and the frailty of human nature.' The Enlightenment view, expressed by Toland, Hutcheson and the Molesworth circle, 'Stressed man's rational capacity for goodness and improvement' (Deane, *A Short History of Irish Literature*, 1986, 52-3). The dominant note of these pamphlets was one of argumentative seriousness, of making a reasoned contribution to the debates on government, ethics and philosophy which were also engaging the attention of thoughtful men in England. Their passion derives from the urgency with which they sought to influence the decisions affecting the economic, civil and intellectual life of both countries.

Jonathan Swift (1667-1745) was the writer who first and most brilliantly combined rhetorical objectives with creative literary form. In the course of his career he wrote seventy-five pamphlets on Irish affairs, the most celebrated of which are *The Drapier's Letters* (1722) and *A Modest Proposal for Preventing the Children of the Poor in Ireland from being Burdensome, and for making them Beneficial* (1729). These texts incorporate the Swiftian strategy of adopting a *persona*, The Drapier, or the Modest Proposer, who elaborates the very position Swift wished to attack. Similarly in *The Battle of the Books* (1704) and *A Tale of a Tub* (1704) the errors of Dissenters, Catholics and Free Thinkers are cloaked in the tones and vocabularies of speakers espousing these false views. This rhetorical impersonation is carried off with such convincing versatility that the reader is in danger of being unable to distinguish the opposition of the author to the prevalence of such views. Swift was a firm supporter of the Anglican Church and a defender of its 'middle position', against the pressure for greater toleration that was being exerted by Dissenting Protestants and Catholics alike. He was also a supporter of the rights of Irish Protestants in matters of trade and commerce, wishing Ireland to enjoy the same freedom in these matters as the English did. Events, both personal and political, soon confirmed Swift's growing disillusionment concerning the possibility of religious and political reform. Instead of securing a bishopric in England, he was appointed Dean of St Patrick's Cathedral in Dublin in 1713. In the following year the return of his political enemies, the Whigs, to power in England separated him from any direct influence on the makers of government policy. In Ireland, however, he wrote the work by which he is best remembered. *Gulliver's Travels* (1726) has survived as one of the central works of eighteenth-century English literature. It incorporates all of Swift's concerns about bad government, misguided human endeavours, the follies of scientists, philosophers, political theorists, economists, as well as the greed and materialism of human kind. The imaginative deployment of a variety of styles, levels of irony, and satirical conventions elevates Gulliver's central concern with the folly of human pride above the squabbles of its own time and place and gives it a universal dimension.

In the eighteenth century, London was not only the focus of political life but also of publishing and theatrical activity. At this time there was no separate literary development in Ireland, any more than there was a separate Irish political life. Therefore, Irish-born writers gravitated to London, as did Irishmen with political ambitions, to exert their influence at the centre of cultural and political power. Sometimes these ambitions were combined, as in the careers of Edmund Burke (1729-97) and Richard Brinsley Sheridan (1751-1816), who were both writers and parliamentarians. Sheridan's plays *The Rivals* (1775), *The School for Scandal* (1777) and *The Critic* (1779) were enormously successful on the London stage, just as the plays of William Congreve (1670-1729) and George

Farquhar (c. 1677-1707) had been earlier. These writers conformed to the expectations of the London audiences. They belong to the English literary tradition even when their approach stretched the limits of its accepted conventions as did Laurence Sterne in *Tristram Shandy* (1759-67). Oliver Goldsmith (1728-74), in his poem *The Deserted Village*, drew upon his memories of childhood in rural Ireland, but his observations are generalised into a lament for the passing of a pastoral golden age. The fate of Auburn was that of many English villages as the Industrial Revolution gathered pace. These writers were not conscious of themselves as contributing to a separate Irish tradition, and did not feel the need to express in their writings an experience different from that of their English contemporaries.

The year 1800 is usually taken as marking a change in this position. It is the date of the Act of Union, and of the publication of *Castle Rackrent* by Maria Edgeworth. With the Act of Union the centre of political and economic power shifted officially from Dublin to London. At the same time the development of Romanticism encouraged an interest in things primitive and rural, in wild scenery and unspoiled people, in folk tales and ancient mythologies, in the periphery rather than the centre. The scene was set for the discovery by the Anglo-Irish of the cultural treasures of the Gaelic past. It is paradoxical that it should have occurred at a time when their own economic dominance was threatened from London by the pressure of reforms, and in Ireland by the various forms of mismanagement which had become endemic. Gaelic culture too was on the brink of collapse after a sustained period of impoverishment and neglect. In particular the Irish language, necessary conduit of Irish poetry, song and story telling, declined throughout the nineteenth century. With the dissemination of English throughout Ireland, the special quality of Irish English, influenced by the syntax and style of the Irish language, attracted the attention of many writers. Maria Edgeworth was the first to make use of these linguistic resources in *Castle Rackrent*. Moreover, she also isolated a question which was to become central throughout the nineteenth century: the relationship of the Protestant landowners to the Catholic peasantry. The friction arising out of this relationship became the central political issue in Ireland once Catholic emancipation had been gained in 1829, and gave rise to a central concern of Protestant writers in the nineteenth century: the effort to reconcile the antagonistic elements of Irish society in a common cultural bond, based on the recognition of a Gaelic culture to which both sides could pay allegiance. Implicit in this endeavour was the expectation that mutual appreciation of the Gaelic past might diffuse the pressures for political reform and reduce the difficulties of governing the country.

The impetus for a reassessment of the native Gaelic culture came from two sources: a growth in scholarly investigation of the literature and music of Gaelic Ireland, and a change in aesthetic standards promoted by the Romantic movement. This prepared writers for the task of disseminating the newly-discovered texts and airs to the general public, and simultaneously prepared the audience to receive them. As early as the 1760s a movement to recover folk poetry had begun in England, stimulated at first by the Ossianic forgeries of James Macpherson and sustained by the scholarly publication of Evan Evans's *Specimens of the Poetry of the Ancient Welsh Bards* (1764), and Thomas Percy's *Reliques of Ancient English Poetry* (1765). To these were added in 1789 Charlotte Brooke's *Reliques of Irish Poetry*. The search for texts which would reveal the secrets of the Gaelic past was paralleled by a developing interest in the ruins and monuments of the Irish countryside which drew the attention of amateur archeologists. Less tangible survivals such as music were also valued, and in 1792 a festival of Irish harpists took place in Belfast which gave an opportunity to Edward Bunting to record the airs they played and initiate his famous *General Collection of the Ancient Music of Ireland* (1796-1840).

Throughout the nineteenth century the work of recovery continued, growing more scholarly and professional as time went on. In the 1830s the Ordnance Survey Office in Dublin began work on a new map of Ireland, which involved a detailed inventory of the countryside and the identification of its topographical features. George Petrie (1790-1866), Eugene O'Curry (1796-1862) and John O'Donovan (1809-61) were involved in this project and also published important works on Irish music, ancient buildings and manuscript materials. Academic interest in the Irish language developed as the language itself went into decline. John O'Donovan published *A Grammar of the Irish Language* in 1845, and the German scholar Zeuss published *Grammatica Celtica* in 1853. Societies devoted to the study of Irish language and literature were founded, from the Gaelic Society in 1807 to the Gaelic League in 1893. Translation of Irish texts was an important element in the popularisation of Gaelic material, as relatively few of those interested in the literature acquired a competence in the language.

Charlotte Brooke in her *Reliques of Irish Poetry* (1780) published original Irish texts and with them her own translations. She thought of the poems as 'sweet ambassadresses of cordial union between two countries that seemed formed by nature to be joined by every bond of interests, and of amity' (*Reliques of Irish Poetry*, viii). She was followed by J.J. Callanan (1795-1829), James Hardiman (1790-1855), and John O'Daly (1800-78), who all endeavoured to make Irish poetry accessible through translation. Samuel Ferguson (1810-86) and James Clarence Mangan (1803-49) raised the art of translation to a new level. Their best work can be read for its intrinsic interest as poetry. This mediation of Gaelic material to an English-speaking audience became the central task of Irish poetry in the nineteenth century. Indeed, an obsessive interest in translation is one of the distinguishing features of Irish poetry in English during this period.

Thomas Moore began the task of popularising Gaelic music and subject matter in his *Irish Melodies* (1807-34). He wrote new lyrics in English to be sung to traditional Irish airs, of the kind collected by Bunting. Moore attempted to convey the spirit of the original in his lyrics, and he interpreted this spirit as one of sorrow and depression tempered by sudden flashes of humour and joy. This interpretation fitted very well with the popular mood of drawing-room music at the time, and contributed to the enormous success of the *Melodies*. Throughout the nineteenth century the audience for Irish poetry included the English reading public, and their taste, to a considerable extent, dictated the form into which Celtic material was transmuted.

The early translators made little effort to capture the rhyme and assonantal patterns of the Gaelic originals in their versions, but Ferguson and Mangan did achieve some success in this. Ferguson was a highly self-conscious translator and published articles on the problems involved in the *Dublin University Magazine* in 1834, in which he argued for a more accurate, scholarly presentation of Gaelic material. He contributed many translations to the Dublin journals, which were eventually consolidated in *Lays of the Western Gael* in 1865. An ambitious version of a long epic poem, *Congal*, appeared in 1872, the *Lays of the Red Branch* in 1897. A Unionist by background and inclination, his poetry explored the common cultural ground on which he hoped to unite the Anglo-Irish and Gaelic peoples of Ireland. The merging of the civilising influence of the Anglo-Irish with the imaginative, intuitive powers of the Gaels would produce, he hoped, a new version of Irish culture and a genuinely unified country within the British Empire.

This vision is unattainable in the poetry of James Clarence Mangan. Though he had little knowledge of Irish, and based his verse translations on prose versions of the originals, his empathy with the laments of the Gaelic poets is born out of a common experience of dispossession, rather than on literary voyeurism. He contributed poems to *The Poets and Poetry of Munster* (1849), edited by John O'Daly. O'Daly saw his task as the restoration to the Irish peasantry of their lost heritage, and therefore he published his collections in cheap pamphlet form, sold at a penny each. The translators who assisted him, Mangan, Edward Walsh, George Sigerson, achieved considerable success in remaining faithful to the originals in verse structure and theme. Mangan himself continues to be regarded as a significant poet, though no collection of his work was published during his lifetime. He adopted the persona of the solitary poet, which genuinely reflected his persistent poverty, and also masked his own misgivings about his poetic gift. His poems were usually presented as 'translations', from German, French and Oriental languages as well as from Irish, and his true gift emerged when the themes of the originals reflected his personal experience of loneliness, despair and disillusionment. While he was very far from participating actively in a national programme of cultural revival his poetry was later co-opted by that movement. His best work is centred on an outcast figure meditating on the present state of desolation, and contrasting it with a previous period of happiness, as in 'O'Hussey's Ode to the Maguire' or 'A Vision of Connaught in the Thirteenth Century'. During the Famine years Mangan wrote poems such as 'The Warning Voice' which were deeply concerned with the fate of his country, but on the whole his sense of pathological isolation and vulnerability is indicative of the larger insecurity which impaired the development of a genuine Irish literature in the nineteenth century.

The scholarship devoted to the retrieval of the Gaelic past, and the debates among the educated Irish about the future direction of the country found an outlet in journals such as the *Dublin University Magazine* (1833-77) and the *Dublin Review* (1836-69). Popular reading material also became available through a series of inexpensive publications, the *Dublin Penny Journal* (1832-6), *The Irish Penny Magazine* (1833-4), and *The Irish Penny Journal* (1840). These contributed to the wide dispersal of popular ballads and songs on topical subjects in the 1830s and early 1840s. The ballads were written in English, to be sung to familiar tunes and airs, and they penetrated to the working people of Ireland in a way that the painstaking translations of Irish poetry were never able to do. When the social and political pressures of the 1840s developed, the wide circulation journal and the emotional appeal of the ballad were combined in yet another dramatic conjunction of literature and politics in Ireland.

The Nation was founded in 1842 by Thomas Davis (1814-45) along with Charles Gavan Duffy (1816-1903) and John Blake Dillon (1816-66) in order to alert people to an urgent sense of national crisis, and they used verse and polemical articles in order to foster a sense of Irish cultural identity which would lead to the repeal of the Act of Union. Davis himself wrote over eighty political ballads, including 'A Nation Once Again' and 'The West's Asleep' which still have power to evoke the aspiration for liberty and cultural self-possession which animated the intellectuals of Young Ireland. After the disappointment of these hopes in 1848, and the agrarian violence which followed the Famine, revolutionary and reformist objectives began to take precedence over literary pursuits with the development of Fenianism and the formation of the Land League (1879). John

Mitchel (1815-75), who was sentenced to transportation after the Young Ireland Rising, left a record of his experience in *Jail Journal* (1854) which contrasts starkly with the sentimentality of the ballads and which contributed to the demand for separation as the only solution to the Irish problem. For the present, however, the growing political awareness of the general population concentrated on land reform rather than political separation as the most immediate and attainable goal.

Although the land tenure system was plainly in need of immediate reform, the Land League's first task was to gain widespread support for its objectives by raising the consciousness of the tenants to the possibilities of combined action. A positive image of the Irish peasant had to be created which would both dispel the servility of the tenants, and mobilise them in a concerted demand for change. The creation of an alternative view of the Irish past was a means to this end: the people had once owned the land of Ireland, and were now reclaiming what was theirs by ancient right. In this version of Irish history the peasantry were the true gentry of Ireland, inherently noble, intelligent, creative and courageous, refined by the fires of adversity into a virtuous, religious and spiritual people. Their oppressors, whether English government or Irish landlord, were by implication or assertion, materialistic, cruel, inhuman, unimaginative and greedy. This vision of the noble peasant was a defensive reaction against the stage-Irish cartoons in *Punch*, and the disparaging references to Irish savages and apes which are to be found in the writings of Disraeli, Froude, Charles Kingsley and Lord Salisbury. The idealisation of Irish rural life was thus political as well as literary. As dissident members of the Anglo-Irish Ascendancy sought common ground with the Catholic Irish based on an appreciation of the rich Gaelic past, the landless people adapted the vision of a glorious past to their own purposes. Since these involved the dismantling of the political and economic power of the landowners, the process became one of separation, rather than of unification. This did not become clear, however, until much later.

In the 1880s and 1890s a change occurred in the use that writers were making of the resources of Gaelic literary and folk material and the subject matter of Irish experience. It did not seem very dramatic at first. Standish O'Grady's energetic and enthusiastic celebration of Irish mythological material in his two volume *History of Ireland* (1878 and 1880) made the scholarly texts available in a popular form to readers without Irish. Yeats's *Wanderings of Oisin* (1889) was a long poem based loosely on available material from the Fenian Cycle. George Moore's novel *A Drama in Muslin* (1886) applied current realistic fictional techniques to the questions of the Land League demands and the rôle of women in Irish Ascendancy society. Somerville and Ross wrote from within that same tradition with such ironic perception that their readers could avoid, if they wished, the serious implications of *The Real Charlotte* (1894) and laugh instead at *Some Experiences of an Irish R.M.* (1898). The Gaelic League, founded by Eoin MacNeill and Douglas Hyde in 1893 appeared to be another in a line of revivalist societies which had been trying to halt the decline of the Irish language. Lady Gregory's collection of stories and legends (later published as *Visions and Beliefs in the West of Ireland*, 1920) and Yeats's *Irish Folk Stories and Fairy Tales* (1888) provided some additional material gathered from the abundant supply of elderly story-tellers. It was a natural step for Yeats to use some of this background in plays such as *The Countess Cathleen* (1892) and *Cathleen Ní Houlihan* (1902). The anthology of young poets called *Poems and Ballads of Young Ireland* (1888) seemed by its title to be looking backwards to the Young Ireland movement of the 1840s, as much as looking forward. Yet out of this disparate range of endeavours was to develop a literary movement which has come to be known as the Irish Literary Revival and which brought Irish writing into the frontline of twentieth-century world literature.

At the time, not all of the writers who are now perceived as contributing to this movement were conscious of belonging to a concerted effort. The Celtic Revival a century earlier had begun with the efforts of scholars to rescue texts and artefacts from oblivion and had influenced a generation of poets and novelists. These had laid the foundation for an acceptance of the value of the Irish cultural heritage which a new generation took for granted and wished to develop. The advice that Yeats and his friends gave to each other was to return to the ancient legends for inspiration, or to explore the resources of contemporary folk material for their own creative purposes. The emphasis shifted from one of preservation and restoration to one of creativity and exploration. The Gaelic material, ancient and modern, should be used for the purpose of throwing new light on the situation of contemporary Ireland, and of encouraging its alteration into a new Ireland, self-aware, self-confident and culturally distinct from England. The procedures adopted had their limitations, however, as John Wilson Foster has pointed out: 'In colonising Gaelic literature the *litterateurs* imposed an urban discourse upon a rural (in the case of folklore), a modern upon an ancient (in the case of bardic literature), an English upon an Irish (in the case of both)' (Foster, 1982, 134).

After the fall of Parnell a separation gradually occurred between those who were working politically and those who were working culturally for change in Ireland. Yeats perceived, for example, that Ireland lacked a native theatre, and set himself to remedy the situation in an effort which culminated in the foundation of the Abbey Theatre in 1904. One of the key achievements of the early years of the Abbey was the production of the plays of Synge. These plays, written by a Protestant Dubliner, and the drama of Lady Gregory, revealed the possibilities of the presentation of rural life on the stage, and encouraged dramatists such as Padraic Colum, T.C. Murray, and George Shiels. Their explorations were not always celebratory, however, and the *Playboy* riots of 1907 were simply a dramatic manifestation of the dissatisfaction of many nationalists with a depiction of peasant life which did not idealise it. For the separatist movement to gain ground, a powerful myth of dispossession of a noble Irish people had been necessary. Literature soon discovered that the reality was more complex, and the ideal of artistic integrity began to supplant the more propagandist aim of national glorification and self-justification. James Joyce's refusal to condemn *The Countess Cathleen* was his first public gesture in defence of the artist's responsibility to his work, rather than to his country.

In the space of a few years, Irish writing progressed beyond the injunction to use Irish subject matter towards a development of form and language which would be especially adapted to the expression of the Irish experience. The several experiments of the Abbey Theatre, with poetic drama, Ibsenite drama, and rural drama created considerable variety in its productions before it was overwhelmed by the popular demand for a predominance of country kitchen plays. Yeats's poetic needs soon caused him to move beyond the use of Celtic myths and legends to the development of a personal symbolism and verse technique. The short story, a genre which builds naturally on the narrative resources of Irish language story-telling, began to attract many of those writers who were close to the pulse of rural and small-town Ireland. They could be published readily in newspapers and journals and find an immediate Irish readership without having to indulge in the explanations and digressions which writers like Carleton, the Banim brothers and Gerald Griffin had been unable to avoid when writing for the English market. Above all, Irish writers no longer felt constrained by a formal English prose style. Writing for an Irish public, the syntactic and verbal resources of Irish English, close to the rhythms and descriptive devices of the Irish language, could be used unselfconsciously on the stage and in fiction. If these efforts were praised in England and America so much the better. Only when the effort of translation, explanation and mediation was abandoned did Irish literature, ironically, become of interest outside Ireland.

It was not possible, of course, for all writers to find acceptance within the confines of close-knit Irish squabbles and opinions. Hardly had Irish writing begun to find its authentic voice than its writers began to feel the need to escape from the constrictions of its social and political pieties. George Moore, having spent some years in

Ireland and been involved in the establishment of the Abbey Theatre, returned to England in 1911 and lived abroad for the rest of his life. James Joyce gave apocalyptic significance to his own departure in 1904 for Europe, finding in his exile no material for fiction, but the freedom to continue his uncompromising examination of Dublin and of life in the 'nicely polished looking-glass' of his novels. The duration of the Irish literary revival is as uncertain as its origins: some critics see it ending in 1916, others see its influence continuing to the death of Yeats in 1939. Its legacy includes the poetry and drama of Yeats, the plays of Synge and O'Casey, the plays, stories and novels of George Moore, and, in reaction, the fiction of James Joyce, together with the work of many other talented writers. By 1900 Irish literature had begun to move beyond the Romantic inheritance which had dominated its development in the nineteenth century, to become an influential participant in twentieth-century Modernism.

FURTHER READING

General Studies of Irish Literature
S. Deane, *A Short History of Irish Literature*, London 1986.
R. Hogan, *The Macmillan Dictionary of Irish Literature*, Connecticut 1978, London 1980.
A.N. Jeffares, *Anglo-Irish Literature*, London 1982.
H. Kosok ed., *Studies in Anglo-Irish Literature*, Bonn 1982.
R. McHugh and M. Harmon eds, *Short History of Anglo-Irish Literature*, Dublin 1982.
A. Martin, *Anglo-Irish Literature*, Dublin 1980.
W. Zach ed., *Literary Interrelations: Ireland, England and the World*, 3 vols, Tübingen 1987.

Nineteenth-century Poetry and Irish Literary Revival
M. Brown, *The Politics of Irish Literature from Thomas Davis to W.B. Yeats*, Seattle and London 1972.
T. Brown, *Northern Voices: Poets from Ulster*, Dublin 1975.
P. Costello, *The Heart Grown Brutal: The Irish Revolution in Literature from Parnell to the Death of Yeats, 1891-1939*, Dublin 1978.
S. Deane, 'The Literary Myths of the Revival' in *Celtic Revivals*, London 1985.
R. Fallis, *The Irish Renaissance: An Introduction to Anglo-Irish Literature*, Syracuse NY, 1977, Dublin 1978.
J.W. Foster, 'The Revival of Saga and Heroic Romance during the Irish Renaissance: The ideology of Cultural Nationalism', in *Studies in Anglo-Irish Literature*, ed. H. Kosok, Bonn 1982.
D. Kiberd, 'The Perils of Nostalgia: a Critique of the Revival', in *Literature and the Changing Ireland*, ed. P. Connolly, Gerrards Cross 1982.
P.L. Marcus, *Yeats and the Beginning of the Irish Renaissance*, Ithaca and London 1970.
C.G. Ó Háinle, 'Towards the Revival. Some Translations of Irish Poetry:

1789-1897', in *Literature and the Changing Ireland*, ed. P. Connolly, Gerrards Cross 1982.

D. Ó Muirithe, *The English Language in Ireland*, Cork 1977.

P. Rafroidi, *Irish Literature in English: The Romantic Period*, 2 vols, Gerrards Cross 1980.

G.J. Watson, *Irish Identity and the Literary Revival*, London 1979.

R. Welch, *Irish Poetry from Moore to Yeats*, Gerrards Cross 1980.

9
FROM UNITED KINGDOM TO DIVIDED ISLAND: ASPECTS OF THE IRISH EXPERIENCE 1850-1922

Gearóid Ó Tuathaigh

IN recent times historians have become rather wary of describing the Great Famine of the 1840s as 'a watershed in Irish history'. They point to the fact that Irish population growth was already slowing down (if indeed it was not already beginning to decline) in the years before 1845, as rising mortality and, in particular, rising emigration rates began to put the brakes on a population which by 1845 was probably approaching 8½ million. Moreover, in more general economic terms, the heavy emphasis on livestock which has been such a prominent feature of Irish agriculture since the Famine (to say nothing of its significance in earlier periods) was already becoming pronounced in the two decades before the 1840s though it needed both the Famine and the agricultural recession 1859-64 to finally put tillage into decisive decline relative to cattle in the Irish agricultural economy. Again, the rise of Belfast as the major centre of a distinct industrial enclave in the north-east was also well under way before the Famine, though here also the post-Famine acceleration of existing trends was so rapid that many commentators would count the Famine as marking a transition of such major consequence as to merit the description 'watershed'.

Even in more general cultural terms it is clear that in the years before the Famine the powerful wave of anglicisation (in speech, customs and habits) was already moving inexorably, if unevenly, across the country from east to west, and, in class terms, was percolating downwards towards the labouring classes in even the more isolated areas. The decimation of the lower levels of rural society in the Famine years had regional and cultural as well as class implications. Casualties were highest among the still largely Gaelic-speaking peasantry of the western half of the country. The Ireland which emerged from the Famine trauma in 1851 was, in every respect, a more anglicised society. The Gaelic element had been decimated. Continuing emigration and the inexorable penetration of the more

126

remote regions by English speech and cultural influence (a complex matter of elementary education and increased literacy, greater travel opportunities and a general trend towards a more 'open' society even in these more isolated areas) further accelerated the attenuation of the Gaelic residuum in the decades after 1850. The full psycho-social implications of this language change in Ireland have not been investigated in any great detail. But it has been suggested that the fervour of Irish religious life in the post-Famine decades was, in some way, a compensation for the loss of a language-bound identity.

Yet even in this area of religious life the precise significance of the Famine has been questioned. The extraordinarily high level of religious conformity and devotional regularity, which were such a feature of Irish Catholicism right up to the 1950s, are now seen as being well under way in the pre-Famine decades as the dominant style of Catholicism in the more anglicised dioceses of the east and south (depending in each case, of course, on the energy, the disposition and the resources available to individual bishops). However, during the post-Famine generation — so the conventional wisdom now has it — this church-centred, clergy-regulated Catholic devotional conformity became the norm throughout most of Catholic Ireland, as Cardinal Paul Cullen's influence became dominant in a church in which an ever-increasing clerical establishment (priests, brothers and nuns) ministered to a constantly diminishing Catholic population in which the comfortable tenant-farmer and the commercial-professional middle-class were increasingly the culturally dominant social classes. Cultural recidivism might still occur from time to time in the more remote western (and still partly Gaelic) dioceses and parishes; but the 'devotional revolution' in Irish Catholicism had triumphed by the turn of the century.

These few opening remarks on the significance of the Famine for socio-economic and more general cultural trends in Irish society — a major watershed or merely a drastic accelerator of trends already in train — may be worth keeping in mind while we consider some of the main developments in Irish society in the period between the Famine and the creation of the 'two states of Ireland' in 1920–22. The basic socio-economic data are clear. By 1851 the population of Ireland stood at c.6.6 million; sixty years later it had fallen to c.4.4 million. Emigration, running ahead of the rate of natural increase, was the main factor in this population decline. The Irish economy in the second half of the nineteenth century was fully integrated into the free-trading, industralised British economy. It had some characteristics of both a developed and an underdeveloped economy. Thus, on the one hand, while the period 1850–1920 saw increased urbanisation in Ireland, on the other, the majority of the population throughout most of the country continued to depend for a living on agriculture.

The agricultural economy itself became increasingly dominated by livestock production in the post-Famine decades. For example, whereas in 1845, as Lee reminds us, 'potatoes, grain and livestock each accounted for about one-third of the value of agricultural output, by 1914 the livestock sector contributed three quarters of the total value.' There were also marked regional variations in agricultural production and, generally, the more commercial farming was to be found in the east, the south, in east Connacht and in parts of Ulster.

Dairy production was especially strong in Munster by the end of the century. In the more extreme westerly zone — and in the hilly inland zone of poor land from Leitrim to Monaghan — the quality of land and consequently the level of agricultural production was generally lower. In the western periphery, in particular, many small-holdings up to the end of the nineteenth century had a significant quasi-subsistence character. On these minute holdings of poor land along the west coast only earnings from seasonal migration, or emigrants' remittances (or a combination of both), plus the relentless export of surplus children, made possible the survival of those who remained. Earnings abroad (whether seasonal or through remittances) effectively supported a problematic social structure on small-holdings not adequate in themselves for the support of the small-holder families.

The state itself, prompted no doubt by the fear of another 'Famine' during the distress caused by the agricultural depression of the late 1870s, intervened to improve this dangerously vulnerable economy, and in 1891 the Conservative government of the day established a special Congested Districts Board to undertake economic and social 'improvements' in designated poorer or 'congested' districts, mostly along the Atlantic seaboard. The Board's activities — the prime objective of which was the relief of congestion on poor land — involved a range of schemes, from the encouragement of cottage industry, arts and crafts, through the provision of vocational education aimed at improving methods of fishing and husbandry, to investment in infrastructure (piers and harbours) and in equipment and machinery. These schemes and activities undoubtedly contributed significantly to improved living standards even in the more remote and least economically endowed areas of the west at the turn of the century. Indeed, the developmental role of the Board was so widely appreciated that the total area under its jurisdiction expanded considerably during its lifetime. At the time of its abolition, immediately after the establishment of the Free State, the Board was active in areas whose total population was over a half-million.

For the more developed zones of Irish agriculture the three decades or so after 1845 were generally years of prosperity. Apart from a

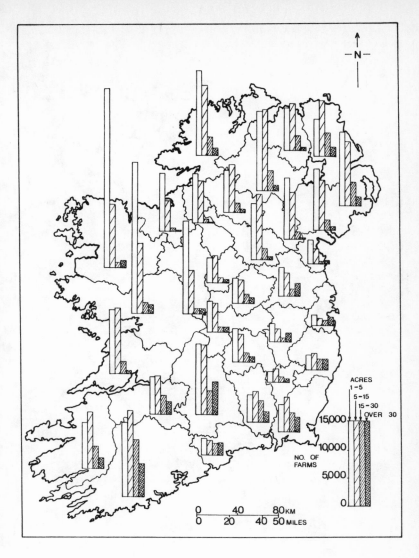

Map 5: Farm size 1841

Source: T.W. Freeman, *Pre-Famine Ireland: a study in historical geography.*
Manchester University Press 1959, 55, Fig. 9.

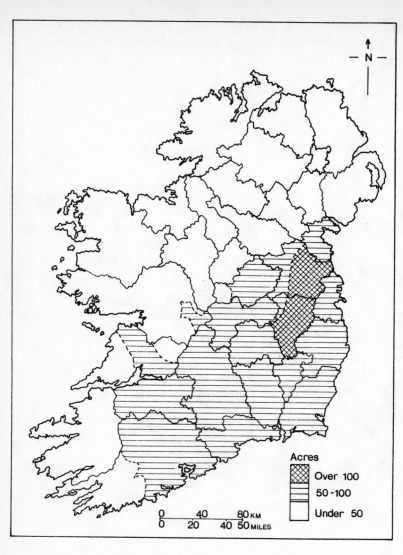

Map 6: Farm size 1936

Source: E. Rumpf and A. Hepburn, *Nationalism and Socialism in Twentieth-Century Ireland*, Liverpool University Press 1977, 46, Fig. 6; T.W. Freeman, *Ireland*, London 1972, 186.

serious depression in the years 1859–64, yields and prices combined to keep the various sectors of Irish agriculture generally buoyant in the mid Victorian decades. The rising tide did indeed lift all boats; but, obviously, some higher than others. It now seems clear that, allowing for exceptional cases, rents did not rise as quickly as prices. This meant that tenants generally got a share in the prosperity of these years; and the more substantial tenant-farmers (especially those with favourable leases) seem to have done particularly well, if their houses, furnishings, general consumption patterns, savings and bank deposits, dowries for their daughters and careers for their sons are anything to go by. Even the smaller farmers improved their living standards (with pigs and poultry bringing in invaluable extra income — especially to women — on small farms.). Moreover, the inexorable decline in the numbers of cottiers and farm labourers (through emigration) gradually eased competition and allowed wages to improve for those who remained. In short, despite marked differences in living standards between the different social classes in rural Ireland, the general experience was that things were improving, and the general expectation was that they would continue to do so. Later, when conditions changed for the worse, reversing or frustrating these rising expectations in the countryside proved to be a difficult and socially explosive business.

It mustn't be thought that all was harmony, sweetness and light in the Irish countryside in the immediate post-Famine decades. Evictions, though far fewer than those 'threatened', and often made as a kind of final notice to force the payment of rent arrears, were always bitterly resented, and frequently resisted. Some were on such a scale as to lead to public outcry and to sustain implacable hostility towards 'landlordism', not only among the actual victims of evictions but also among the tenants as a whole. This general resentment against 'evicting landlords' was especially strong among those 'forced to emigrate'.

The drastic changes in social structure caused by the Famine (the decimation of labourers, cottiers and small-holders) were not reversed in later decades. There was, it is true, a resumption of some aspects of the pre-Famine economic and social patterns in the poor peripheral western areas. But, generally, the relentless decline of the labourer, cottier and small-farmer class and the consolidation of very small holdings so as to bring about a modest but socially significant increase in the number of holdings between, let us say, 50 and 150 acres, were the principal features of post-Famine rural society. This was the pattern of occupancy and social change on the land in the period between 1850 and 1920 (Maps 5, 6).

So far as economic performance (as distinct from ownership or social structure) is concerned, Irish agriculture, given the structure of occupancy of Irish land, was neither particularly efficient nor notably backward in responding to the market conditions in which it found itself, as part of a free-trading, industrialised British state where cheap food was a prime consideration of economic policy. Landlord re-investment in land was, it seems, low by British standards. Food processing, and in particular the provision of breakfast-table produce for an expanding urban society with changing consumption demands in food, was disappointingly underdeveloped in Ireland, compared with the performance of the Danes and the Dutch. Indeed, in the general area of maximising added value to primary foodstuffs the Irish agricultural sector was not a notable success. But on the other hand the internal system in Ireland for producing, rearing and selling cattle to Britain was well developed, as were the transport and communications systems (a dense railway network was completed between c.1850 and 1880), and so too were the appropriate institutions for banking and credit. In sum, given soil, climate, market conditions, structure of occupancy and the return on labour and other inputs, Irish farmers seem to have behaved quite rationally as individuals. They clearly did not think in wider terms of added value or employment through food processing. But what made good sense for the individual farmer was not necessarily the best option for optimising the economic returns from Irish agriculture as a whole.

The fact that 'the flight from the land' in later nineteenth-century Ireland usually meant emigration to Boston, New York, Liverpool or Glasgow, prompts the question of why Irish towns and cities were not absorbing the surplus labour of rural Ireland. The answer is that the majority of Irish towns were incapable of absorbing surplus rural labour because they were themselves economically depressed (and, in the eyes of many, socially and culturally stagnant) in the second half of the century. There were, of course, some exceptions. Dublin, the 'deposed capital' as Mary Daly has called it, continued to function as a major centre for distribution, trade and commerce, as well as being the administrative centre for state and corporate institutional activity. But Dublin's successful manufacturing base was quite limited — brewing, distilling and confectionery carried the flag almost entirely for the city's main exports. For the rest, the craftsmen and skilled tradesmen of the city during the later nineteenth century found themselves constantly on the retreat before British competition in consumer goods (especially as mechanisation continued to advance in hardware products in the middle third of the century). Thus, even though the city experienced only a modest growth in population in the period 1850–1920, by the early twentieth century it had a depressed working class, with a housing problem and a public health record among the worst in urban Europe. The tenement conditions in which the unemployed and underemployed of Edwardian Dublin — Joyce's 'centre of paralysis' — lived and suffered, excited the passionate political activism of the socialists Larkin and Connolly, and sparked the indignation of many writers, including the young Sean O'Casey.

If Dublin presented the picture of a once prosperous capital — 'the second city of the empire' — now fallen on hard times, then for contrast Belfast was the obvious, indeed the sole, candidate among Irish cities. In sheer growth terms Belfast was the spectacular success story of Irish urban history in the Victorian and early Edwardian era. Between 1851 and 1914 its population grew from 100,000 to 400,000. The economic surge which sustained this urban growth was based, in the first instance, on the revival of the city's staple industry, linen, in the middle third of the century, together with the ancillary industries generated by mechanised textile production. But from the 1860s onwards shipbuilding began to assume a growing rôle in Belfast's economic progress. On the eve of the First World War the Belfast shipyards were building the largest vessels afloat (including the *Titanic*), with some 12,000 men involved directly in shipbuilding, to say nothing of the thousands employed in support or spin-off industries.

As often happens, success breeds success. Belfast's manufacturing base by the early twentieth century included many products, for example in food and drink, which were in no way related to linen, shipbuilding or engineering, but which probably owed their success, in part at least, to the general climate of entrepreneurial and business dynamism which the major industries undoubtedly generated. Whether the contrast between Belfast's 'success' and Dublin's relative 'failure' in manufacturing growth is ultimately attributable to differences in the supply (and quality) of entrepreneurial resources between the business elites of the two cities, and whether such differences were themselves predictable (in the light of key cultural/educational determinants) or random and accidental, are matters about which historians have long argued, and continue to argue. But there can be no argument about the fact that, in growth terms, Belfast prospered under the Union while Dublin, in general, did not.

Furthermore, while Ireland was a more urbanised society in 1914 than it had been sixty years earlier (a rise from 15 per cent to 35 per cent living in towns), the growth of Belfast and the slower growth of Dublin, together with rural depopulation, were the main causes of the relative growth in urban Ireland in the seventy years before 1920. Most other Irish towns did not experience any significant growth, in population or prosperity. A limited range of manufacturers (with a food-related staple often crucial); some administrative and commercial services; a retail sector increasingly trading in imported goods; a diminishing (though at an uneven pace) number of local craftsmen; these were the most common features of town life throughout most of Ireland as the nineteenth century advanced. Small wonder that a rash of industrial exhibitions and 'Buy-Irish' activities accompanied the nationalist cultural revival at the turn of the century.

Not surprisingly, this economic base in Irish towns produced a social structure with a high petit-bourgeois, trading sector (shop-keepers and publicans), a middle class decidedly more commercial and professional than industrial, and a working class which in only a limited number of towns was sufficiently large and concentrated (at factory or trade level) to encourage thinking and organisation along class lines. By the later nineteenth century, however, the spread of 'new unionism' (and a dash of syndicalism) among unskilled workers combined with the political activism of a number of committed socialists, notably James Connolly, to produce a more radical and agg-ressive mood among sections of the Irish working class, especially in the larger cities and towns. The great Dublin strike and lock-out of 1913 — in which the employers under William Martin Murphy sought to break the growing power of the major general union, the Irish Transport and General Workers Union — was a long and bitter episode, and marked a key moment in the history of the Irish labour movement and of class politics in modern Ireland.

In view of its developed industrial base, Belfast might have been expected to provide the most advanced class consciousness and the most organised working class in Ireland. Class politics and trade union militancy did indeed feature prominently in Edwardian Belfast. However, such class politics were irreparably riven by the deep and bitter animosity along politico-sectarian lines that infected every aspect of life in the north-east. As Belfast expanded spectacularly between 1850 and 1914 migrants from the countryside brought with them from their rural homes in Ulster their fears and their prejudices. Deep-rooted sectarian attitudes made the transition from their largely rural setting (the world of early Orangeism, Defenderism and secret combinations of all kinds) to the heartland of an urban industrial landscape, with little loss of intensity. To the familiar social problems of a rapidly expanding industrial city, were added the par-ticular inter-communal tensions generated by the different ghettoes of the Protestant and Catholic workers — distinct, discrete, but yet in dangerous proximity to each other. Urban community conflict of a sectarian kind inevitably developed its own forms and rituals, its own 'style' as it were, in Belfast. Just as inevitably its incidence had its own rhythms and regularity, with changes in the general economic climate, alterations in work practices and opportunities, threatened shifts in the denominational balance of different zones or neighbour-hoods, the exceptional excitement generated by various waves of religious revivalism, each and all likely to trigger off a riot or a longer period of inter-communal violence.

But it was political controversies, and in particular controversy arising from the central question of the constitutional status of Ireland, which provoked the widest mobilisation, the most acute polarisation, and the most sustained excitement among the different communities in Ulster, especially in the Belfast area. What caused this political tension to reach a crisis-point in the early twentieth century can only be understood in the context of political developments in Ireland as a whole in the decades after the Famine.

The trauma of the Famine years finally buried the Repeal crusade of O'Connell. In the political vacuum that followed the death of O'Connell himself in 1847 and the demise of the mass movement he had directed for more than twenty years, there were several groups seeking to set the political agenda for the next generation. Broadly speaking we can identify two main tendencies, the reformist and the revolutionary, within the majority Irish nationalist tradition. They were not, however, in ideas or personnel separate or mutually exclusive. Most Irish nationalists shared certain basic ideas and beliefs: first, that the source of most of Ireland's economic and social problems lay ultimately in the 'subordinate' constitutional status of Ireland; second, that the 'undoing' of the Act of Union which was the instrument of this subordination was a prerequisite for Irish economic revival and social regeneration; and finally that some form of autonomous Irish state was consistent with the 'historical destiny' of Ireland, and with the sense of distinct identity felt by most Irish people. With different nuances and emphases these were the shared assumptions of most Irish nationalists.

However, when we move beyond these assumptions, matters become more complicated. How autonomous or independent should the Irish national state be? Should it be — as a republican separatist tradition asserted — a completely separate entity from Britain? Or a kingdom co-equal in status with Britain, having its own parliament, but under the one monarch — as the Repeal demand had insisted? Or should it be something less than an 'equal' kingdom; a subsidiary unit of the United Kingdom, with a devolved but subsidiary parliament and institutions — as Home Rule later came to mean? Perhaps even more basic and perplexing than these questions concerning the precise form which an Irish national state should take, was the matter of what constituted the distinct Irish identity for which a national state was being sought? What were the distinguishing marks of the nation now demanding its own state?

On all of these questions there were differing — at times contradictory — views among Irish nationalists. And, on the thorny question of the means permissible in achieving an Irish national state,

Irish nationalists cannot be easily divided into revolutionary/physical force goats and constitutional/pacifist sheep. Some constitutional nationalists were not opposed in principle or on moral grounds to the use of force in the struggle for freedom, but they rejected the 'armed revolutionary' route to political independence on the grounds that it was unnecessary or that it was unlikely to succeed. On the other hand, in the decades after 1850 Irish 'revolutionaries' — essentially Fenians under various titles — had difficulty on more than one occasion in deciding what their attitude should be to major social movements (for example, the Land War) or constitutional demands (for example, Home Rule) which the majority of Irish people of a nationalist view seemed quite prepared to welcome, but which fell considerably short of a separate, independent Irish Republic.

The generation which followed the Famine provided plenty of evidence of these complexities in Irish nationalist thinking. Not surprisingly, the Famine calamity forced the land question to the top of the agenda of Irish problems. A movement to strengthen the legal position of tenants looked promising for a time during the 1850s. Its leaders — including the former Young Irelander, Charles Gavan Duffy — sought to make 'tenant-right' the issue which would unite tenants 'north and south', mindful no doubt of the failure of O'Connell's Repeal crusade to make any appreciable impression on the Protestant community in Ireland as a whole, and in particular on the Orangemen in Ulster. Public opinion in Britain was inclined to lay heavy blame for the Famine on the Irish landlords, and among the British intelligentsia the debate had already begun which was soon to lead to questioning (by, among others, John Stuart Mill) of the applicability or appropriateness of English land law to Ireland, in particular the laws relating to property rights. However, the tenant right movement of the fifties came too soon. Political factionalism and the general prosperity of Irish agriculture during most of the fifties sapped the energies of the movement. Other questions called for more immediate attention.

Among these, a number of specifically 'Catholic' demands formed the programme of a reformist group of politicians for whom Cardinal Paul Cullen — the most influential figure in the Catholic hierarchy — acted as client, conscience and co-ordinator. The most significant reform of this largely confessional agenda was the disestablishment of the (Anglican) Church of Ireland, a demand which became more insistent as the gradual advance of the 'representative' (if not yet the democratic) idea made the notion that the church of a minority should be the established and endowed state church increasingly difficult to defend. In pressing for the disestablishment of the Church of Ireland, Irish Catholic lobbyists found firm allies among British nonconformists, and the nonconformist vote was a crucial element in the electoral triumph of Gladstonian Liberalism in the 1868 general election. Disestablishment in Ireland followed almost immediately; but further Gladstonian reforms during the years 1868 to 1874 (in the areas of tenant-right and university education) were less satisfactory to the clericalist/liberal-reformist 'alliance' in Ireland.

It is part of the conventional wisdom that Gladstone's reform package for Ireland was the result of his shock and anxiety in the face of Fenian 'outrage' in the 1860s. Certainly, Fenianism — in all its labyrinthine complexity — is crucial to any understanding of Irish politics between the Famine and 1922. However bewildering the details of its long history, the essential facts about Fenianism are quite clear. It was born out of the fiasco of the Young Ireland 'rising' of 1848-9. Its founders were survivors of the fiasco, and they were determined that there would be another day. Fenianism (or the Irish Republican Brotherhood as it was styled in Ireland) was nurtured on both sides of the Atlantic by the immediate and bitter memory of the Famine, and by the rather longer memories of Irish historical grievances in general. It was implacably opposed to 'English rule in Ireland'. Separatist, republican, and clandestine, the IRB was committed to the idea that the use of all means, including force, was justified in the struggle to end British rule in Ireland. The particular intensity of this Fenian spirit among Irish exiles in the cities of America and Britain has been seen by historians as largely the response of the overwhelmingly poor immigrant Irish to the difficulties and prejudices they encountered within their new host countries. This may indeed have been a major factor in producing that intense nationalism (with a fierce hostility to England) which has been such a marked feature of Irish nationalism 'in exile' since the Famine.

However, there are one or two other aspects of Fenianism in Ireland which had certain long-term consequences and which are worthy of notice. First, its rank and file membership (which, for a secret, oath-bound society, was quite considerable at its peak) was more heavily drawn from the artisan, petit-bourgeois, and proletarian elements of the cities and towns than was the case with any earlier constitutional or revolutionary movement in Ireland. In the case of some Fenians this probably strengthened the basically egalitarian rhetoric of social justice which had been part of the radical republican tradition since the 1790s. Second, no Irish organisation received such trenchant condemnation from the Catholic bishops as a whole as did the Fenians. Of course, Irish republicanism from its inception in the 1790s (due, in part at least, to the French revolutionary connection) had encountered suspicion and hostility from the Catholic hierarchy. The clandestine, oath-bound basis of Fenianism was anathema to Catholic churchmen. Accordingly, from the movement's beginnings in the

1850s the Fenians were threatened with excommunication and sub-jected to the relentless public condemnation of churchmen. That many thousands of shop assistants, teachers, labourers, tradesmen and soldiers did, nevertheless, take the secret oath did not necessarily mean that they were rejecting Catholicism. There is ample evidence that many Fenians continued to be, in conscience and practice, devout Catholics, notwithstanding the denunciation of the clergy. But their defiance of the threat of excommunication indicated a toughness on the part of ordinary Fenians in the face of clerical hostility which was to prove an enduring part of the Fenian legacy to later republicans. This was no simple anti-clericalism (along continental lines), but rather a peculiar tradition of Catholic dissent in Irish political culture.

There is a final point concerning Fenianism in Ireland which merits comment, however brief. It has been suggested that Fenianism — with its rituals, its secrecy, its heady rhetoric of over-throwing a mighty empire — lent excitement and a vicarious sense of importance to social groups (the lowly-anchored, immobile elements of a stagnant economy) whose lives would otherwise have been spent in quiet desperation. No doubt there are many determinants of political activism, especially activism in clandestine organisations. But to reduce to the relief of boredom the steely determination, the political stamina, and the willingness to endure severe privations and imprisonment shown by committed Fenians, is to risk missing most of the significant aspects of the movement.

What cannot be denied, of course, is the fact that the actual attempts made by Fenians in arms to dislodge Britain from political control in Ireland were not immediately successful. The belief that 'England's difficulty is Ireland's opportunity' may have been reason-able enough. But identifying and acting upon the opportune moment proved rather difficult. Leadership rivalries, disagreements and mis-understandings between the Irish and the American 'wings' of the movement on strategy, tactics and timing, poor internal security, poor planning, and, ultimately, poor weather, all contributed to the com-prehensive failure of the Fenian rising in Ireland in 1867. American Fenian 'raids' on Canada served only to emphasise the disarray of American Fenianism and the failure of its leadership to calculate accurately the priorities of American foreign policy.

The activities of the Fenians in Britain — mainly attempted rescues of prisoners — brought casualties and fear to British cities. The belief that it was these Fenian outrages in British cities that forced Gladstone to confront Irish discontent reinforced an older conviction (not confined to militant nationalists) that Britain was more likely to listen to the argument of force than to the force of argument. This has been a recurring maxim in successive turbulent phases in Anglo-Irish relations ever since.

138

After the failure of the 1867 rising there followed the predictable bout of recriminations. But far more interesting were the regroupings which also followed. In America, after an interlude of internal squabbling, Clan na Gael (under the shrewd direction of John Devoy) emerged as the main successor organisation of American Fenianism, and it was to play a vital rôle in all subsequent phases of the struggle for an Irish national state up to 1922. The IRB itself, as an organisation, survived the '67 debacle, and in the decades that followed it maintained a shadowy but continuous existence. Its ageing leaders might not have been able to influence seriously the course of political events in Ireland, but yet they remained the steadfast custodians of the republican separatist faith until, at the turn of the century, new men saw new opportunities for revitalising the old Fenian ideal and structures.

In the short term, however, perhaps the most interesting development of all was the way in which some Fenians (or ex-Fenians) became involved in more routine, non-revolutionary, lobby politics. Some lost their political virginity, so to speak, while co-operating with humanitarian lawyers and others in committees lobbying for amnesty for Fenian prisoners. Others became involved in tenant-right activities in various localities. Others still — a small number, in fact, — became involved in an organisation called the Home Government Association — later to be called the Home Rule Association. This association had a curious pedigree. Founded by Isaac Butt — a lawyer and one time Conservative champion of the Union — one strand in the founding of the Home Rule movement in 1870 was the disgust of some Protestant Conservatives at the treachery, as they saw it, of the Westminster parliament in disestablishing their church. This spurred some of them to wonder whether they might not be better off under some form of devolved Irish parliament than under the seemingly uncaring (and certainly unreliable) single United Kingdom parliament at Westminster. But the influence of this Protestant Conservative constituency soon waned, as the more traditional Catholic response to grievance politics asserted itself, and they began to rally to the Home Rule flag — the latest flag-of-convenience for the Irish nationalist demand for some form of autonomous Irish state.

The early Home Rule movement was but a pale shadow of O'Connell's Repeal campaign. For one thing, the Home Rule demand itself (basically an imprecise devolution scheme within an overall Union context) was a considerable dilution of the Repeal demand. Moreover, the ageing Butt was no O'Connell. The movement lacked a mass membership in Ireland, and under Butt, seemed unlikely to make any great impression at Westminster. However, just as O'Connell had attracted some younger and more impatient nationalists in the Young Ireland group, so too Butt's Home Rule vehicle attracted some Fenian fellow-travellers as well as a few MPs. These latter, soon impatient with Butt's leadership style, began to attract attention for their aggressive, 'obstructionist' behaviour in the House of Commons. Among these obstructionists was the young Wicklow landlord — scion of a noted Anglo-Irish family — Charles Stewart Parnell. The more abuse hurled at the obstructionists by the British political establishment the more honest and admirable they appeared in Irish nationalist eyes. Under Parnellite auspices 'Home Rule' began to sound and to seem more militantly 'green' than it actually was. Yet, for all the notoriety of Parnell and his fellow-obstructionists, Home Rule might well have merited no more than a brief mention in Irish political history, were it not for the transformation of the political landscape brought about by the 'land war' in Ireland in the late 1870s.

It is easier to describe the 'context' in which the land war erupted than to explain satisfactorily why it took the particular form and course that it did. A general crisis in Irish agricultural incomes — the product of a combination of successive bad seasons, low yields and depressed prices — and a potential subsistence crisis for poorer small-holders in the West, led to the founding of a tenants' protection organisation, or Land League, in Mayo in 1879. Originally reflecting the demands of radical smallholders in the West, in that it advocated redistribution of land as well as rent reduction, as the Land League became a nationwide body it became increasingly dominated by, and eventually came to reflect, the demands of the more comfortable tenant-farmers. Its agenda of reforms narrowed to the 'Three Fs' (Fair Rent; Fixity of Tenure while these fair rents were being paid; and Freedom of Sale, with due compensation for improvements, whenever the tenant-farmer might wish). The agitation, which was intense in the years 1879 to 1882, used a variety of techniques, legal and illegal (threats, intimidation, assault, damage to property: the established repertoire of secret societies), and added a new word (Boycott) to an old weapon — the social ostracisation of the person ignoring or breaking the rules of the moral community. The Liberal government of Gladstone, while handing out plenty of coercive legis-lation to uphold law and order in Ireland, had, by 1881, effectively given in to the agitation of the tenant-farmers.

The 1881 Land Act may be seen, in retrospect, as the crucial turning point of the land war. By establishing a land commission to establish fair rents — in effect an arbitration court to adjudicate on disputes between landlords and tenants regarding rents — the 1881 Act dealt a fatal blow to the notion of rents being settled by 'free contract' between landlord and tenant. The short-term impact of the land commission's decisions — once the troublesome issue of out-standing arrears had been settled in 1882 — was almost universally to the advantage of the tenant, the new fixed or 'judicial' rents being, on average, 20 per cent lower than the old rent. And yet, significant as these reductions were in taking the steam out of the first and decisive phase of the land war, the long-term implications of the 1881 act were still more significant. The judicial rents fixed by the land commission were to be unalterable for fifteen years. In the event, they were not. When a further crisis hit agricultural incomes in the mid-1880s there was renewed agitation; and, again, rents — including judicial rents — were revised downwards. The message was clear for Irish landlords: there was no longer a secure and predictable income from Irish land. If there were to be an agrarian agitation for rent reductions every time agricultural prices/yields suffered a set-back; and if (as now seemed the case) the government of the day could not be relied upon to 'stand firm' in defence of contracts or agreed rents, clearly the economically sensible thing for landlords was to get out of Irish land and find new ventures where their capital was more likely to yield a better and less uncertain return. In short, it made good economic sense to sell their Irish land, provided, of course, the price was right. Here was the rub.

The tenants, too, might have been expected to favour buying out their landlords and becoming owner-occupiers of their holdings. But again the price would have to be right. Getting the price right for both parties was, in essence, the objective of the succession of land-purchase acts introduced by successive governments between 1881 and 1909. Pledging government credit to create farmer-ownership in Ireland was the ultimate British solution to the Irish land question. But it took some time to find the terms which would be sufficiently attractive to both buyer and seller, the tenant and the landlord. The 1903 land purchase act (Wyndham's) finally found the formula which enticed the bulk of the landlords and tenants to embark on the transfer of ownership to the occupiers. There followed a dramatic change in land ownership in Ireland. In 1870 it is estimated that only 3 per cent of the occupiers of agricultural holdings in Ireland were owners of their farms; by 1914 upwards of 60 per cent of the occupiers were either owners already or were involved in purchase schemes which would ultimately leave them so.

A number of questions concerning 'the land struggle' continue to intrigue and divide historians. Why did the land war happen when it did? To say that it was in response to an agricultural depression is not enough. A deep depression between 1859 and 1864 had not produced a land league or a land war. The fact that the Irish agricultural crisis of the late 1870s coincided with an industrial recession in America and Britain is undoubtedly relevant; a temporary fall-off in Irish emigration to the industrial cities meant that there was a back-up of impatient, would-be emigrants (the raw materials for agitation) in the Irish countryside in 1879. Leadership was crucial in mobilising popular discontent. How crucial was the Fenian (or ex-Fenian) influence in this mobilisation? Was the land war a 'defensive' or an 'offensive' campaign by the tenants? These and other, related, questions continue to provoke debate. Certainly, after a long period of almost uninterrupted improvement and rising prosperity, it was understandable that tenant-farmers of every degree would fight hard to hold on to their hard-won gains, and that western smallholders in particular, haunted by the memory of the Famine, would respond to exhortations not to allow themselves to be plunged back to a repetition of the late forties. Improved communications and rising literacy levels facilitated political mobilisation, and there is evidence of the rising self-confidence and assertiveness of the Catholic middle class (in town and country) in their drive for control of the Boards of Guardians of the Poor Law Unions in the years immediately preceding the land war. Deference, therefore, to the landlords and their allies in the Ascendancy may well have been weakening before the onset of the land war. But the Land League — which the more comfortable farmers came to dominate after it became a nationwide movement — dealt a fatal blow to whatever may have remained in the late 1870s of deference to landlord power and social rank.

And what of the Fenian influence? Undoubtedly there were ex-Fenians who, frustrated at the seeming irrelevance of the old conspiratorial, rebellion-plotting antics of the IRB, threw their weight behind the land agitation because it was intrinsically 'an issue of the people'. Michael Davitt, whose family had emigrated to Lancashire after eviction in Mayo in the Famine years, and who was himself a crucial figure in the founding of the Land League, was one of these former Fenians who gave whole-hearted support to the land agitation for its own sake, so to speak. Davitt's solution to the Irish land question — nationalisation — was not the solution finally adopted. Yet he could celebrate the victory of the tenant-farmers over the landlords as 'the fall of feudalism in Ireland'. Notwithstanding the rejection of his own nationalisation proposals, Davitt saw the land war in longer historical context, and welcomed the defeat of landlordism as the repayment of an historical debt.

Other Fenians who backed the land war, such as Devoy, made more complex calculations. Convinced that the government would be unable to concede the demands of the tenants, these Fenians supported the land war as a way of forcing confrontation between the government and the mass of the tenantry. From such a confrontation they hoped for the politicisation necessary for a separatist revolt. That this was a miscalculation did not prevent such Fenian 'moles' from getting their own particular satisfaction from the defeat of the landlord class. And, of course, there were some Fenians — notably the old guard on the ruling

142

council of the IRB — who refused to have anything to do with the land war, seeing it as a dangerous distraction from the single, pure aim of planning the revolution which would establish an Irish Republic; ever-vigilant for the right revolutionary moment, they decided to sit out the land war.

A final question on the land war and its consequences: was it a social revolution? In the sense that it produced a massive transfer of land ownership it clearly was a force for major social change. But in a more fundamental sense the outcome of the land war may be seen as conservative, not to say counter-revolutionary. Private ownership in land was strengthened, not weakened, by the defeat of the old landlords and by the creation of a vast number of owner-occupiers. Structural inequalities (in size and quality of holdings) were effectively frozen at the sub-landlord level. No major redistribution of land took place. In short, the land war and its outcome constituted a 'social revolution' only for those whose social declensions derived from the particularity of the Irish historical experience of land ownership and confiscation, of plantation and dispossession.

The land war proved to be the making of Parnell and the salvation of the Home Rule movement. Parnell had put himself at the head of the land agitation — in parliament and in the country — even though it cost him considerable financial loss personally. But when the first phase of the land war closed in 1882 — its end hastened by Parnell's impatience to move on to a political movement in which, with the land question 'solved', the more prescient and patriotic landlords would assume a leading rôle — Parnell was the dominant figure on the Irish political landscape. The revitalisation of the Home Rule movement — grafting it on to the Land League branch structure and establishing a disciplined parliamentary party — was completed by 1885. By this stage the Home Rule party — dominated at local level by farmers, shopkeepers, publicans, merchants and solicitors — was politically and socially a conservative party, enjoying the confidence and support of most of the Catholic hierarchy. Indeed, it has been argued that the accommodation which had been reached by 1885 between the Catholic Church and the Home Rule party was, in effect, a kind of concordat between the Church and the embryonic Irish national state; with the church giving its support to the Irish National 'state' in return for having the primacy of its influence in such crucial areas as education accepted by the Home Rule leaders. In short, it is suggested that by the mid 1880s a model of Church-State relations was already established which was to apply formally in the Irish Free State after 1922.

Be that as it may, the mid 1880s may be considered vital years in the political history of modern Ireland. The 1884 Electoral Reform Act, increasing the electorate and creating almost everywhere throughout Ireland single-seat constituencies, paved the way for the spectacular

143

Home Rule triumph in the 1885 general election. The party of Parnell won 85 of the 103 seats in Ireland, and held the balance between the Liberal and Conservative parties at Westminster. By year's end Gladstone — for a complex set of reasons, not exclusively, perhaps not primarily, related to the situation in Ireland — announced his conversion to Home Rule. In 1886 he introduced a Home Rule bill: his party split and the bill was heavily defeated. The Conservative and Unionist party at once entered into what was to become twenty years of almost uninterrupted office and power. It would be difficult to exaggerate the underlying significance of the events of 1885–86. The general election of 1885 in effect settled the electoral map of Ireland for a generation. It also revealed starkly what came to be described later as 'the Ulster question'. Both of these statements need to be amplified a little.

Notwithstanding the bitter divisions and factionalism which followed the traumatic downfall and death of Parnell in 1891, the total nationalist representation at Westminster did not change very much in the twenty years after 1885, remaining at over four-fifths of the total Irish representation. The class, regional and denominational features of the representation — that is, the state of public opinion on Home Rule — was, likewise, remarkably stable. Throughout most of the country the anti-Home Rule or Unionist view was disproportionately concentrated among those of rank and wealth in society, and was heavily Protestant. But it was, in most of the country, a minority view electorally. The one exception was in Ulster, where the popular vote for Unionism comprised Protestants of all social classes, from landed aristocrats to petit-bourgeois and artisan levels, where the vote was substantial, and where it was electorally the dominant view throughout the eastern half of the province. The long-term historical forces which shaped community identities and attitudes in Ulster along ethno-religious lines are too well-known to need elaboration here. But what does require clarification is the precise nature of the 'Ulster problem' during the Home Rule crisis of the late nineteenth and early twentieth centuries. The 'Ulster problem' of the period 1885–1910 was not simply that Ulster as a whole was uniformly (or even overwhelmingly) electorally Unionist, while the other three provinces were overwhelmingly Nationalist. It is rather that Ulster was *evenly divided* between Home Rule and Unionist voters. In the fateful general election of 1885 the representation of Ulster was divided almost evenly between Home Rule and Unionist MPs. In the two decades that followed no substantial change occurred. The essential point, then, regarding the state of Irish opinion, is that any analysis of the special problem of Ulster, within the overall context of a changing framework for Anglo-Irish relations, must begin by recognising the fact that the 'Ulster problem' was not that Ulster was *different* but that Ulster was *divided*. This was already clear in 1885.

What also emerged — perhaps not quite so clearly — in the year 1886 was the fact that Ulster Unionists were already prepared to contemplate any and all options for the defeat of Home Rule. Already in 1886 there was talk of arms; already there was evidence that Ulster Unionism — with its popular base — was more uncompromising and more extreme in its determination to resist Home Rule, than the more patrician or haute bourgeois versions of Unionism so prominent in the other provinces. Already, also, the Conservative party — or at least key sections of it — were indicating their willingness to give a virtual blank cheque to the Ulster Unionists in deciding on a strategy of resistance to Home Rule. It is worth pointing out, however, that the Ulster Unionist show of strength in rejecting Home Rule in 1885-6 was not yet tied to a secessionist or partitionist option for themselves; rather was it an attempt to prevent the granting of Home Rule to any part of Ireland by showing that Ulster was an insuperable obstacle 'blocking the way'.

The nature and intensity of Ulster Unionism over the past century or so has interested historians and social scientists in recent years. As with modern Irish nationalism, or indeed any deeply-held political belief, Ulster Unionism is a mixture of sense and sentiment. The sentiment combined an emotional attachment to a particular set of symbols and traditions perceived as part of a common British inheritance; a version of the Protestant concept of liberty of conscience which incorporated a deep suspicion of and hostility to Roman Catholicism (feared and reviled not just as authoritarian but as heretical as well); and a distinct sense of identity rooted in their origins as a planter community. The most powerful and pervasive element of this Ulster Unionist *mentalité* was its hostility to Roman Catholicism, on intellectual, theological and indeed philosophical grounds. This sense of Protestant righteousness, combined with planter historical consciousness, undoubtedly made for resolute political convictions. But it also encouraged attitudes of superiority and mastery which were less attractive and which, ultimately, were less useful politically as community assets. The more easily arguable grounds for Unionist opposition to Home Rule was largely economic: the reasonable fear that a Home Rule parliament would adopt economic policies (for example, protectionism) adverse both to the interests of Belfast's empire-orientated industrial base, and to the economic interests of the region as a whole.

In the event, Ulster Unionist resistance to Home Rule did not have to approach the brink in 1885-6, or for more than twenty years thereafter. The Conservative-Unionist party was in office almost uninterruptedly up to 1906. Gladstone's successors as leaders of the Liberal party did not share his enthusiasm for Home Rule, but none of them openly repudiated the party's general commitment to Ireland. Devolved Home Rule for Ireland — whatever the details — would only have to wait, it seemed, until a Liberal government was returned to office. This did not happen until 1906. Even then the Liberal government of 1906 was sufficiently strong in parliament not to need the support of John Redmond's Irish Nationalists to stay in office. Only with the two general elections of 1910 (which greatly reduced the number of Liberal MPs) did the Irish Nationalists recover the parliamentary leverage which forced Home Rule to the top of the new Liberal government's agenda.

However, while Irish parliamentary politics of the period 1886 to 1910 may indeed appear relatively dull and uninteresting (enlivened only by the venom with which the leaders of the various nationalist factions abused each other), political activity in the wider context in Ireland in these years was extremely rich and varied, and full of interesting developments. Major legislation on land, local government and regional development indicated a Conservative determination to demonstrate that Home Rule was not a prerequisite for good government and sensible reform in Ireland. Many prominent Irish Unionists busied themselves in conferences with nationalist leaders (for example, on the land question) aimed at a kind of conciliar version of problem-solving within the Union framework. Some took even more striking initiatives; for example, Horace Plunkett strove to win converts to 'the co-operative ideal' as the way forward in improving land use and general agricultural efficiency and prosperity in Ireland. Within the nationalist ranks, also, there were significant new departures. The extraordinary blossoming of cultural debate — the founding of the Gaelic League, the Irish Literary Revival, the rash of literary magazines and of *journaux de combat* — and the vibrant nativism in sport and athletics (as evidenced by the founding of the GAA), whether we view all this activity as a reaction to the sterility of parliamentary political debate or as an attempt to define or elaborate on the distinct sense of Irish nationality for which a national stage was being sought — greatly extended the debate on Irish nationalism well beyond the single issue of 'when' or 'how much' Home Rule would come to Ireland.

More explicitly political — and more directly challenging to Home Rule — were the activities of a plethora of propagandists (such as D.P. Moran, W.P. Ryan, Bulmer Hobson and Arthur Griffith) writing for newspapers, holding meetings and establishing societies and organisations with astonishing rapidity. Griffith was especially prolific in floating political ideas as an alternative to Home Rule. His most settled and comprehensive set of proposals, grouped under the eminently apt title *Sinn Féin*, called for a constitutional arrangement between Britain and Ireland along the lines of the Austro-Hungarian dual monarchy (which Griffith understood less than perfectly); the abstention of Irish MPs from Westminster and their constituting themselves an Irish parliament in Dublin whose policies would rest on

146

full-blooded protectionism aimed at achieving the maximum degree of economic (and indeed intellectual) self-sufficiency. Griffith's *Sinn Féin* organisation (formally constituted from several smaller political groups in 1905) attracted an assortment of advanced nationalists dissatisfied with the limited scope of Home Rule or impatient at the lack of progress towards an Irish state. A number of young republicans also gave Sinn Féin some support, and it was this same group of young republicans who effectively took over and began to re-organise the almost moribund IRB secret organisation in the years after 1908. Among the new members recruited in the years between 1908 and 1914 was Patrick Pearse.

Yet, for all the activities, the writings, the resolutions, and the intellectual excitement generated by these various nationalist groups, they all seemed destined for the footnotes of Irish political history when in late 1910 Home Rule became once again the dominant 'live' political issue. The balance of power in Westminster lay with Redmond's party. Asquith's government had no option but to introduce a Home Rule bill in 1912. With the power of the House of Lords now limited to a delaying prerogative, it seemed certain that Ireland would have some kind of devolved Home Rule parliament by 1914, unless something drastic intervened. Of course, something drastic did indeed intervene during 1912-14. The Ulster Unionists, led by the Dublin lawyer Edward Carson, mobilised in large numbers, formed and partly armed a volunteer army, in order, as they claimed, 'to defeat the present conspiracy to set up a Home Rule parliament in Ireland. And in the event of such a parliament being forced upon us we further solemnly and mutually pledge ourselves to refuse to recognise its authority.' This effectively translated as: we refuse to accept the decision of the parliament of the United Kingdom; we are armed to resist Home Rule; and if we cannot prevent the conferring of Home Rule on any part of Ireland, our second option is to ensure that we will be excluded from the jurisdiction of the Home Rule parliament.

The militarisation of the Ulster Unionist challenge to Home Rule provoked a predictable response on the nationalist side; a body of Irish Volunteers was established (its leadership heavily infiltrated from the outset by IRB activists) with Redmond only belatedly (and never satisfactorily) assuming titular authority over the new body. Confronted with the proliferation of volunteer armies in Ireland (the Dublin workers had formed their own Irish Citizen Army after the confrontation with police during the bitter labour lock-out of 1913); faced with indications that senior officers of the 'real' (i.e. British) army in Ireland would be unwilling 'to coerce Ulster' into accepting Home Rule; and all too aware that unconditional support was being offered to the Ulster Unionists by leaders of the Conservative party, the Liberal government not surprisingly began to look for a compromise. Beset by many other problems, Asquith's cabinet had no stomach for confrontation with the Ulster Unionists. Inexorably the partition option moved to the top of the agenda. Redmond was outraged. Carson, too, must have begun to feel the initiative slipping away from him; after all, he had seen and stoked Ulster's intransigence as a way of defeating Home Rule for Ireland as a whole, not as a device to secure partition. But by the time the war broke out in 1914 — with a Home Rule Act finally passed by parliament but with its implementation suspended until the end of hostilities and the resolution of the Ulster impasse — some form of partition was accepted as inevitable by all the major players, even if the territory and the duration of the partition arrangement remained to be settled.

The sequence of events by which the Home Rule impasse of 1914 became the two states of Ireland in 1920-22 is rich and complex in its detail. Predictably, it has attracted a good deal of scholarly attention and has inspired an impressive body of historical writing. This allows us to ask a number of pertinent questions regarding the solutions — to the Irish and the Ulster 'problems' — reached in these years. It has become a cliché to say that the final arrangements of 1920-22 satisfied none of the main parties in Ireland. This verdict may be a bit too glib. The Ulster Unionist leader, James Craig, may indeed have been correct in stating that in accepting a devolved parliament for the six Ulster counties which comprised Northern Ireland, the Ulster Unionists were accepting that which they had not sought. Yet the partition settlement must have given a measure of satisfaction to most Ulster Unionists (at least those within the new Northern Ireland). After all, their tactics had paid substantial dividends. They remained outside the Irish national state, with a devolved Home Rule of their own within the United Kingdom. Territorially, they controlled the largest possible area of Ulster consistent with a substantial and dependable majority for the Union. The nationalist minority within Northern Ireland was, of course, fairly large — about one-third of the population. But had the unit of exclusion been the historic province of Ulster then the very slight overall Unionist majority would have been precarious, and community divisions might well have produced a conflict of such magnitude that Northern Ireland could have collapsed before very long. On the other hand, a smaller territorial unit (even if it coincided with greater political and religious homogeneity) would have raised doubts as to its economic and general institutional viability. All in all, the Ulster Unionist had least cause for dissatisfaction with the settlements of the years 1910 to 1922.

The balance sheet for nationalist Ireland is more difficult to assess. Partition — which became the main nationalist grievance in the decades after 1922 — was no less distasteful to John Redmond and his fellow Home Rule leaders than it was to the largely republican popular-front Sinn Féin party which replaced Redmond's old party as the voice of nationalist Ireland after the general election of 1918. But it is a measure of the impact of the 1916 Rising and its aftermath (the execution of the leaders and the subsequent miscalculations of the British government, culminating in the disastrous proposal to extend conscription to Ireland) on nationalist opinion that, from the establishment of the secessionist Dáil Éireann in early 1919 to the final terms of the Treaty at the end of 1921, what was at stake was the precise status and sovereignty of the Irish national state. More importantly, the demand now being made by the political leaders of nationalist Ireland — in negotiations, in propaganda, and in arms in the guerilla 'war of independence' — was for a fully sovereign, independent, Irish republic. This was a far cry from the Home Rule terms which were the basis for the reconstruction of Anglo-Irish relations in the years before 1914. And, while the republic (even a twenty-six county republic) had to give way to a dominion-status Free State, as the best offer that Griffith and Collins and their fellow negotiators could extract from Britain in the 1921 treaty negotiations, the constitutional powers and status of the new Free State itself were a major advance on any Home Rule terms offered in the pre-war days. These new terms — and the retreat from the demand for a fully independent, separate, Irish republic — were so disappointing and unacceptable to a large section of the Irish nationalist movement that a bitter civil war was fought over them. The majority — in the Dáil and in the twenty-six county areas designated as the new Irish Free State — was prepared to accept the terms of the 1921 Anglo-Irish treaty. But a sizeable minority refused to accept the terms, and resorted to arms in an attempt to prevent the 'retreat from the republic'.

The bitter civil war of 1922-3 (in which more than six hundred lives were lost) undoubtedly clouded the opening years — indeed the first generation — of the new Irish state. That the war was fought over the substance — and the symbols — of the sovereignty of the Irish state rather than its territorial extent (as was frequently suggested in later years, when partition became the main grievance of successive Irish governments and of Irish nationalists in general) is striking evidence of the rise in political expectations within nationalist Ireland in the short interval between 1914 and 1921.

The IRB had, perhaps, most reason for feeling gratified at this hardening of attitudes, or at least the raising of political demands, within the leadership of nationalist Ireland. After all, it had been IRB activists who had infiltrated and manipulated the Irish Volunteers; it was they who had controlled the minority of the Volunteers who elected to remain at home in 1914, refusing to answer Redmond's call

149

to join the colours and fight in the Great War for the rights of small nations; and it was an IRB group (notably Clarke and McDermott) which had recruited the vital personnel (including Pearse and Connolly), laid the plans, and carried out the 1916 rebellion. Though the rising itself was initially most unpopular with the ordinary citizens of Dublin (and, it would seem, in the country as a whole), the IRB had the resilience to have its activists to the fore in the regrouping of the nationalist ranks under de Valera's leadership in the reconstructed Sinn Féin after 1917. Indeed, even after Dáil Éireann claimed the allegiance of all Irishmen (including members of the guerilla army, the Irish Republican Army), the IRB did not cease to exercise a vital influence, having members involved in vital positions at all levels of the nationalist movement. The Treaty of 1921 may indeed have fallen short of the pure Fenian demand for an Irish republic totally separate from Britain. But when compared with the best terms on offer in 1914 the Treaty could certainly be seen as a major step along the way to the republic — as the IRB man Michael Collins fervently argued. Perhaps, then, it was not altogether surprising that among the early visitors received by the leaders of the new Free State — signifying his approval as it were — was the old Fenian, John Devoy.

A word by way of conclusion. The leadership in both political jurisdictions in partitioned Ireland faced difficult, but radically different, challenges after 1922. Within Northern Ireland the main challenge lay in finding a way of accommodating a large, disaffected nationalist minority, who refused to acknowledge any allegiance to the symbols, ethos or legitimacy of the state in which they now found themselves. In short, the main task facing the Unionist leadership in Northern Ireland (in an economic environment which deteriorated after 1920) was to convince the nationalist minority to accept the fact that what was done was done and could not be undone, and that Northern Ireland would continue to be a part of the United Kingdom for the foreseeable future.

The tasks facing the leaders of the new Free State were rather different to those facing the Unionist government in Belfast. The Free State did not have a large disaffected Unionist minority. Indeed, once it became clear that private property rights were not to be threatened by the new regime in Dublin, most former Unionists chose the path of political quietism, and made a hard-nosed if generally unenthusiastic accommodation with the new rulers. This was not without its strains and bruises. Some found the accommodation too difficult, and emigrated. But those who stayed also found aspects of the new Irish state hard to accept. The Unionist minority in the Free State was mainly Protestant, while the dominant ethos (and the social legislation) of the Free State reflected the conservative and staunchly Catholic views of the dominant social groups in the new state — the Catholic bourgeoisie of the towns and the strong farmers of the countryside.

The immediate task for the leaders of the Free State was obviously to staunch the wounds of civil war and to establish firmly the institutions of the new Irish state. The constitutional transformation of the dominion Free State into the twenty-six county Irish Republic would come later. But the fundamental challenge facing successive governments in the independent Irish state was deeper and more daunting. This challenge was the vindication of the assumptions, the ideas, the very credo of generations of Irish nationalists that Ireland would prosper — economically, socially and culturally — under an independent, native Irish government, as it had not done and could never do under British rule. Realising the creative possibilities of political sovereignty, as enshrined in nationalist ideology and rhetoric, was the main challenge facing the leadership of the modern Irish independent state.

In the decades after 1922 the political leaders of the 'two Irelands', North and South, were to find their respective challenges very daunting indeed.

FURTHER READING

For details: F.S.L. Lyons, *Ireland Since the Famine*, London 1971.
For ideas: J.J. Lee, *The Modernisation of Irish Society 1848-1918*, Dublin 1973.
Other works of interpretation worth consulting are:
D.G. Boyce, *Nationalism in Ireland*, Dublin 1982.
S. Clark and J.S. Donnelly Jr eds, *Irish Peasants: Violence and Political Unrest 1780-1914*, Dublin 1988.
P. Corish, *The Irish Catholic Experience*, Dublin 1985.
O. MacDonagh, *States of Mind: A Study of Anglo-Irish Conflict 1780-1980*, London 1983.
C. Townshend, *Political Violence in Ireland*, London 1982.

10
POLITICS AND SOCIETY IN POST-INDEPENDENCE IRELAND

Tom Boylan, Chris Curtin, Liam O'Dowd

THE establishment of the Irish Free State in 1922 represented a partial success for Irish nationalism. Although the goal of a thirty-two county republic had not been realised, over most of the island the majority of the population was no longer obliged to live in a state run by an alien power. Nationalists had placed most of the blame for Irish social and economic ills on British rule. Now, however, they had the opportunity to manage their own affairs. Northern Unionists had also something to celebrate. In control of even more territory than they had hoped for and apparently secure in their numerical dominance over the Catholic population, they could create a state in tune with their values and aspirations.

How the two states evolved: what types of political institutions and groupings emerged; what economic policies were pursued and what kinds of societies were fashioned in the decades after partition are the questions addressed in this chapter.

I
POLITICAL INSTITUTIONS AND GROUPINGS

The Treaty gave dominion status to the twenty-six counties, leaving them in a similar relationship to the British crown as Canada. To all intents and purposes the leaders of the new state were given a free hand; the position of Governor-General was only of symbolic significance and the crown's right to veto legislation was never actually exercised. The Oath of Allegiance to the crown was, in fact, removed in 1932 and shortly afterwards the office of Governor-General was abolished. The External Relations Act (1936) further weakened the formal British connection, while the 1937 Constitution was ratified by public referendum without reference to the crown. Finally, the twenty-six counties were given the official status of a republic with the passing of the Republic of Ireland Act (1948).

With the heady days of revolution over and the effective ending of British rule, nationalists now had an opportunity to choose their own form of government. The occasion was not used to innovate and the institutions recommended in the 1922 Constitution and confirmed again in the 1937 Constitution, generally followed the British pattern. Its main features were a parliament (Oireachtas) composed of two houses, Dáil Éireann and Seanad Éireann, the former elected by universal suffrage and the latter by a variety of socio-political panels and by direct political appointment. The government and its leader the Taoiseach (Prime Minister) supported by the dominant party or parties in the Dáil became, as in the British cabinet system, the dominant institution, and in combination with top-level civil servants effectively made and executed public policy. Parliament, despite expectations in the Constitution, did not in practice constitute a serious check on government activities. The office of President introduced in the 1937 Constitution possessed little real power.

If Free State political institutions lacked the element of novelty, the same could not be said for the electoral system. Every election in the south since independence has been held under the almost unique process of a Single Transferable Vote (STV) in multi-member constituencies. (This electoral system is used in only one other sovereign state, Malta). STV was favoured by both the nationalist elite and the British government who saw it as ensuring maximum representation for minorities such as Protestant Unionists. More than anything else however this system was adopted in Ireland because it found favour with, and was vigorously promoted by, British electoral reformers.

A concern for institutions at the local level was not evident in the new state. Local bodies such as the Poor Law Guardians and Rural District Councils were quickly dismantled. The power of the County Councils which replaced these bodies was increasingly eroded and the position of local elected representatives was undermined with the growth in central bureaucratic control. By the 1950s local government, as a distinct political process, had given way to the idea of local authorities as outposts of central government. Significantly, the new ruling group, despite the anti-British nature of its nationalism, looked no further than the British for models to manage public issues. As a consequence, the political institutions of the Free State emerged almost as a direct copy of the colonial past.

The Free State enjoyed a remarkable degree of political stability. Unlike the vast majority of elected governments in Europe in the 1920s that of W.T. Cosgrave enjoyed ten years of unbroken power. The defeated republican forces — those who remained committed to the republican ideal as proclaimed by Pearse — did question its legitimacy for a number of years but they had little success in their efforts to establish their own 'republican' institutions. The transfer of power to Fianna Fáil in 1932 was relatively peaceful; it withstood the challenge in the 1930s from both the radical republicans and the fascist-like Blueshirts and the party enjoyed sixteen successive years at the helm. Stability was certainly aided by the fact that partition removed the possibility of a challenge from a large, disruptive Protestant minority. A Unionist party did not emerge in the Free State where in 1926 non-Catholics only represented 8 per cent of the population. After the Treaty some Protestants who held government positions transferred to the new Northern Ireland civil service, but those who remained suffered few material disadvantages and showed no lack of loyalty to the Free State administration. The fact that large numbers of civil servants went on to work for both Irish regimes clearly assisted the smooth transfer of authority.

The main division that emerged in southern Irish politics in the 1920s was not along class, ethnic or regional lines, but rather hinged on attitudes and approaches towards Britain and the partition issue. Many people continued to cast their vote for or against the Treaty as represented by the two main parties, Fine Gael and Fianna Fáil, and the civil war split dominated elections and party politics. The clear left/right division that was typical of most western European politics did not emerge in the Free State. Indeed the combined vote for left-wing parties rarely exceeded 16 per cent. Farmers' parties did emerge in the 1920s and 1940s but though their support for government proved at times crucial, they never succeeded in making major electoral inroads. The two major parties succeeded in drawing support from all sections of the population. Support for Fine Gael was strongest along the east coast and in the Midlands among business people and large farmers. Fianna Fáil support was initially strongest in the western counties amongst small farmers but it also found favour with the Dublin working class. In power, Fianna Fáil became more moderate and by the 1940s it had made significant progress in winning votes from middle-class and business interests, justifiably meriting its catchall label.

In 1920, the Government of Ireland Act had established two parliaments in Ireland. The planned parliament of Southern Ireland (twenty-six counties) quickly became a dead letter as a result of Sinn Féin opposition and was later superseded by Dáil Éireann, established under the terms of the Anglo-Irish Treaty. The parliament of Northern Ireland (six counties) was duly opened in 1921 and continued to function as a subordinate parliament within the United Kingdom until its abolition in 1972. When the Anglo-Irish Treaty of 1921 established the Irish Free State the partition of Ireland was complete. On the other side of the border, the emergence of Northern Ireland was the outcome of over four decades of intense Ulster Protestant opposition to Irish Home Rule. Ulster Unionists wished to avoid at all costs becoming a minority in a Catholic-dominated Irish state. For them Home Rule meant 'Rome Rule'. Since the 1880s, Ulster Unionists had planned to resist nationalist agitation for Home Rule by force if necessary. In this

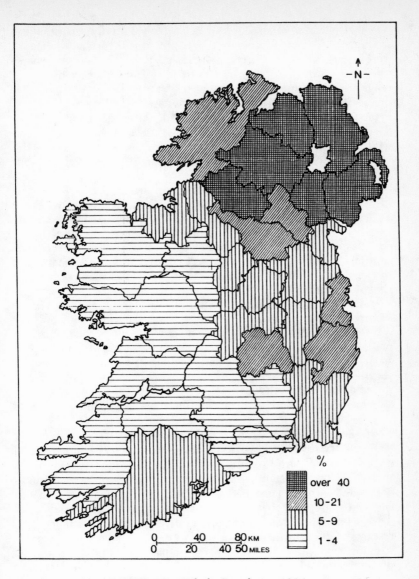

Map 7: Non-Catholic Population 1926

Source: E. Rumpf and A. Hepburn, *Nationalism and Socialism in Twentieth-Century Ireland*, Liverpool University Press 1977, 45, Fig. 5.

they had important advantages. They controlled the only major industrial region in Ireland in which the vast majority of Irish Protestants were concentrated; they had key allies in the British Army and Conservative party; and the Orange Order provided a convenient political and religious framework for an army of resistance. Moreover, the Order united Protestants of different denominations and classes — Presbyterians, Church of Ireland, the landed gentry, merchants, industrialists, farmers and the urban working classes. It was this cohesion which ensured the survival of Northern Ireland in the midst of the violence, bloodshed and intimidation which marked its establishment in the years 1920 to 1922.

The new Northern Ireland statelet comprised those districts Ulster Protestants could control militarily and within which they would have a permanent and unassailable majority. They had failed to retain the whole of Ireland within the United Kingdom, and even abandoned three counties of the historic province of Ulster in which there were substantial Protestant minorities. Nevertheless, it still proved impossible to establish a homogeneous Protestant Northern Ireland within the six-county framework finally adopted.

Half a million Catholics (one-third of the population) were incorporated into Northern Ireland against their will. Many of these were located in the west and south of the six counties. Strong advocates of a united independent Ireland, they bitterly resented their new status as a permanent and powerless minority in a Protestant and Unionist state — a state which regarded them as a perpetual source of dissaffection and disloyalty.

While the Partition settlement was seen as an interim measure by many British and southern politicians on the way to a permanent North-South accommodation, it was viewed very differently by Ulster Unionists. Many Unionists would have preferred to be administered directly from Westminster but they quickly came to see the merits of their own Northern state as a permanent bulwark against enemies both within and without. These included the disloyal nationalist minority in the North, southern political parties agitating for a united Ireland, and British politicians who might be tempted to betray Northern Protestants by doing a deal with the South. The Unionist party, which was to enjoy fifty uninterrupted years of one-party rule until the abolition of the Northern Ireland parliament in 1972, was able to identify itself with the very existence of the state. Any potential Protestant challenge to its dominance was marginalised by portraying it as a threat to the Union.

External factors also helped to ensure the survival of Northern Ireland in its precarious early years. The civil war in the south (1922-3) between nationalists over the Anglo-Irish Treaty greatly weakened the IRA's attacks on the new regime in the North. Furthermore, a

Boundary Commission established under the Anglo-Irish Treaty to readjust the border between Northern Ireland and the Irish Free State collapsed in 1925, thus effectively confirming the existing border. This gave Unionists the chance to consolidate both militarily and administratively. Nationalists had expected that this commission would render Northern Ireland non-viable by ceding to the Free State large areas of the new political unit.

The new state in the North was seen by Unionists as a means of preserving the status quo rather than as a vehicle for radical new departures. The Northern Ireland parliament was modelled on Westminster with its own Prime Minister, a bi-cameral legislature and civil service. There were fifty-two seats in the local parliament while Northern Ireland representatives continued to occupy twelve seats in the Westminster parliament. Northern Ireland also inherited over seventy local authorities dating from the reform of Irish local government in 1898. With a population of only one and a quarter million people, the province certainly did not lack political institutions! What it did lack, however, was the type of consensus which underpinned competitive representative democracies in other countries.

From the outset, Northern politics were dominated by the Partition question. Each election was a plebiscite on the nature, even on the existence, of the state. It was also in large part a sectarian headcount, with Catholics voting for parties opposed to the Union and Protestants voting for the Unionist Party. The abolition of the Proportional Representation electoral system by the Unionists in 1929 further reduced the prospects of minority parties and independents. Partition divided the potential constituency of Irish Labour and marginalised any left-wing opposition to conservative parties in both parts of Ireland.

Nationalists did not formally sit in the Belfast parliament until 1927 and did not accept the rôle of official opposition until 1965. They were in any case in a hopeless minority with no prospect of forming an alternative government. Gerrymandering at local level ensured that nationalists did not even control local government areas in which they had a majority. Nationalist politicians, denied any political influence by Unionists, tended to oscillate between ritual denunciations of the Northern Ireland state and boycott of state institutions. The anti-Partition League sought to enlist the support of southern political parties and British Labour politicians in the 1940s and 1950s but this proved to be a miserable failure. The IRA launched a sporadic and abortive offensive between 1956–62 which gained little support from Northern nationalists.

Although the Northern parliament had much of the trappings and protocol of the Westminster parliament, it had limited powers. It could only raise 20 per cent, at most, of its own revenue. It had more scope in administering expenditure, although Northern Ireland's declining economy and British policy limited the room for manoeuvre here. In any case, Unionists were seldom interested in using their administrative powers to initiate policies distinctive to Northern Ireland. This lack of initiative, together with built-in sectarian majorities, ensured that almost 50 per cent of seats were uncontested in Northern Ireland general elections between 1929 and 1969. Parliament generally met for only two months of the year, largely to endorse the policy of the government.

The most distinctive element of the Northern Ireland administration was the Unionist party's direct control both of the police and the Ulster Special Constabulary. The latter was an entirely Protestant part-time paramilitary force which could be expanded quickly to meet any threat from republicans. Under a draconian Special Powers Act, the invariably Unionist Minister for Home Affairs could authorise arrest without charge, internment without trial, flogging, execution, and the banning of meetings, organisations or publications. These powers were aimed almost exclusively at the dissident minority community. The identification of the security forces with the Protestant Unionist community was to remain the key indicator of the endemic lack of consensus over the existence of the state as well as a reminder of the civil strife and turmoil which attended its birth.

II
ECONOMIC POLICY AND PERFORMANCE

In 1922, in so far as a strategy for the economic development of the newly-established state existed, it was based on Sinn Féin's philosophy of self-sufficiency. This strategy, if vigorously pursued, would have implied a radical restructuring of the Free State's economy along with a renegotiation of its economic relationship with the United Kingdom. For many of those involved in the struggle for political independence the pursuit of economic self-sufficiency was an integral part of the nationalist ideology, and they would have looked to its implementation from the outset.

However, for the first administration charged with the task of managing the economic fortunes of the fledgling Free State, the constraints imposed by inherited economic structures, notwithstanding the benign rhetoric of nationalist aspirations, looked very formidable indeed. With the benefit of hindsight we can see that these structures reveal the now familiar classic features of a relatively underdeveloped colonial economy. These included the predominance of agriculture, in which the pattern of production had been dictated over the previous two centuries by changing conditions in the United Kingdom markets; and an underdeveloped industrial sector which had been exposed to the rigours of free trade with British industry since the Act of Union in

1800. In 1926, the first year for which comprehensive statistics are available, agriculture accounted for 53 per cent of total employment and 32 per cent of Gross Domestic Product (GDP). By contrast, industry accounted for a mere 13 per cent of employment and 18 per cent of GDP, while the service sector (mainly public sector) shares were 33 and 50 per cent respectively. Between them, the agricultural and service sectors accounted for 86 and 82 per cent of the Free State's employment and output respectively, reflecting an extreme sectoral imbalance within the economy. As a comparatively small economy by international standards, possessing a very limited natural resource base (with the exception of land) the new state was of necessity heavily dependent on international trade. Not surprisingly the pattern of this trade was dominated by trading relationships with the United Kingdom. In 1926 Great Britain supplied just over 65 per cent of total imports, while in the same year 83 per cent of our total exports (mainly agricultural) went to that country. If Northern Ireland is included in these calculations then in 1926 the United Kingdom (Great Britain and Northern Ireland) supplied 76 per cent of imports while 97 per cent of exports went to that market. From an economic perspective, therefore the new Irish Free State was an extremely small, trade-dependent economy, heavily reliant on its agricultural sector as the major source of wealth creation, and characterised by a weak and unevenly developed industrial sector.

The nationalist ideology of economic self-sufficiency dictated the pursuit of industrial development through protection once political independence had been attained. But this was not the economic strategy adopted by the first Free State government under the leadership of W.T. Cosgrave. From the outset the new government was committed to the development of agriculture and agricultural policy consequently dominated public policy discussions. More specifically, the main concern was to regain for Irish agricultural products the ground lost in United Kingdom markets following the First World War. During that war Irish agriculture had virtually monopolised the supply of food to the United Kingdom market, and this in turn had permitted Irish farmers to adopt a cavalier attitude to such matters as the quality or standard of their product. Consequently, when trade relations were normalised after the war British consumers looked to alternative suppliers and Irish producers experienced a serious fall in their share of the United Kingdom market. This market loss was exacerbated by a serious slump in agricultural prices after 1920 and when the Free State was established, Irish agriculture was in the depths of a severe recession. The immediate objectives of agricultural policy were purely economic; the achievement of increased output and productive efficiency, with its corollary of lower unit costs and higher profits for producers, buttressed by an attempt to implement proper marketing procedures to

159

ensure the quality and standard of Irish produce. The pursuit of these objectives was reflected in the work of the Commission on Agriculture which was appointed in 1922 and which reported in 1924. Following the recommendations of the Commission a number of legislative measures were implemented during the 1920s with the aim of ensuring high standards of quality and presentation of agricultural produce. The short-term impact of these measures was remarkably effective. By the end of the 1920s Irish agricultural exports had largely retrieved their previous shares of the United Kingdom market. By the same token, however, the earlier colonial pattern of Irish economic production and trade, dominated by agriculture and directed almost exclusively to the United Kingdom market, was not only maintained but effectively enhanced. In the economic area continuity rather than change was the preferred option for the first Irish administration.

This same continuity is evident when we come to consider industrial strategy. It was in this area of economic activity that many expected the most radical changes in economic policy. However the tone of future industrial policy was struck in the reports of the Fiscal Inquiry Committee, which reported in November 1923. Contrary to expectations, in certain segments of industry at least, the Committee opposed the introduction of protection for Irish industry. Not that industry had ever been unanimous in its demands for protection. The small number of industries which had survived free trade and now pursued a successful export business actively opposed the introduction of protective measures, as did the major agricultural groups. Nevertheless, for the remainder of its term of office, the government implemented what W.T. Cosgrave termed 'a policy of selective protection' — but 'selective' was the operative word. The budgets of 1924, 1925 and 1926 introduced a limited number of protective duties and in 1926 the Tariff Commission was established which provided the framework for guiding and implementing the policy of 'selective protection'. The limited nature of protection policy as pursued by the Cosgrave administration was reflected by the fact that over the seven-year period 1926-32 only fifteen industries made application for protective duties. In 1932, the end of the term of office of the Cosgrave administration, Ireland was still effectively in a free trading relationship with the United Kingdom.

There remains the question as to why the first Irish administration steadfastly refused to pursue the accepted nationalist strategy of economic development. A number of contending explanations have been put forward, between whcih historians continue the difficult task of abritration. First, it has been argued that in the immediate aftermath of a vicious civil war, the main priority was to re-establish stability within the community and this militated against radical innovations in economic strategy. Second, in attempting to bring

160

about political viability the new administration relied heavily on the support, moral rather than material, of the British government. Third, the social elements which dominated the new administration were representative of the most conservative groups in Irish society. Protection offered no clear benefit to them, and hence they could not be expected to push for it.

These considerations explain the direction of economic strategy of the 1920s but when Mr de Valera came to power in 1932 he sought to pursue a diametrically opposed strategy. If economic issues had dominated relations between the United Kingdom and the Irish administration during the 1920s then political considerations would regain their primacy under de Valera, but they would have far-reaching economic implications. So far as de Valera was concerned there remained much unfinished political business with the United Kingdom. The central objective of his political career was the quest for sovereignty and this meant undermining the British connection as enshrined in the Treaty, so that Ireland might achieve the kind of independence he envisaged and had argued for since 1922. In the economic domain this would lead to de Valera launching a major experiment in economic nationalism, underpinned by a philosophy of self-sufficiency.

In carrying out this experiment de Valera was greatly helped by the world-wide economic depression. By 1930 the Depression had taken grip in all of the major industrial countries including Britain. In October 1931 the victory of a National Government in the United Kingdom, along with the further deepening of the Depression, made it clear that the United Kingdom, in common with most other countries, would be forced to implement protective tariffs in an attempt to protect its domestic markets. This was expected to lead to a rush by other countries to export goods to the British market before the imposition of the tariffs. It was envisaged that this would lead to unprecedented dumping of goods onto the Irish market, and in order to protect Irish industry legislation was quickly introduced in November 1931 to allow the imposition of extensive customs duties. Even before the general election of 1932 protection policy had became a major issue as a result of external developments and this was singularly fortuitous for de Valera and his party, given their commitment to a strategy of self-sufficiency.

Additional support for de Valera's policy of comprehensive protection arose from the dispute between the Irish and English governments over the payment of the land annuities. These represented payments due to the British government as a result of the land acts of the late nineteenth and early twentieth centuries. Shortly after coming to power de Valera ceased payment of these annuities. By way of retaliation the British government imposed substantial duties on Irish

161

exports of livestock and other agricultural produce. In addition, quotas which limited the exports of Irish livestock and other produce to Britain were imposed at the beginning of 1934. The Irish government responded in turn with penal tariffs on certain British imports. This trade dispute between the two countries, popularly known as the 'Economic War', lasted from 1932 to 1938. It was undoubtedly disruptive economically but the Economic War served de Valera's purpose admirably by marshalling the political support which facilitated his pursuit of political sovereignty, including his experiment in economic nationalism.

The pursuit of self-sufficiency dominated policy in all the major sectors of the economy. In agriculture a dramatic reversal of policies took place. In contrast to the policies pursued by the earlier administration the Fianna Fáil agricultural strategy was aimed at achieving self-sufficiency and increasing the numbers living on the land. This involved the expansion of tillage production at the expense of grazing; the provision of guaranteed prices for wheat and sugar-beet producers; and the imposition of prohibitive tariffs on butter and bacon imports.

If this represented a major re-orientation of previous policy, an even greater reversal was planned for the industrial sector. Within months of taking office the Fianna Fáil government imposed tariffs on a large array of industrial products, and prompted by the outbreak of the Economic War in 1932 it quickly passed various acts which implemented its strategy of import substitution for industrial goods. As a result the Free State made a rapid transition from a free-trade economy to one of extreme protection by international standards.

The economic policies pursued after 1932 contributed significantly to widespread structural change in the economy. The share of agriculture in both employment and output fell from its 1926 levels of 53 and 32 per cent respectively to 48 per cent of total employment and 27 per cent of output by 1938. In absolute terms this represented a loss of over 64,000 jobs in agriculture between 1926 and 1938. However this was more than compensated for by the increase in industrial and service employment where an additional 69,000 jobs were created. The most spectacular increase came within the industrial sector where just over 55,000 new jobs were created by 1938. By this date, industry and services combined had displaced agriculture as the primary source of employment. These changes in the sectoral composition of employment and output were seen as vindicating in no small way the general policy of self-sufficiency. Moreover, the self-sufficiency achieved during the 1930s proved especially valuable with the onset of the Second World War.

Achieving self-sufficiency through a strategy of import substitution is, from an economic perspective, an elusive objective and Ireland's experience was no different to others in this respect. With hindsight it

162

could be argued that the impact of import substitution had already been exhausted by the late 1930s. The disruption of the international economy caused by the war may have exaggerated the benefits of continuing with this policy. Similarly, the economic boom in the immediate post-war years (between 1946 and 1949 Irish industrial production increased by almost 50 per cent) may have concealed the long-term damaging effects of a sustained policy of import substitution. By the early 1950s these consequences were becoming evident.

The 1950s represented a most difficult period for the Irish economy. There were a series of balance of payments crises during the course of the decade and stringent measures to rectify them further restricted the level of economic activity. Unemployment increased dramatically and emigration became the major economic and social problem. Emigration averaged 40,000 a year over the decade and overall almost half a million people emigrated. Altogether the trauma of these developments led to a protracted re-evaluation of economic strategy and by the end of the 1950s the main elements of a new direction for economic policy had been formulated. The experiment in economic nationalism had now clearly failed and a new strategy based on export-led growth was pronounced to be the best way forward.

The economic development of Northern Ireland presents both similarities and contrasts to that of the Irish Free State. The similarities rest largely on the common experiences of two economies which had a close relationship with Britain over a protracted period. The contrasts arise from the different economic structures inherited by both parts of the country from the nineteenth century along with the different trajectories followed by both economies after 1922. The principal difference in inherited economic structure was undoubtedly the more developed industrial base of Northern Ireland compared with that of the Free State. Northern Ireland's industrial base was highly specialised and was concentrated on shipbuilding, textiles, engineering and a number of ancillary industries. This difference in the industrial structures of both parts of the country was reflected in the figures for industrial employment in 1912. By this date over two-thirds of all Irish industrial workers were in north-east Ulster, mainly centred in and around Belfast.

It was a similar story where agriculture was concerned. In 1926 agriculture in Northern Ireland accounted for just over 25 per cent of the labour force, but in the Free State it accounted for over 50 per cent. However, it should be noted that in both the Free State and in Northern Ireland agriculture was the single largest source of employment. Farms in Northern Ireland were on balance smaller than in the Free State, but a higher proportion of their area was devoted to tillage production. During the 1920s agricultural policy in Northern Ireland pursued a broadly similar line of development to that of the Free State. The main emphasis was on upgrading the quality of agricultural produce through the extension of agricultural education, the provision of increased credit facilities for agricultural producers, and the development of agricultural co-operatives.

As in the Free State, redirection of agricultural policy changed in Northern Ireland around 1931, mainly in response to initiatives by the British government. These were aimed at stimulating domestic agricultural production and involved the use of tariffs against imported agricultural goods and the establishment of state marketing boards to co-ordinate the sale of agricultural produce in the British market. In addition Northern Ireland farmers gained from the provision of British subsidies to agricultural producers. The combined effects of these measures was to provide Northern Ireland agriculture with an elaborate support system which contributed to its successful performance especially when compared to that of the Free State. The war years further stimulated agricultural production to meet the demands for food.

The immediate post-war years saw the continued expansion of agricultural production in Northern Ireland. Increased production was mainly concentrated in poultry and pig farming in order to meet the food shortages that persisted in the United Kingdom for some years after the war. As these food shortages eased and trade relations between the United Kingdom and the rest of the world were restored, Northern Ireland's agriculture was forced to compete with low-cost agricultural imports, a result of the celebrated cheap food policy of the British government. On balance, however, in the post-war period Northern Ireland farmers felt themselves to be at a disadvantage compared with their counterparts in England and Scotland because of their distance from the United Kingdom and other markets. Special subsidies overcame this difficulty and Northern Ireland agriculture has since enjoyed a secure position within the United Kingdom market.

When Northern Ireland was established its industrial base was experiencing serious difficulties. Industries such as shipbuilding and linen, which had brought so much prosperity to the region during the nineteenth century, were by the 1920s in decline. Shipbuilding, which had employed over 15,000 in 1913 was by 1924 providing employment for only 7,500; employment in linen declined from 74,000 in 1924 to 55,000 in 1930. By the mid-1920s unemployment in Northern Ireland averaged 24 per cent and by 1931 had risen to 28 per cent.

The response to this industrial crisis was the introduction of a wide range of measures aimed at stimulating production and promoting sales among existing industries. Steps were also taken to attract new industries. These included the setting-up of the Ulster Industrial

Development Association with the objective of encouraging people to purchase native products. Beginning in 1932 a novel programme to attract new industries was launched which provided rentals to new firms for up to twenty years, exempted them from rates, subsidised the costs of sites, provided tax remission on profits and made available interest-free loans. These measures made a real, if modest, contribution during the 1930s to stimulating industrial development. Northern Ireland was thus even ahead of Great Britain at this time in the use of such policy measures, and twenty years ahead of the Irish Free State. However the real solution to the industrial crisis of the 1920s and '30s was provided by the outbreak of the Second World War: in the shipbuilding industry employment rose to 30,000 at its peak of war-time production.

After the war, strategy was again focused on the development of new industry to replace the declining traditional sectors. Efforts were also made to re-equip and modernise existing industries, and in 1956 the Northern Ireland Development Company was established to attract new overseas investment. Its efforts met with considerable success and on balance the 1950s and early 1960s were years of economic progress. Between 1950 and 1962 industrial production increased by 50 per cent and Northern Ireland's growth rate surpassed that of the United Kingdom as a whole and greatly exceeded that of the Republic of Ireland. Notwithstanding this progress, unemployment remained the central problem for Northern Ireland's economy, and this was to present a major challenge during the 1960s.

III

SOCIAL STRUCTURE, INSTITUTIONS AND PROCESSES

Independence for the South, then, did not lead to wide-ranging institutional or administrative innovation nor did it usher in an era of economic prosperity: similarly little attempt was made to use the opportunity offered by independence to initiate social change. As one commentator has remarked: 'the Irish social revolution — the transfer of land ownership, the undoing of the confiscation of the seventeenth century — had already been carried out before the political revolution began ... The Free State was basically too poor, too contented and too conservative to engage in any radical transformation of its society' (Laffan, 1984, 33-4). Consequently there is again remarkable continuity in social trends and attitudes between the pre- and post-independence periods.

The long-term trend of depopulation continued from the 1920s through to the 1950s. Population decline was not, however, evenly distributed and the population of urban areas actually increased. Population decline in rural areas, and in the west of Ireland in particular, reflected the continuing impact of emigration. The average annual rate of natural increase was high and was actually greater in the 1950s than at any decade since the 1860s, and higher than most European countries. A high rate of natural increase combined with a declining population was one unique feature of southern Irish demography. Others included the very low marriage rate and the late age of marriage; as late as 1961 more than 70 per cent of males aged between twenty-five and thirty-four were unmarried. Non-marriage for many represented an alternative to emigration. By remaining single a person could continue to live in Ireland and maintain a standard of living which, while less than that available through emigration, was still acceptable. Those who did marry, on the other hand, were remarkably fertile. In the mid-1940s two out of every five families had between six and nine children. Mainly as a consequence of emigration, the Free State continued to have a very high proportion of its population in dependent age groups.

Demographic trends reflected very much the rural character of the Free State. Even in the 1950s, more than 30 per cent of the population was employed in agriculture and the figure was 60 per cent or more in a number of western counties. Fewer than one worker in four was employed in manufacturing industry, mostly in small firms. The industrial base for the establishment of a substantial working class had not yet emerged. Society was dominated by people of property and by their preoccupation with social status and differentials. While considerable differences existed between farmers (in terms of income and farm size), nevertheless they all enjoyed positions of high social standing and authority by virtue of their ownership of land. A class hierarchy also existed in the towns extending from the professionals and the shopkeepers — big and small — down to the tradesmen and the labourers. This hierarchy revealed itself in material possessions, attitudes, beliefs and recreational activities. It was a rigid system and opportunities for social mobility were extremely limited.

Family life on the farm was characterised by a rigid division of labour along age and sex lines. There were clear sets of 'male' and 'female' tasks. Most of the heavy farm work was undertaken by the father, while his wife dominated activities within the household. All major decisions concerning the farm and the family finances were typically taken by the father. Sons, even those in middle age, had little say in farm activities and were still referred to as 'boys'. Wives had control over whatever income they could earn from such enterprises as the sale of butter and eggs and were free to make all decisions about the training and education of children. The typical form of marriage until the 1950s, for medium and large farmers in particular, was the 'match'. This was an arranged marriage for the son who was nominated to succeed to the family farm, and for those daughters for whom partners could be found locally. The main features of the match were that it reflected parental control and that the woman 'marrying in' brought a dowry or 'fortune' with her. This in turn was used to support the other children in the household, usually to assist their emigration. The high birth rate in farm families reflected the desire for children who were viewed as a basis for generational continuity, a source of labour, and as an insurance against old age. Boy children were preferred over girls who 'were favoured neither by father nor mother and accepted only on sufferance. They were loved but not thought of as of any great importance' (McNabb, 1962, 40).

Women had been prominent in political activity during the revolutionary period but after independence their public rôle diminished. There were fewer women involved in electoral politics in the 1950s than the 1920s. The 1937 Constitution only referred explicitly to women's special position within the home and there was generally little political or ideological encouragement given to women to pursue a public rôle. Yet women did enter the labour force in considerable numbers. In 1951 they comprised 30 per cent of the work force and were heavily concentrated in the low-skill food industries. At this time only 5 per cent of 'working' women were married, reflecting both the ideological pressure to conform to the ideal of full-time motherhood, and the practical obstacles in the way of the 'working' wife (such as the marriage bar for women teachers, only removed in 1958).

Nationalism had found strong allies among the Catholic clergy and the nationalist movement had been closely linked with the demands of Catholics for full civil and political rights. Thus, it is perhaps not surprising that apart from an early skirmish with the opponents of the Treaty the Catholic hierarchy, and indeed all levels of clergy, enjoyed a close relationship with politicians of all persuasions. In the early decades of the Free State the clergy were preoccupied with sexual morality and there were numerous pronouncements on the dangers presented by the cinema, dance halls, 'dirty' books, and foreign dress. The state proved only too willing to play its part in curbing these 'occasions of sin' and legislation was introduced setting up a censorship board, prohibiting divorce, banning contraceptives and licensing dance halls. The 1937 Constitution incorporated Catholic social teaching into sections on the family, private property and church-state relations. Primary and secondary education, although state financed, was under clerical control. When church and state did come into conflict, the state usually yielded. Thus the Catholic hierarchy successfully opposed the introduction of the Mother and Child Scheme in 1951 (designed to provide free medical care for pregnant women and for children) on the grounds that it represented undue interference by the state into the privacy of the family, and this forced the resignation of the then Minister for Health, Noel Browne. Until the 1950s authors such as Hemingway, Steinbeck and even Graham Greene were banned. During the 1950s, however, direct intervention by the Catholic church in public life diminished considerably.

A national language and culture are invariably considered amongst the most important building blocks of the nation/state. Independence offered the possibility of translating the Gaelic ideal, an 'Irish Ireland', into something approaching reality. Gaelic sports — hurling and football — flourished with little or no state assistance, but Irish music and song remained very much minority interests. However, a major effort was made to revive the Irish language as the everyday language of the people. In this respect, hopes for the restoration of Irish as the common language of the country were very much pinned on education. In primary schools it was recommended that all instruction for infants should be through Irish and that in the higher classes a minimum of one hour's instruction per day was to be in Irish. After some years, this policy was firmly opposed by the Irish National Teachers Organisation and was relaxed from the late 1940s onwards. In the secondary schools the government relied more on the carrot than the stick and offered inducements such as extra grants for schools, salary increments for teachers and bonus examination marks for pupils using Irish as the medium of instruction and expression. In most secondary schools, however, Irish simply became another subject of study with the added negative value of having to be passed by examination before the final qualification (Leaving Certificate) could be awarded. Some knowledge of Irish was also made compulsory for state officials but overall these policies met with only limited success, and English remained the language of everyday work and recreation for the majority of the population.

The new state thus faced considerable difficulties in restoring Irish as the first language of the country. It also made little progress with the task of keeping it alive in the *Gaeltacht* (Irish speaking) areas. The *Gaeltacht* (an agreed geographical definition was not available until 1956) was composed not of one unit but was spread mostly along parts of the western seaboard, with outposts in a small area of Co. Waterford and two tiny colonies transplanted to Co. Meath as part of the land reform programme. The western *Gaeltacht* was one of the most underdeveloped parts of Ireland and was marked by very high emigration and acute depopulation. The Commission on the *Gaeltacht* (1926) had highlighted the need for a comprehensive socio-economic policy to stem the tide of people leaving because of economic necessity. However, there was little action for decades and it was not until 1956 that a special state department was established with specific responsibility for the area. Gaeltarra Eireann, a state sponsored body, was set up in 1958 as a development agency for the

Gaeltacht and by the early 1960s had succeeded in creating 700 full-time and 1,000 part-time jobs. Pious platitudes had at last been replaced by practical action.

Outside the *Gaeltacht* as well as within, poverty continued to be very much in evidence but the decades after independence were not notable for the expansion of social services by the state. Secondary and third-level education operated mainly on a fee-paying basis and consequently was availed of mostly by the children of the better off. Of the 57,000 children who completed their primary education in 1957 only 10,000 stayed on to do their Leaving Certificate and less than 2,000 found their way to university. Everywhere there were large numbers of people living in sub-standard and overcrowded living conditions. There was little government action on this front in the 1920s but a drive against slum housing got underway in the 1930s and over 80,000 new dwellings were built. Those in employment could hope to benefit from both new and expanded social insurance schemes, but the position of the unemployed remained precarious, though the Unemployment Assistance Act (1933) provided for some financial support for all unemployed males. The poor and the destitute had to rely on charitable organisations, run principally by religious orders.

Two decades after independence the Irish Free State had one of the worst health records in Europe. Tuberculosis had fallen at a slower rate than in most other European countries and the rate actually increased between 1939 and 1947. Infant mortality also rose in these years. The resources of the local authorities responsible for health services had remained unaltered and there was little available to those who could not afford to pay. Both the Poor Law system and the mentality that went with it — that poverty was the fault of the poor — still held firm. In 1947, however, a separate Department of Health was established and state funding increased dramatically. A major hospital building and reconstruction programme was undertaken and the impact was quickly felt, particularly in the eradication of tuberculosis. Specialist health services and benefits such as maternity cash grants and disablement allowances were also made available to the poor and those on low incomes.

In Northern Ireland the fundamental divide between Catholic Nationalist and Protestant Unionist persisted and became ever more institutionalised. The attempts to establish a wholly Catholic state in the South were matched by a desire on the part of the Orange Order and Protestant activists to ensure that Northern Ireland would have a Protestant ethos. After Partition, a renewed evangelical movement preached anti-Catholicism, espoused temperance, and advocated strict sabbatarianism. Ironically, it shared with Catholic fundmentalists an obsession with sexual morality. While there was less censorship formally enshrined in legislation than in the south, it

169

existed nevertheless in powerful covert and pervasive forms. Radio and television closely reflected the prevailing Unionist ethic, largely ignoring Irish culture and excluding political dissent. Northern newspapers were divided on Unionist-Nationalist lines both in terms of ownership and readership.

In 1930, after an early attempt at integrated education, the Northern Ireland government conceded to Protestant agitation for 'Bible-teaching in schools' and 'Protestant teachers for Protestant pupils'. The Catholic church also maintained its own schools which remained outside the Protestant state system but were partially funded by the state.

Schooling was only one institutional manifestation of the depth of the communal divide in Northern Ireland. Communal affiliation influenced and in many cases determined where people lived, worked and worshipped. It shaped the sports they played, the businesses they patronised and even dictated their choice of marriage partner. However, Protestants and Catholics also had much in common and frequently interacted with each other, especially in rural areas. But they mingled with an awareness of their differences — differences which were expressed in the existence and institutions of the northern state itself.

At the core of Unionist politics was the concern to maintain a permanent pro-Union, Protestant, majority in Northern Ireland. Indeed, the Catholic proportion of the population remained remarkably stable for fifty years after Partition at one-third of the total. Although Catholic birth rates were substantially higher than Protestant, Catholic emigrants outnumbered Protestants by two to one. Membership of the Orange Order was a requirement for success in Unionist politics and the Order worked to ensure that Protestants got preference over Catholics in jobs, houses, and business contracts. By 1943, only 6 per cent of the Northern Ireland civil service was Catholic and the top fifty-five posts were all in Protestant hands. There was little significant change in the composition of the civil service until the 1970s. Allocation of housing by local authorities was also a major bone of contention. Allegations of discrimination against Catholics were well founded, especially in western and southern areas where the sectarian headcount approached parity. Unionists were anxious to prevent any of the Border areas falling into the hands of the 'enemies of the state'.

The territorial dimension to the communal divide was most important. Northern Ireland was a mosaic of distinct but interlocking Catholic and Protestant areas which were in large part a product of seventeenth-century patterns of settlement. Partition had ensured that these internal boundaries now assumed the status of 'national' borders. Flags, parades, marches and occasional rioting

170

marked many of these boundaries. In small tightly-knit communities where kinship was of major importance, division was accentuated by the absence of inter-marriage between Catholics and Protestants. Furthermore, there were considerable differences in the social structure of both communities. A small professional Catholic middle class of priests, teachers, doctors, lawyers and shopkeepers existed largely to service their own community. Catholics were disproportionately represented among small farmers in poorer upland areas, among the unemployed and in unskilled and semi-skilled occupations. Protestants, on the other hand, had a more differentiated class structure. Large landowners, factory owners, merchants, and a professional class which serviced the whole community were largely Protestant. Protestants controlled the skilled manufacturing jobs in shipbuilding and engineering in Belfast. Many small farmers, unskilled workers and unemployed were also Protestant and shared many common problems with their Catholic neighbours. Nevertheless, their conviction that Northern Ireland was their state, and that its existence guaranteed them preferential treatment over Catholics helped prevent sustained political co-operation between both communities. Catholics, for their part, lacked economic and political power and saw little prospect of remedy within the existing political structures.

In both communities, substantial numbers of women worked in manufacturing industry, notably in the linen and clothing sector. Low pay and poor conditions characterised the linen industry which was controlled by approximately 400 local linen families. The rapid contraction of this sector in the 1950s and 60s marked a move away from paternalism and Protestant control of indigenous industry. Thereafter employment was to expand with a growing number of jobs for women in services. The 1950s also marked the extension to Northern Ireland of the new British Welfare State measures. Northern Catholics now became significantly better-off in material terms than their co-religionists south of the Border. Thus, despite much higher rates of emigration than Protestants, they were still less likely to emigrate than southern Catholics in the 1950s.

CONCLUSION

The stability of the Free State after independence contrasts favourably with the experience of many new states in the twentieth century and even with the periodic turmoil of its northern neighbour. Power was successfully transferred to a native government in 1922 and to an opposition party in 1932. Irishmen were now at the helm and this in itself was an immense source of satisfaction. Sovereignty could be developed and exercised as indeed it was by the adoption of a neutral stance during the Second World War. In most other respects the impact of independence was limited and life continued much as before. There was little in the way of political innovation or economic progress; emigration and depopulation continued and independence made little difference to the poor. The Free State was in many respects an archaic and backward-looking polity, preoccupied ideologically with a mythical folk past but making little effort to tackle the very real problems of underdevelopment. However, it was demonstrated in the 1960s that a native government could lay the foundation for economic and social change and even a modicum of prosperity. Northern Ireland, by contrast, inherited a similar political and rather different economic structure, which notwithstanding some modification and change, provided a substantially higher level of prosperity than that of the Free State. But religious tensions from the outset facilitated and encouraged the creation of a deeply-divided sectarian society. The marginal improvement in the standing of the Catholics in the 1950s and 1960s, brought about mainly by the introduction to Northern Ireland of British Welfare State measures, only served to highlight their grievances in the areas of law and security, voting rights, housing allocation and employment. Thus the scene was set for the Civil Rights agitation of the 1960s and the Protestant backlash which was to usher in the current Northern Ireland conflict and force the British government to reassert direct control over Northern Ireland in 1972.

REFERENCES
M. Laffan, 'Two Irish States', *Crane Bag*, vol. 8, no. 4, 1984, 26-40.
P. McNabb, 'Social Structure', *Limerick Rural Survey*, ed. Newman, Tipperary 1962.

FURTHER READING
T. Brown, *Ireland: A Social and Cultural History 1922-1973*, London 1981.
P. Buckland, *The Factory of Grievances: Devolved Government in Northern Ireland, 1921-39*, Dublin 1979
M.E. Daly, *Social and Economic History of Ireland since 1800*, Dublin 1981.
R. Fanning, *Independent Ireland*, Dublin 1982.
M. Farrell, *Northern Ireland: The Orange State*, London 1976.
T. Garvin, *The Evolution of Irish Nationalist Politics*, Dublin 1981.
D. Johnson, *The Interior Economy in Ireland*, Dublin 1985.
F.S.L. Lyons, *Ireland Since the Famine*, London 1973.
J. Meenan, *The Irish Economy Since 1922*, Liverpool 1970.
F. Rumpf and A. Hepburn, *Nationalism and Socialism in Twentieth-Century Ireland*, Liverpool 1977.

11
TWENTIETH-CENTURY IRISH LITERATURE

Gerald Dawe, D.E.S. Maxwell, Riana O'Dwyer

THE universal recognition of literature from Ireland as a major force owes a great deal to the capacity for innovation and experimentation displayed by its major modern writers. Yeats, Joyce and Beckett extended the resources of poetry, fiction and drama in a way which influenced writers from other cultures and languages, and extended the influence of Irish writing far beyond the limits of parochialism or provincialism. In the early years of the century the desire to find appropriate forms to express the particularity of Irish experience led to the Irish Literary Theatre's experiments with drama, Joyce's expansion of the novel and Yeats's development of the resources of the lyric form. The consequence of such individual efforts was the revelation to other Irish writers of the availability of their experience as a subject for literature, and an indication of some of the means which they might use to express it. The resulting corpus of poetry, plays, novels and short stories, each developing along different lines, and through the efforts of many writers, represents a formidable creative literary achievement, which is examined through its major genres in this chapter.

I
POETRY

The international standing of Irish poetry in the twentieth century is mainly due to W.B. Yeats (1865-1939). His achievement, principally as a poet but also as a critic, dramatist and polemicist for Irish cultural nationalism, is the pivotal point around which the direction of Irish poetry is most often drawn. Yet there is a contradiction involved. For in spite of the tremendous influence Yeats exerted throughout his own lifetime — in Ireland, Europe, the United States and across language barriers world-wide — his poetic legacy within Ireland has been fiercely debated by critics but rarely acknowledged by contemporary poets.

During his long life, however, W.B. Yeats transformed Irish poetry in the English language from its uncertain beginnings in the nineteenth century — the sprawling mythological epics of Sir Samuel Ferguson (1810-86), the martial ballads of Thomas Davis (1814-45), James Clarence Mangan's (1803-49) exotic and introverted auto-biographical masques — into a language of what he was to call 'passionate syntax'.[1] In 'To Ireland in the Coming Times' (*The Rose*, 1893) Yeats proclaims his allegiance to the company of Davis, Mangan and Ferguson as poets who

> ... sang, to sweeten Ireland's wrong,
> Ballad and story, rann and song;
> Nor be I any less of them,
> Because of the red-rose-bordered hem
> Of her, whose history began
> Before God made the angelic clan,
> Trails all about the written page.

During the turbulent years ahead Yeats continuously redefined this allegiance as Ireland lurched first into class struggle (the 1913 lockout), rebellion and executions (Easter 1916) then into the War of Independence (1919-21) and finally the Civil War (1922-3) before the state was actually founded, albeit within a partitioned country. Some of Yeats's greatest poems came out of this imaginative struggle for national identity as he questioned the meaning of history, both in terms of his own life and his family's, but also as regards his strife-torn country.

'September 1913', for instance, opens with a powerful sense of dis-illusionment that the high, lofty ideals of nationalists such as Yeats's friend and mentor, John O'Leary, had ignominiously dwindled into grasping religiosity and commercial self-interest:

> What need you, being come to sense,
> But fumble in a greasy till
> And add the half-pence to the pence
> And prayer to shivering prayer, until
> You have dried the marrow from the bone?
> For men were born to pray and save:
> Romantic Ireland's dead and gone,
> It's with O'Leary in the grave.

Most critics agree that it was in the collection from which this poem comes, *Responsibilities* (1914), that the diction and rhythm of Yeats's poetry took on a much more clearly-defined edge. Probably under the influence of his friend Ezra Pound who was acting as a sec-retary to him during this time (1913-14), Yeats broke from the customary crepuscular ambiguities which had characterised the earlier poetry and created in collections such as *Responsibilities* and *The Wild Swans at Coole* (1917) a stark imagistic simplicity unburdened with literary conceit:

174

The trees are in their autumn beauty
The woodland paths are dry,
Under the October twilight the water
Mirrors a still sky;
Upon the brimming water among the stones
Are nine-and-fifty swans.

The remaining twenty years of his life were to prove remarkably creative for Yeats the poet. He pursued his own intuitive needs into the supernatural, an obsession since he was a young man, and simultaneously proposed a view of civilisation and history in poetry and prose that, while verging toward the fascist movements current in the late 1920s and 30s, insisted upon the essential integrity and significance of the poetic imagination to the modern world.

In poems such as 'The Fisherman' and 'Ego Dominus Tuus' (*The Wild Swans at Coole*) Yeats explored his ambition, as he says in the first poem, to write 'one/Poem maybe as cold/And passionate as the dawn', conscious, all the while, as he stated in the second poem, that

> art
> Is but a vision of reality.
> What portion in the world can the artist have
> Who has awakened from the common dream
> But dissipation and despair?

It is the rhetorical question which Yeats's poetry constantly sought to answer, sometimes in an over-elaborate symbolic construction, like 'The Phases of the Moon' (*The Wild Swans at Coole*) but also in the naturalistic style of 'Easter 1916' or 'Sixteen Dead Men' where contemporary life becomes art.

Never far from Yeats's mind, though, was his particular sense of himself as a poet and the need to *create* a suitable landscape and vision of life which could house his imagination and the bounty it brings. In 'Sailing to Byzantium' (*The Tower*, 1928) Yeats wishes to repose, figuratively, in 'the artifice of eternity', celebrating with an almost Keatsian sensuousness, the glorious Byzantine world, 'to sing .../Of what is past, or passing, or to come'. This desire always gives way in Yeats's poetry to a rigorous refusal to give up on the world and while there are many poems in which Yeats bestows a curse upon the modern world and what he sees as its graceless and glum unheroic failings, he returns to that 'real' world, often with a vengeance:

> There, on blood-saturated ground, have stood
> Soldier, assassin, executioner,
> Whether from daily pittance, or in blind fear,
> Or out of abstract hatred, and shed blood.

175

In sequences such as 'The Tower', 'Meditations in Time of Civil War', 'Nineteen Hundred and Nineteen' — all published in *The Tower*, 1928 — and 'Blood and the Moon' (*The Winding Stair and other poems*, 1933) from which the above quotation is taken, Yeats set down powerfully forthright terms of reference for those poets who were publishing or beginning their writing careers at this time. This ensured that in his *Last Poems* (1936-9), Yeats spoke with an indisputable authority not only on the recent history of his country, a history which he and friends like Lady Gregory had in part shaped, but, more crucially, of the place which he had confirmed for poetry in Irish life, and *vice versa*. When Yeats summoned the literary and political figures (O'Leary, Standish O'Grady, Maud Gonne) associated with his past as 'All the Olympians: a thing never known again', the implicit judgment on the world he was soon to leave was quite clear. It did not measure up to *his* expectations and consequently, as he says in 'The Statues' (*Last Poems*):

> We Irish, born into that ancient sect
> But thrown upon this filthy modern tide
> And by its formless spawning fury wrecked,
> Climb to our proper dark, that we may trace
> The lineaments of a plummet-measured face.

Yeats's influence, both during his life and for some time after, was to elevate 'We Irish' into finding an appropriate place ('our proper dark') in the world which would, by example, reject the modern tide's 'formless spawning'. The impressive scope, idealistic ambition and imaginative demands of such a vision encouraged other poets such as F.R. Higgins (1896-1941) unwisely to emulate it with little artistic success. Higgins's poet-friend, Austin Clarke (1896-1974) also started by imitating Yeats's epic range, then slowly and steadily realised after a period of artistic silence, bracketed by *Night and Morning* (1938) and *Ancient Lights* (1955) that the poet must follow his own imaginative light and not bask in one as powerful as Yeats's.

Patrick Kavanagh (1904-67), even at some remove, was greatly influenced by the cultural ideals and literary dominance of Yeats's writing. In some of his earlier work one hears the strain of Irish pastoralism which Yeats had promoted, but Kavanagh grew to despise 'Irishness' and rejected out-of-hand what he saw as the suffocating provincialism of the Irish literary scene, still caught in the spider's web of Yeats's writing or looking over its collective shoulder for approval in London.

In poems like 'Shancoduff', Kavanagh asserted a literally more down-to-earth vision of Irish life, dismissing the exemplary haughty idealism of Yeats while adamantly retaining the subjective emphasis, naming of places and vernacular speech that was so distinctive in Yeats's poetry:

176

The sleety winds fondle the rushy beards of
    Shancoduff
While the cattle-drovers sheltering in the
    Featherna Bush
Look up and say: 'Who owns them hungry hills
That the water-hen and snipe must have forsaken?
A poet? Then by heavens he must be poor.'
I hear and is my heart not badly shaken?

Kavanagh displayed, in his poems as much as in life, the local, per-
sonalised ways of reading experience by focusing upon what he saw as
the actual conditions of living in the country:

At the cross-roads the crowd had thinned out:
Last words are uttered. There is no to-morrow;
No future but only time stretched for the
    mowing of the hay
Or putting an axle in the turf-barrow.

Patrick Maguire went home and made cocoa
And broke a chunk off the loaf of wheaten bread;
His mother called down to him to look again
And make sure that the hen-house was locked. His
    Sister grunted in bed.

The sound of a sow taking up a new position.
Pat opened his trousers wide over the ashes
And dreamt himself to lewd sleepiness.
The clock ticked on. Time passes.

While he came to consider that there was 'something
wrong ... some kinetic vulgarity'[2] with the poem from which this
quotation comes, *The Great Hunger* (1942), Kavanagh rarely lost
sight of, or belief in, his love of his rural origins. Often inspired by his
aggressive unease and unwillingness to be part of what he called 'the
synthetic Irish thing',[3] Kavanagh's poems after *The Great Hunger*
often celebrated the life he knew as a child ('A Christmas Childhood'),
its customs ('Spraying the Potatoes') or the eventual reconciliation
which he made with a hard life, trying to make ends meet as a poet in
spite of poverty, illness and bitterness:

O unworn world enrapture me, encapture me in
    a web
Of fabulous grass and eternal voices by a beech,
Feed the gaping need of my senses, give me ad lib
To pray unselfconsciously with overflowing speech

177

For this soul needs to be honoured with a new
   dress woven
From green and blue things and arguments that
   cannot be proven.

('Canal Bank Walk')

Taking their roots from the Modernist poets Ezra Pound and T.S. Eliot, the artistic discipline of James Joyce and drawing upon continental literary movements such as surrealism and on French poetry, the intellectual orientation of poets Denis Devlin (1908-59) and Brian Coffey (b. 1905) had little in common with the pre-eminence of Yeats or his immediate descendants like Clarke or Kavanagh. They sought, instead, to create a literature that was, in its sophistication and allusive concentration, free from overtly regional or national bearings. Introspection, an intense observing of 'the self' in relation to an other marks the poise and grace of these two poets, as in Devlin's 'Memoirs of a Turcoman Diplomat' or Brian Coffey's meditative 'Missouri Sequence' (1962). Devlin's *Collected Poems*, published five years after his death in 1959 at the age of fifty-one, was edited by his friend Brian Coffey. Coffey's own work is marvellously diverse and from his first publication, a joint collection with Denis Devlin published in 1930, to his most recent collection, the magnificent long poem, *Death of Hektor*, it defies any easy assimilation with 'the' tradition of Irish poetry and casts doubts upon the existence of such a mighty monolith.

Indeed it could be said that with the death of Yeats and throughout the immediate aftermath of the Second World War, Ireland was cut off from the necessary wider cosmopolitan audience upon which a poet like Coffey or Devlin depends. Ireland's policy of neutrality, however, confounded the English-based northern Irish poet, Louis MacNeice (1907-63) and drove a metaphorical wedge between the two parts of the country, re-inforcing the seemingly different and contrasting paths Northern Ireland and the Republic of Ireland were to follow. This strengthened the claims of poets such as John Hewitt (1907-87) in seeing Northern Ireland as a separate and distinctive region within the entire country, laying down the imaginative possibility in the 1940s and '50s for a renaissance of poetry in the province later on. When this actually did come about, in the 1960s and '70s in the North, the stimulus came not alone from MacNeice and Hewitt, but included the vigorous self-awareness and colloquial manner of Patrick Kavanagh, who was brought up along the border in Co. Monaghan, and John Montague's (b. 1929) re-imagining of Ulster in global terms.

Roughly during this same period of the 1950s and '60s, the poetry of Thomas Kinsella (b. 1928) was charting its own course, highly-mannered, austere and very conscious of the great changes which had taken place, *outside* Ireland, in the writing of poetry. If W.H. Auden and Pound sound through Kinsella's early work, it is in no sense merely derivative. In a poem such as 'Nightwalker' (1968), Kinsella successfully weds the modernist tone of analytical scrutiny with his own, and his country's, experience. His understanding, too, of the mythic dimensions of ordinary life are never forced ('Ancestor', *New Poems*, 1973), and Kinsella resists the traditional imagery of the Irish landscape by penetrating through its lyrical surfaces to the historico-mythological deposits underneath, as in 'A Country Walk' (*Downstream*, 1962). This is also the case with poets such as Pearse Hutchinson (b. 1927) and Brendan Kennelly (b. 1936), two 'southern' poets noted for their engagement with the tragic discrepancies between ideal and reality in Irish life and history. Desmond O'Grady (b. 1935), on the other hand, seeks to transcend these inbred problems through a poetry of physical celebration and an exuberant embrace of foreign landscapes and literatures.

At the heart of what Richard Murphy (b. 1927) writes there is a troubled confrontation between past and present but what marks Murphy out is the refined equipoise of his poetry, derived in part from his southern Anglo-Irish background and its inherited sense of being caught, time-locked, between two worlds — at once grandly imperial but also marooned and decaying. This abiding tension is finely contained by Murphy's formally distant, architectural designs, most noticeably in his latest collection, *The Price of Stone* (1985). It is also present in the earlier work, *Sailing to an Island* (1965) and in the historical mosaic of *The Battle of Aughrim* (1968).

It was on the redrawn battle-ground of Irish history that shifted northwards from the historical site of Aughrim, Co. Galway in the seventeenth century, to the housing estates and public highways of Belfast, Derry and a dozen other places in Northern Ireland that world-wide attention was focused during the late 1960s. With such media attention on 'The Troubles', and given the then current state of contemporary English poetry which seemed drained of vitality, poets in their early thirties from both Catholic and Protestant backgrounds, found themselves in a brief few years the centre of critical attention. Seamus Heaney (b. 1939), James Simmons (b. 1933), Michael Longley (b. 1939), Seamus Deane (b. 1940) and Derek Mahon (b. 1941) have had to define their art, no more than Yeats, in a time of great social disturbance, reacting against the pressures of their time as best they could. It has been a difficult task. Of the five poets mentioned above, Seamus Heaney, the best known internationally, and Seamus Deane, also one of the country's leading critics, have probed through their poetry the complex social and cultural roots of their Catholic-Irish background in the hostile environment of Northern Ireland. Emphasising the order and control which art can make of

179

such unreasonable states, Michael Longley and Derek Mahon have maintained an equivocal distance from their own backgrounds in Protestant Belfast. Their poetry, one feels, is tautened by a self-consciousness of how the dominant and domineering attitudes inherent in their domestic cultural roots eventually led to the 'Troubles' erupting in the late 1960s. James Simmons, often seen as the jester in the pack, has remained totally committed to a highly-charged, almost defiant belief in the supremacy of the individual's emotional and sexual experience. Yet running through his poetry there is a call for tolerance and for the rights of ordinary men and women to live their lives without religious or cultural hindrance.

Whether or not these poets, and others, constitute a 'school' or 'group' is debatable. The distinguished critic, and himself a Northerner, Terence Brown, examined the issue at some length in *Northern Voices* (1975) and in an interview with Derek Mahon, published in *Poetry Ireland Review* (No. 14 Autumn 1985, p. 13), asked the poet about poetry from the North. Mahon commented:

> ...the so-called Ulster poetry that ill-informed people in England are so excited about, I don't see it lasting much more than another generation and then probably it'll never happen again. It hadn't happened before, despite your own intriguing researches into Northern voices of the past, therefore it had to happen sometime and now it has happened: and I've a suspicion that it isn't going to happen again, that the next wave of Irish poetry will again be a Southern wave; this is only a hunch.

Imaginative initiative, in other words, is volatile and cannot be focused for any great length of time upon a given place or region. Southern poets such as Michael Hartnett (b. 1941), Eilean Ní Chuilleanain (b. 1942), Paul Durcan (b. 1944) and Eavan Boland (b. 1945) adjusted their individual vision to the radically altered conditions in the Ireland of the 1970s and 1980s, bearing in mind the deadly turn events had taken in the North during the same period.

The condition of poetry in Ireland then, in the past twenty years or so has reflected deepening shifts and cracks in the political and social life of the country as a whole. This has not been a passive mirroring process. One of the distinguishing features of contemporary Irish poetry has been the public perception of poetry as having a directly interpretative bearing upon recent events. This assumption is, in turn, the result of Yeats's cultural nationalism which has had a profound influence throughout the country both during and after the foundation of the state.

With poets from Northern Ireland, such as those mentioned but also including younger poets such as Paul Muldoon (b. 1951), Tom Paulin (b. 1949) and Medbh McGuckian (b. 1950) receiving massive exposure in the literary and public media in Ireland, Britain and further afield, an understandable reaction has emerged in recent years with the parallel generation in the Republic of Ireland such as Harry Clifton (b. 1952), Matthew Sweeney (b. 1952), Thomas McCarthy (b. 1954) and Dermot Bolger (b. 1956) asserting their own imaginative independence. Their poems depict the interior world of the country as it actually is, rather than how it has been traditionally interpreted in literary, cultural and political terms. In taking on such a difficult challenge, these and other young poets can call upon the rich and divergent poetic resources of a tradition that, despite the occasional lapses into complacent chauvinism, is rooted in the complicated ambition and unique achievement of its founding father, William Butler Yeats.

II
DRAMA

There is no equivalent in Gaelic culture to the European development of drama from the church to the secular stage. The drama cultivated by the Protestant Ascendancy, the Anglo-Irish, was detached from the population outside its enclaves. Theatres were built in Dublin, the most celebrated, the Smock Alley, in 1622; and eventually in the provincial, mainly garrison, towns. It was essentially a coloniser's theatre. English companies toured English plays.

Irish players became celebrated, notably Thomas Dogget (1660-1721), Peg Woffington (1714-60) and Charles Macklin (1697-1797). Their profession necessarily took them to England, where London was the magnet for Irish dramatists too — or rather, for playwrights of Irish birth. Although one may catch an accent from their native country in the work of Farquhar, Congreve, Goldsmith, Sheridan, Wilde and Shaw, it is rooted in the English dramatic tradition.

The beginnings of an indigenous Irish drama can be dated quite precisely. In 1897 W.B. Yeats and two landowners in the West of Ireland, Augusta Lady Gregory and Edward Martyn, conceived the idea of the Irish Literary Theatre. Shortly afterwards the novelist George Moore joined the trio. The venture allied itself with, in Douglas Hyde's phrase, 'the necessity for de-Anglicising Ireland', though it proposed a drama written in English. The long intercourse between Gaelic and English had produced a Hibernicised English. Recognisably a distinctive speech, it was an appropriate medium through which 'to build up', as the Theatre's prospectus put it, 'a Celtic and Irish school of dramatic literature'. The founders shared a contempt for English commercial theatre and, lacking any native precedent, took to a number of not always compatible approaches.

181

Yeats saw a dramatic potential in Lady Gregory's translations of Irish heroic legend and folk tales, versions of Irish life to supplant the 'stage Irishman' of the popular stage. He was ambitious to revive verse in a poetic, non-realist drama, 'the theatre of Shakespeare or rather perhaps of Sophocles'. Moore and Martyn advocated the example of Ibsen. While Yeats did not openly dissent, he considered Ibsen a passing fashion in realist theatre. His preference was the symbolist drama of Villiers de l'Isle Adam's *Axel* (1894). Such aesthetic disputes were of less concern to the theatre's prospective audience than the requirements of nationalist politics. These required of an Irish theatre, as a corrective to English disparagement, faithful, indeed idealised, portrayals of Irish life and character.

In the Irish Literary Theatre's three Dublin seasons (1899-1901), heroic verse drama was represented, for example, by Yeats's *The Countess Cathleen;* Ibsenite realism by Martyn's *The Heather Field*, a travesty of his model; and peasant comedy by Douglas Hyde's *The Twisting of the Rope*. The experiment sketched an outline of possibilities.

Resentful of Yeats's increasingly evident indifference to encouraging the continental realist style, Martyn withdrew. Moore tired of the enterprise and went back to London. The brothers Frank and Willy Fay replaced them. They had trained a company of amateur players and agreed with Yeats that speech should be the dominant presence on stage. In 1903 they joined Yeats and Lady Gregory to form the Irish National Theatre Society. This, as the Irish National Theatre Society Ltd, acquired a home in 1904 in Abbey Street: the Abbey Theatre. 1903 had seen the production of Yeats's *The Hour Glass* and *The King's Threshold*, Lady Gregory's first play *Twenty-Five* and, most significant for the Abbey's development, Padraic Colum's *Broken Soil* and J.M. Synge's *In the Shadow of the Glen*.

Colum and Synge herald a decisive move from Yeats's ideals for verse drama to plays written in prose and with a peasant or, increasingly, a small-town background. Both playwrights were, in their different ways, realist. Synge demanded authenticity of sets and properties and used the Abbey's conventional proscenium stage. But the dramatic rhetoric of his prose, though derived from the vernaculars of Wicklow and the western islands, was an elaborately stylised version of peasant speech. It has a poetic power which Yeats acknowledged, and endows its scenes with the force of legend and fable. So the story of Christy in *The Playboy of the Western World*, without losing any of its immediacy, becomes a parable of the artist/outcast's dangerous, emancipating invasion of communal stability.

Colum's prose is plainer. Yeats thought it incapable of accommodating any poetic vision. It is true that his plays are more fully identified with the circumstances of a particular time and place than are Synge's. Yet they have their own, more subdued poetic cadence.

Though Yeats tried to break down its constrictions, as he saw them, by incorporating into his plays such devices as masks, music and dance, most Irish dramatists accepted the nineteenth-century proscenium stage available to them. Colum's successors established its dominance in the realist manner. William Boyle (*The Building Fund*, 1905) and T.C. Murray (*Birthright*, 1910) wrote plays that turned upon contemporary social issues, the speech of their characters close to that of their models in real life. Lennox Robinson (*The Cross Roads*, 1909), who was accomplished in a variety of styles, was most at home in social comedy. A couple of interesting exceptions to this pattern were the fantasy plays, quirky, exuberant, nightmarish of George Fitzmaurice (*The Pie-Dish*, 1908) and the verse plays of Austin Clarke (*The Son of Learning*, 1927).

Within this run of realist drama, however, its best practitioners do question the solidity of the convention, the assumption that it is the business of theatre to reflect as closely and accurately as possible the particulars of daily life: rooms that are replicas of real rooms inhabited by characters conforming to the manners and behaviour of their background and period and placed in a situation comprehensible in those terms. The undermining of these intentions is particularly noticeable in the early plays of Sean O'Casey (*The Shadow of a Gunman*, 1923) and Denis Johnston (*The Old Lady Says 'No'*, 1929).

Many of Denis Johnston's plays, such as *The Moon in the Yellow River* (1931) are ostensibly realist. But he was attracted to the techniques of German expressionism and much of his work, like *The Old Lady*, is highly experimental in form. So too are O'Casey's later writings, although his first plays, the 'Dublin trilogy', are apparently quite traditional, using orthodox sets and dealing with contemporary political subjects. His tenements, however, in fact constitute a knockabout world of farce, of absurd unreliability, collapsing objects that mirror collapsing ideals and relationships.

In both these dramatists, as in Synge, language challenges the claims both of realist theatre and of reality itself. The purpose of language is not just to report, to reflect, reality. It creates a world of its own, a fiction with an equal claim to truth, which may displace or alter the world of facts. A feeling of the 'sovereignty of words' — Yeats's phrase — though not unique to Irish drama is characteristic of it. That the language used is English is itself a political consequence, the outcome of bargaining between imagination and circumstance. English is given an indigenous place by its gaelicised nature.

In Irish drama, the subjects on which it bears are often political too. O'Casey's are overtly so, as is much of Yeats, Johnston, and most

183

recently, Brian Friel. Samuel Beckett's bleak landscapes, though not specifically localised, open here and there on disinherited Irish hinterlands — 'Kov [Cobh?] beyond the gulf'. A language which is in a sense politicised turns to political matter.

The work of George Shiels (*Paul Twyning*, 1922) and Paul Vincent Carroll (*Shadow and Substance*, 1937) is, in a broad sense, political commentary on post-independence Ireland. The society that concerns them is an inheritance from Victorian notions of respectability, ubiquitous in the northern small business middle class, Shiels's subject, and in the south as a Catholic bourgeoisie consolidated itself. Carroll conducts rather an indecisive crusade against hypocritical pieties encouraged by clerical authority. Shiels achieves a strangely modernist effect by his quite disinterested portrayal of a society where cheating and self-seeking are the norms of behaviour.

The 1940s and 1950s saw few new dramatists of interest, M.J. Molloy (*The King of Friday's Men*, 1948) excepted. In 1954, however the tiny Pike Theatre established in Dublin by Alan Simpson and Carolyn Swift, presented Brendan Behan's *The Quare Fellow*, and in 1955 shared the English-language première of Beckett's *Waiting for Godot*. Although they caused no immediate upsurge, these productions were perhaps harbingers of revival.

It is tempting, but probably misguided, to suggest some common source for the dramatic revival of the mid 1960s and the assault at the end of the decade on the claims and assumptions of the northern state. Certainly, behind the domestic settings and individual lives created by contemporary Irish dramatists lies the instability of social and political inheritances no longer sure of themselves. Sam Thompson (*Over the Bridge*, 1960) and John Boyd (*The Assassin*, 1969) address directly political issues. Tom Murphy (*A Whistle in the Dark*, 1961), Eugene McCabe (*King of the Castle*, 1964), Brian Friel (*Philadelphia, Here I Come*, 1964), Thomas Kilroy (*The Death and Resurrection of Mr Roche*, 1968) anatomise private lives whose despairs bear an imprint of political and social futilities. An underlying and pervasive question, what is 'home'?, invites answers at once satisfying and disheartening.

The Field Day Theatre Company, founded by Brian Friel and others in Derry in 1980, has as its aim to foster the dramatic expression of such concerns. His own *Translations* (1980) takes as its central metaphor the anglicising of Irish place names in the survey of the 1830s. Among a diverse set of entrances into the same territory are Stewart Parker's *Northern Star* (1984), Murphy's *The Gigli Concert* (1983), Kilroy's *Double Cross* (1986) and Frank McGuinness's *Observe the Sons of Ulster Marching towards the Somme* (1985).

It is remarkable in the development of Irish drama how much it emerges from an indigenous experience and imagination. It has evolved manners of stage presentation which, within a broadly realist convention, move away from narrowly imitative portrayal.

The experimental drama of Europe was known in Ireland at the turn of the century. In Ireland it was suggestive not prescriptive. Synge rejected it. It interested Yeats, but he drew upon it, as he did upon the Japanese Noh plays, arbitrarily, to satisfy his own predilections. Denis Johnston, perhaps the most consciously receptive to the drama abroad, gave to his borrowings from German expressionism a distinctively Irish inflection. These are autocratic alliances within a self-sufficiency that persists to the present day, still informed by the sense of language as the agent of other realities than the sensible particulars of daily life.

III
FICTION

The twentieth-century Irish novel has become identified in the public mind with the achievement of James Joyce (1882-1941) who deformed and transformed the conventions and language of the established realistic novel in an effort to express the essence of his experience of life and history. *Dubliners* (1914), his first major publication, was based on the presumption of realism, on the assertion that 'he is a very bold man who dares to alter in the presentment, still more to deform, whatever he has seen and heard.'[4] It also excluded all narrative commentary, all explication, and anything which did not contribute to the recreation of reality. The stories rarely deal with dramatic events, do not have heroes or changes of fortune for better, for worse. The life they depict is made bearable by the strategies of moral blindness, muteness and inaction which enable the Dubliners to survive in an oppressive, limiting and poverty-stricken physical and intellectual environment. Excessive suffering can be avoided in this way. It is only when the repressed desires are explored and examined that the pain of existence flares, as when Gabriel Conroy, in *The Dead*, faces the limitations of his capacity for love. Conversely, in *Portrait of the Artist as a Young Man* (1916) the development of the consciousness of Stephen is from blindness to light, from silence to eloquence, from passivity to action, from home to exile. The process is expressed through the use of motif and stylistic modulation, in a setting which has shifted from the Dublin exterior, to the interior of Stephen's mind. This process might serve as a paradigm for the changing relationship of the Irish novel to Irish society in the twentieth century, as it moved from a descriptive relationship to an analytic one. The earlier need to reveal for the first time the manner of Irish living, in a spirit of unity and conformity with what was being described, gave way to the necessity to underline the duplicity and insufficiency of the Irish society that was developing.

This was not, of course, part of a programme of reform, but arose from the writer's perception of the gap that soon came to exist between the official ideology of the new Irish Ireland and the reality of living in it. Joyce, who left Ireland in 1904, made Dublin the setting for *Ulysses* (1922) and *Finnegans Wake* (1939), while transforming both the novel form and the English language. His depiction of contemporary Ireland and its history became an image of the twentieth-century modernist dilemma: to find forms of artistic expression adequate to a sense of separation and alienation rather than of community and conformity. Early readers of *Ulysses* were shocked at the identification between the middle-aged, ineffective advertising agent Bloom and the heroic, resourceful leader Ulysses. The anti-hero, however, soon became a stock-figure of twentieth-century fiction. HCE, the central character of *Finnegans Wake*, was able, by his very ordinariness, to incorporate in himself the achievements and failures of kings, patriots, and the common man. He is a hero because he is representative, not because he is exceptional. Joyce's technical virtuosity released the novel from its association with the conscious imitation of reality and enabled it to incorporate also the intuitions of the unconscious, of fantasy, of dream, of myth and of language.

Many of Joyce's preoccupations had also been those of George Moore (1852–1933), whose father's death when he was only eighteen gave him an estate in Mayo and first-hand experience of the difficulties of the Irish landlords. *A Drama in Muslin* (1886) reveals pitilessly the insecurity of the landlord's situation and the lack of purpose in the entire system, where men cowered in fear of assassination and financial ruin and women battled with each other for suitable marriages. Alice Barton, the central figure, perceives the injustice of 'each big house being surrounded by a hundred small ones, all working to keep it in sloth and luxury,' and escapes from Ireland through the discovery of her talent as a writer. She is also rewarded in the conventional novel way by a suitable marriage, for a woman making her way in the world by writing alone was not yet a possibility. None the less, Alice's departure anticipates Stephen Dedalus's, as George Moore's collection of short stories, *The Untilled Field* (1903) anticipates Joyce's *Dubliners* in their theme of suppression by Irish society of the individual need for freedom and self-expression. *The Lake* (1905) develops this theme through the growth in self-awareness of Father Oliver Gogarty, a Catholic priest in a rural parish, whose discovery of his hidden needs leads him also to choose exile as an alternative to the restrictions of his rôle and environment.

Realism, however, was a strategy which had its limitations in the context of Ireland in the early twentieth century. The definition of a new Ireland, which could achieve cultural and political independence, relied heavily on the creation of the myth of a glorious Gaelic past.

This was in marked contrast to rural and urban reality at the time. The dichotomy is exemplified in the duality of technique in the novels of James Stephens (1882-1950). *The Crock of Gold* (1912) creates a pastoral world of Celtic innocence, peopled by gods, philosophers, tinkers and leprechauns. *The Charwoman's Daughter* (1912) is set in the Dublin slums where Mary Makebelieve endures her drab surroundings by escape into dreaming and fantasy. Fantasy as a grotesque parody of human endeavours is also the dominating technique of the fiction of Flann O'Brien (Brian O'Nolan, 1911-66). In his most successful novel, *At Swim-Two-Birds* (1939), writing is no longer capable of revealing the patterns of experience, because it is itself conceived as an authoritarian imposition upon it. The nature of the novel is itself under discussion, with a choice of four beginnings, and the development of three interwoven narratives, in one of which the characters themselves discuss their existence as characters and their servile relationship to the despotic author. The modernist insistence on the novel as a fiction which is separate from life is here made explicit.

In some circumstances, however, fiction is necessary in order to verify the fact of life. In the novels of Samuel Beckett (b. 1906), especially his trilogy, *Molloy, Malone Dies, The Unnamable* (1947-9), life is reduced to a tale told about it. There is no conventional chronology, no narrative development, no existence except the voice which speaks and no termination except extinction. The only activity in life is to talk about it, the only release from talking is death, at which time the narrative will cease, whether it has taken shape or not. The fiction, like the characters, moves away from external reality into a confrontation with itself. With the development towards monologue, the form used in the trilogy, the reader lacks any comparative fictional points of reference. External reality is irrelevant to Beckett's fiction; the only reality is fiction itself.

Isolation is also explored by Francis Stuart (b. 1902) in *Black List/Section H* (1971). Stuart has written twenty-two novels, of which the latest are the most powerful. *Black List* remakes the facts of autobiography into a quest for the self, which can only succeed by achieving total isolation. The central character is displaced historically, socially and personally into successive states of suffering and humiliation, by means of which he is purified and redeemed. John Banville (b. 1945) has carried out a similar quest through quite a different novel technique. He has turned in his tetralogy, *Copernicus* (1976), *Kepler* (1981), *The Newton Letter* (1983) and *Mephisto* (1986) to the discrepancy between the sordidness of actual existence and the complexity of the universal systems and patterns discovered by the great physicists. Kepler made his discoveries about the movements of the planet while engaged in the pursuit of a theory which

187

proved to be false. Similarly in the other novels, an underlying truth is revealed by the search for an illusion, epitomised in the lost twin motif in *Mephisto*. The surface of the novels creates an impression of vibrant human activity, a recreation in realistic terms of a historical place and time. Beneath this surface lurks a tissue of literary, philosophical and scientific allusion which insists that these are fictions, not documentary re-creations. Underlying all of them is the question of the relationship of creativity to actuality, art to life, which Yeats initiated as a central question of modern writing.

In *Birchwood* (1973) and *The Newton Letter* (1983) John Banville used the setting of the Irish Big House for an exploration of misconception and misguided quests, for seeing significance where none any longer exists. At this stage in the twentieth century the Big House has become synonymous with decline and decay, the extinction of a way of life which was oppressive or civilised, depending on one's point of view. The Big House theme has been the most exclusively Irish topic to emerge in fiction, since *Castle Rackrent* was published in 1800. Edith Oenone Somerville (1858-1949) and Violet Martin (Ross, 1862-1915) were exploring the lifestyles and social interactions of the landlord families at the same time as George Moore and Joyce were writing. Though they did not attempt any experiments in technique, several of their novels, especially *The Real Charlotte* (1894) and *The Big House at Inver* (1925) used traditional methods of character and plot development to analyse the inevitable downfall of their own way of life. Elizabeth Bowen (1899-1973) in *The Last September* (1929) described the last stages of existence of such a Big House, culminating in its spectacular burning. A similar holocaust is described by John McGahern in his story, 'Old Fashioned', from *High Ground* (1985). The fires which consumed so many fine buildings in the 1920s, and the decay which overcame many others, were powerful metaphors for the shift in political power away from the Ascendancy class after the foundation of the Irish Free State in 1922. Even in ruin or decay the houses remained potent symbols of the past and the focus of a fictional reassessment of the legacy they represented, for example in *Langrishe Go Down* (1966) by Aidan Higgins (b. 1927), and several novels by Jennifer Johnston (b. 1930): *The Gates* (1973), *The Captains and the Kings* (1972), *How Many Miles to Babylon* (1974) and *The Old Jest* (1979).

Not all Irish writers have felt the need to expand the limits of the novel's conventions by experimentation. Many of the severest critics of Ireland's limitations since 1922 have used realistic fictional modes for their explorations of experience. Two writers from Cork, Sean O'Faolain (b. 1900) and Frank O'Connor (1903-66) participated in the idealistic endeavour to create a new republican Ireland in their twenties, only to be shocked and disillusioned by the censorship and narrowness that characterised the 1930s and '40s. They and many others found their work banned in Ireland and their primary readership denied to them. Sean O'Faolain founded *The Bell* magazine in 1940 and edited it until 1946, writing many articles against the provincialism and puritanism that was stifling any prospect of personal and creative freedom. In his novels and short stories O'Faolain explored the relationship between the value of tradition and the necessity of adaptation. The progress of Irish families from rural hardship to middle-class respectability in *A Nest of Simple Folk* (1934) and *Bird Alone* (1936) is won at the expense of submission to narrow notions of respectability. The republican hero of *Come Back to Erin* (1940) is out of place in a bourgeois Ireland which has no further use for his idealism. Frank O'Connor's short stories explore the value of tradition and its shortcomings. He was drawn to the sustaining power of community relationships, which his stories portray vividly, but was also conscious of the limitations which can be imposed on the individual. Liam O'Flaherty (1896-1984) returns to the landscape of the west for his most powerful novels, *Skerrett* (1932), *Famine* (1937) and *Land* (1946), which concentrate on the basic powers of endurance evoked by the necessities of subsistence living, and which are contrasted to the corrupting effects of the city in *The Informer* (1925). Peadar O'Donnell (1893-1986) who edited *The Bell* from 1946 to 1954, drew upon similar experiences of life in Donegal for his novels *Storm* (1925), *Islanders* (1928), and *Adrigoole* (1929). The harsh realities of traditional life in the west contrasted sharply with the official idealisation of their culture and language. Unfortunately economic improvement could not come without damaging this fragile lifestyle, and many of these novels and stories record a way of life which was on the point of disappearing.

The expectations of Irish women were also beginning to change as they too became conscious of the possibility of achieving individual fulfilment. Kate O'Brien (1897-1974) took up the theme of the rôles allocated to Irish women, which had not received much literary attention since *A Drama in Muslin* (1886). The desire of her heroines to break away is usually stimulated initially by the desire to follow some forbidden love, as in *The Anteroom* (1934) and *Mary Lavelle* (1936), but in the process they discover a wider prospect of possibility than that presented by marriage alone. In *The Land of Spices* (1941) the question of careers as a permissible option for girls is faced directly. A woman who became a nun might obtain a good education and wield power equivalent to a bishop's, while a girl who wished for a secular career had to defy the expectations of family and society. These novels anticipated the explorations of traditional Irish rôles and how to escape from them which became central fictional themes in the 1960s and '70s. Mary Lavin (b. 1912), in her short stories, has

189

continued the identification and probing of these moments of crisis and decision. Brian Moore (b. 1921) set his first four novels in the Belfast of his youth and explored the restrictions which its social structures placed on its people. His powerful first novel, *The Lonely Passion of Judith Hearne* (1955) explores the dilemma of a devout middle-aged Catholic spinster, who has conformed to the religious and social expectations of her society only to discover that neither religion nor friends will support her emotional needs. Elizabeth, the dying woman in *The Barracks* (1963) by John McGahern (b. 1934), makes a similar discovery of her own isolation. For both of them the realisation comes too late. In *The Dark* (1965) by John McGahern, and in the trilogy by Enda O'Brien (b. 1930), *The Country Girls*, *The Girl with the Green Eyes* and *Girls in their Married Bliss* (1960–4) young people are shown exploring their sexual and emotional needs in adolescence, as part of the process of separation from their families. The choices which face them involve the rejection of the rural-based lifestyles of their parents as the price for attaining individual freedom. John McGahern has gone on to explore the social and personal aspects of betrayal, a sense of loss as well as a sense of gain, a countryside deserted by young people and condemned to atrophy, farms being run by old people without successors, traditions and customs which will die out when they do.

The 1970s and '80s have seen the entry of many young writers on the scene. They include Neil Jordan, Des Hogan, Clare Boylan, Bernard McLaverty, to make a random selection. They are continuing the process of interrogation of the direction Ireland is taking, the search for fictional means to express a changing reality, which has characterised the development of Irish fiction in the twentieth century.

REFERENCES
1. Quoted in T. Parkinson, *W.B. Yeats: The Later Poems*, London 1964, 185.
2. Patrick Kavanagh, *Collected Poems*, London 1972, author's note xiv.
3. Patrick Kavanagh, *Collected Pruse*, London 1973, 227.
4. James Joyce, *Letters*, II, 134 (5.5 1906).

FURTHER READING
See the General Studies listed after Chapters 6 and 8. The following titles address specific areas of interest.

1. Poetry: Criticism
Seamus Deane, *A Short History of Irish Literature*, London 1986.
Douglas Dunn ed., *Two Decades of Irish Writing*, Manchester 1975.
Dillon Johnston, *Irish Poetry After Joyce*, Dublin/Notre Dame 1985.
Sean Lucy, *Irish Poets in English*, Cork 1972.

Poetry: Anthologies

Sebastian Barry ed., *Inherited Boundaries: Younger Poets from the Republic of Ireland*, Dublin 1986.
Gerald Dawe ed., *The Younger Irish Poets*, Belfast 1982.
Maurice Harmon ed., *Irish Poetry After Yeats: Seven Poets*, Dublin 1981.
John Montague ed., *The Faber Book of Irish Verse*, London 1978.
Frank Ormsby, *Poets from the North of Ireland*, Belfast 1979.

The two outstanding poetry magazines in Ireland are *Cyphers* (Dublin) and *The Honest Ulsterman* (Belfast) to which can be added recent publications *Krino* and *The Salmon* (both from Galway), *North* (Belfast) and literary reviews such as the *Irish University Review* (Dublin), *The Irish Review* (Cork) and *Graph* (Dublin) all of which contain material directly related to poetry in Ireland. The most important Irish-language poetry publications are *Innti* (Dublin) and *An Tonn Geal: The Bright Wave*, an anthology of Irish poetry in translation, edited by Dermot Bolger (Dublin 1986).

2. Drama

S.H. Bell, *The Theatre in Ulster: A Survey of the Dramatic Movement in Ulster from 1902 to the present day*, Dublin 1972.
U. Ellis-Fermor, *The Irish Dramatic Movement*, London, rev. edn 1954.
A. Gregory, *Our Irish Theatre*, 1914; enlarged edn Gerrards Cross 1973.
R. Hogan, *After the Irish Renaissance: A Critical History of Irish Drama Since 'The Plough and the Stars'*, Minneapolis 1967; London 1968.
R. Hogan ed., *Modern Irish Drama*, 4 vols, Dublin, 1975-9.
H. Hunt, *The Abbey, Ireland's National Theatre, 1904-1979*, Dublin 1979.
D.E.S. Maxwell, *Modern Irish Drama: 1891-1980*, Cambridge 1985.
K. Worth, *The Irish Drama of Europe from Yeats to Beckett*, New Jersey 1978.
W.B. Yeats, 'A People's Theatre,' in Bentley ed., *The Theory of the Modern Stage*, Harmondsworth 1968.

3. Fiction

D. Averill, *The Irish Short Story from George Moore to Frank O'Connor*, New York and London 1982.
D. Dunn ed., *Two Decades of Irish Writing*, Cheadle Hulme 1975.
J.W. Foster, *Fictions of the Irish Literary Revival: a changeling art*, Dublin 1987.
J.W. Foster, *Forces and Themes in Ulster Fiction*, Dublin 1974.
R.M. Kain, *Dublin in the Age of William Butler Yeats and James Joyce*, Oklahoma 1962; Newton Abbot 1972.
H. Kenner, *A Colder Eye: The Modern Irish Writers*, New York 1983.
A. Martin ed, *The Genius of Irish Prose*, Cork 1984.
P. Rafroidi and T. Brown eds, *The Irish Short Story*, Gerrards Cross 1979.
P. Rafroidi and M. Harmon eds, *The Irish Novel in Our Time*, Lille 1976.

12
A CHANGING SOCIETY: IRELAND SINCE THE 1960s

Tom Boylan, Chris Curtin, Michael Laver

IF post-independence Ireland can be characterised as insular and con-servative, preoccupied with stability rather than progress, then the 1960s may be said to have witnessed change and a certain libera-lisation in Irish society. This theme of change was most pronounced in the economic domain, when for the first time since independence substantial economic growth was recorded, particularly in the Republic. Significant changes in social values, attitudes and behaviour quickly followed in the wake of the new-found economic prosperity. Nevertheless many of the issues which currently preoccupy Irish society are reminiscent of the earlier period. In the Republic, the familiar themes of unemployment and emigration are again to the fore, while in Northern Ireland the sectarian conflict seems as intractable as ever. The changing Ireland might best be seen as an attempt to mix 'home made and imported issues in old bottles'. The resulting mixture is potentially explosive.

ECONOMIC GROWTH AND INTEGRATION: THE IRISH ECONOMIES POST 1958

The trauma of the 1950s, characterised by economic stagnation and high levels of emigration, was replaced in the 1960s by an equally dramatic change of direction in the fortunes of the southern Irish economy. Economic stagnation gave way to an impressive per-formance in industrial growth which transformed the material standard of living in Ireland. Demographic decline was stabilised and during the 1970s Ireland experienced a net migration of people back to the country. This represented the reversal of a trend that had characterised Irish demography since the mid nineteenth century. At this time also the marked dependence on the United Kingdom market was substantially lessened and the process of diversifying the markets for exports was initiated. In short, the sustained economic growth of the 1960s and early '70s conferred a new liberation on Irish society; releasing it from its oppressively low standards of living and forced emigration, and facilitating new initiatives in economic policy making. What was responsible for this radical change in Ireland's economic development?

As on previous occasions, it was the combination of a stringent critique of domestic policy in conjunction with major external developments which forced a fundamental re-orientation of economic policy. This questioning was in part a reaction to the abysmal performance of the economy during the 1950s but it was also the culmination of a critique of de Valera's experiment in economic nationalism that had started as early as the late 1940s and that had continued relentlessly through the 1950s. In 1947 for instance, Sean Lemass, the Minister for Industry and Commerce, and later the major political architect of the new economic strategy, drafted a bill which highlighted the consequences of prolonged indiscriminate protection as the major obstacles to future industrial development. Similar criticisms were contained in a number of reports, which were undertaken by external consultants on behalf of the Irish government during the early 1950s. For example the influential report of the Commission on Emigration of 1959, which examined in great detail the causes and consequences of the high levels of emigration, also stressed the need to re-evaluate the existing strategy on export development with its corollary of a more open economy. This line of argument also found favour with academic economists and public servants, as it did in the reports of a number of government appointed committees such as the Capital Investment Advisory Committee. By the end of the decade there was already in existence an extensive body of thought which provided a critique of the existing economic strategy. Thus when T.K. Whitaker's study *Economic Development* was published in 1958 it represented both the culmination of a protracted period of critical re-evaluation and also the beginning of the process of re-orientating Irish economic policy.

The principal component of the new strategy of economic development was the need to re-orientate domestic industry away from its focus on a stagnant domestic market and to exploit the opportunities of expanding foreign markets. This meant in effect the abandonment of protection and its replacement by a strategy of export-led growth based on a policy of trade liberalisation. It was envisaged that domestic industry, after almost thirty years of protection from international competition, would encounter considerable difficulties in making the transition from comprehensive protection to free trade conditions. Consequently the attraction of foreign companies became a critical part of the new strategy. These new foreign companies, it was argued, would act as major catalysts of change and development, and the industrial sector was clearly seen as the major 'engine of growth' within the new programme. Current investment policy was also critically examined. Not only did the volume of investment need to be increased, but its composition also came under scrutiny. In particular it was argued that the emphasis needed to be shifted from 'social' to more 'productive' type investments.

This emphasis on the need to abandon protection and adopt trade liberalisation reflected in turn external developments. Part of the larger adjustment in post-war Western Europe was the movement towards trade liberalisation. By the later 1950s this had taken the form of two large trading blocs; one represented by the European Economic Community (EEC) which was established as an economic customs union by the Treaty of Rome in 1957; the other a less ambitious entity but based on the same principles, namely, the European Free Trade Association (EFTA). By 1960 the environment which defined the context for the Republic's trading relations was firmly based on the principles of free trade organised around these large trading blocs. It was realised that in order to reap the benefits of producing for, and selling to, large foreign markets it would be necessary to participate in one of these trading areas. These considerations were to exert a profound influence on the thinking behind Irish economic policy throughout the 1960s and '70s and it reinforced the lessons which were already apparent from the failure of protection.

Just as the main components of the new strategy were articulated and refined during the 1950s, so too it was during this period that the principal institutional and legislative measure, which provided the foundation for future industrial expansion, were implemented. The Industrial Development Authority (IDA) came into operation in 1950 and Córas Trachtála (The Irish Export Board) in 1952 and as their names suggest they were given the task of attracting foreign investment, and stimulating Irish exports. Legislation such as the Underdeveloped Areas Act (1952) and the Industrial Grants Act (1956) introduced a wide range of grants and tax reliefs to industry, including the Exports Profits Tax Relief, the most significant of the measures for the promotion of industrial exports. In addition, the Industrial Development (Encouragement of External Investment) Act of 1958 reflected the reversal of policy towards foreign direct investment. The Industrial Grants Act of 1959 further extended the scope of grants available for new industries. As a result of these developments, most of the important measures which provided the basis for the industrial expansion of the 1960s were securely in place by the end of the 1950s.

The formal end to protection was clearly signalled when Ireland, following the United Kingdom, applied for membership of the EEC in 1961. Political differences between France and the United Kingdom delayed membership of the EEC for a further twelve years, but it was clearly just a matter of time before free trade became a reality. From this time on industrial policy in particular was increasingly concerned with preparing domestic industry for free trade conditions and encouraging new export-oriented industries. As part of this movement, two unilateral tariff reductions of 10 per cent were implemented in 1963 and 1964. In December 1965, as part of the preparation of the Irish economy for participation in the EEC, the Anglo-Irish Free Trade Area Agreement with the United Kingdom was signed which provided for the elimination of all protective duties between the two countries by 1975. This represented a return to the historically close links between the two economies. However, the motivation on this occasion was not to return to an over-arching dependence on the United Kingdom market, but rather to secure the best possible terms for both Irish agricultural and industrial products in what was still Ireland's single largest market. Moreover, the agreement with the United Kingdom would provide the Irish economy with a 'trial-run' at operating under free trade conditions. In the event, the Anglo-Irish Free Trade Area Agreement was overshadowed by developments in Europe, and both Ireland and the United Kingdom acceded to EEC membership in 1973. The agreed arrangements between Ireland and the EEC provided for a five-year transition period, at the end of which Ireland would enter into full free trade arrangements with the rest of the EEC member states. The period 1958-78 therefore represented the completion of Ireland's transition from protection to free trade.

As a result of this re-orientation, there were dramatic changes in the volume and composition of Ireland's trade. In 1960 the ratio of imports to Gross Domestic Product (GDP) stood at 35 per cent and the ratio of exports to GDP was 25 per cent, but by 1983 the latter had risen to 60 per cent. The comparable figures for the EEC as a whole recorded an increase from 19 to 28 in the case of the import/GDP ratio and an increase from 19 to 29 per cent in the case of the export/GDP ratio. Ireland's trade dependence, as a result of the change in its policy, was therefore among one of the highest of the EEC member-states between 1960 and 1983.

While the Republic's trade dependence or 'degree of openness' greatly increased over the 1960s and '70s the composition of trade also changed dramatically. The five-fold increase in the volume of trade over the last twenty-year period was largely the result of the expansion of manufactured exports. Starting from a very low base in the early 1950s, these amounted to a mere 18 per cent of total exports by 1961, but by 1983 they accounted for a massive 63 per cent. By contrast, the proportion of agricultural exports, in the form of live animals and food, dropped from a level of 61 per cent of total exports in 1961 to 25 per cent in 1983. It was during this period that the Republic finally shed its historic dependence on primary product exports; in 1983 almost two-thirds of its exports fell into the manufactured category. This dramatic increase in exports was largely achieved through the grant-aided foreign firms involved in the final assembly of manufactured products.

A third dimension to the changing economy concerned the trading pattern with the United Kingdom. While remaining Ireland's single largest customer, the share of Irish exports going to the United Kingdom fell from 75 per cent of total exports in 1960 to 37 per cent in 1983. This decreased dependence on the United Kingdom has been replaced by a greater concentration on EEC markets and on wider world markets. In 1960, for instance, the EEC countries, excluding the United Kingdom, accounted for a mere 6 per cent of Irish exports. By 1983 however, just over 32 per cent of the Republic's exports went to EEC countries. And it was a similar story for markets outside the EEC. In 1960 they accounted for 19 per cent of exports but by 1983 over 31 per cent of exports went to these markets. Viewed from an alternative perspective, the United Kingdom's share of Irish exports is a mere 5 per cent ahead of the share of other countries in the EEC, or 6 per cent ahead of countries outside the EEC. On the import side, however, the pattern of diversification has remained considerably more stable with the United Kingdom's share of Irish imports decreasing from 49 to 45 per cent between 1960 and 1983, the EEC's share increasing from 14 to 22 per cent, and the rest of the world's share decreasing from 37 to 33 per cent over the same period. In short, membership of the EEC has led in the Republic's case to considerable trade diversification and has consequently altered quite dramatically the nature of our trading relationships.

The main reasons for the diversification of the Republic's export markets can be quickly listed: the mixed ('stop-go') performance of the United Kingdom economy in the 1960s and '70s; the impact of the foreign companies attracted to Ireland which had already established both European and wider market outlets; the accession of Ireland to the EEC which provided new market outlets for agricultural produce in particular, albeit mainly in the form of sales to intervention; and the development of new markets in different parts of the world, particularly in the Middle East, and in less developed countries. While this diversification of trade can be welcomed from an economic viewpoint, in so far as it protects the country from the effects of a severe recession in any one particular market, it is none the less undeniable that the dependence of Irish economic growth on development in foreign markets is still massive. Diversification has clearly redistributed the form of dependence, and therefore to some extent the risk, but has not altered its extent.

A novel feature of Irish economic policy after 1958 was the introduction of a series of 'programmes' or 'plans' for economic expansion. These covered the period from 1958 to 1972 and represented the Republic's commitment to a form of economic planning. The First Programme for Economic Expansion, which was based on

T.K. Whitaker's document *Economic Development*, was introduced in 1958 and covered the years 1959 to 1963. The First Programme (it could not be called a plan; in fact the term 'plan' was studiously avoided) did not contain any numerical targets. The emphasis throughout was on the failure of past policies and the need for an overall co-ordinated approach to a new set of policies. During the period of the First Programme the growth in the volume of Gross National Product (GNP) amounted to over 4 per cent a year, which was considerably faster than anything that had been expected.

Encouraged by these results, the government launched a Second Programme for Economic Expansion to cover the years 1964–70. This was an altogether more elaborate exercise. It was modelled on the principles of French indicative planning and involved widespread consultations with the 'social partners', i.e. the trade unions and employer groups. The objective here was to reach agreement on the contribution that different sectors of the economy would have to make if the overall growth targets of the Second Programme were to be achieved. The growth targets were taken from the Organisation for Economic Co-operation and Development (OECD), which put forward the idea that standards of living in the member states should increase by 50 per cent over the decade 1960–70. This objective, when translated into the Second Programme's time horizon, implied a 4 per cent per annum rate of growth. This target was in fact attained and the 1960s witnessed a more sustained period of economic growth than in any previous phase of the Republic's history.

The contribution of economic planning to the sustained growth of the 1960s remains unclear. Even though the overall targets were achieved, it became clear, as the decade progressed that many of the detailed sectoral projections were inconsistent. Three areas in particular stand out. One was the extent to which imports outstripped the projected levels in the Second Programme, and this led to a balance of payments crisis in 1966. However the government, as a result of enlarged private capital inflows, avoided the over-reaction which had characterised the previous decade. The second area of disappointment from the planners' point of view was the poor contribution of agriculture to overall national growth. Instead of the Second Programme's projection of an annual average rate of growth of 4 per cent in agricultural output, the actual recorded rate was less than 1 per cent. However the most disappointing feature of the economic planning exercise as undertaken in the Republic lay in the failure to achieve employment targets. The Second Programme set a goal of 81,000 net new jobs between 1963 and 1970. As the plan progressed, it became evident that the numbers leaving agriculture were greater than anticipated and at the same time the growth of industrial and service sector employment was lower than required. In other words, increased productivity rather than increased employment was responsible for most of the growth in output. The net effect was a decline in employment of 18,000, which in turn contributed to a short-fall of almost 100,000 compared to the projection contained in the Second Programme.

A Third Programme for Economic and Social Development was introduced in 1969 to replace the Second Programme, which had been abandoned in 1967, and this new Programme was to cover the period up to 1972. It addressed itself to the problems of achieving full employment but it disappeared without trace, overwhelmed by the dynamics of Irish demography and by the fact that in the late 1960s Ireland became a net recipient of population from inward migration for the first time since the Famine.

After 1973 economic planning was declared inappropriate because of the increased uncertainty in the external environment, and Ireland attempted to adjust to the world of rising oil prices. Economic growth became highly erratic and was sustained for brief periods in the late 1970s only through massive government borrowing. This latter subsequently became a major problem and since 1981 economic growth has virtually stagnated. This in turn has generated extremely high levels of unemployment. In addition, long-term structural problems in the Republic's economy have emerged more clearly into focus. The failure to re-direct large sections of domestic industry into successful export-oriented industries has greatly constrained the contribution of the industrial economy to overall economic growth. Similarly, the weakness of an industrial strategy based on foreign investment has now, after twenty-five years, become much more visible. The classic problems of low linkage between foreign-firms and the domestic economy; the comparatively low value-added activities of these firms; the problems of transfer pricing and the repatriation of surplus profits; all these have now emerged as major problems in the Irish context and have become the focus of intense examination. Industrial policy is once again undergoing a re-orientation to find solutions to these problems. On the agricultural front, the dismantling of the Common Agricultural Policy (which had provided guaranteed prices for the principal agricultural goods), in conjunction with the implementation of production quotas on certain goods, will greatly limit the contribution that the agricultural economy can make to overall economic growth. The integration of the Irish economy into the wider world economy must be deemed a mixed blessing. While there have been undoubted benefits, the Republic's participation has also highlighted both the greater sensitivity of a small open economy to world economic fluctuations and the decreasing ability of the small nation state to pursue autonomous economic policies within larger trading blocs. These difficulties constitute the major challenges to the

Irish Republic's economy in the late 1980s.

In Northern Ireland the 1950s and early 1960s were on balance years of steady economic progress. Between 1950 and 1962 the level of industrial production increased by over 50 per cent, which represented a substantially better performance than the Republic, and even surpassed that of the rest of the United Kingdom. From 1960, Northern Ireland's main preoccupation became, as in the Republic, the provision of additional employment to meet the demand of an expanding labour force. The growth of manufacturing industry was seen as the major source of future growth and development. The expansion of the industrial sector was seen as necessary in order first to absorb the surplus labour which was migrating from the agricultural sector, and second to renew the industrial base of the economy as large segments of traditional industries such as shipbuilding and engineering went into decline.

The tradition of government intervention in Northern Ireland to promote industrial development can be traced to the 1930s, when the policy framework which provided for grants, interest-free loans and exemption from rates, was first established. These measures were, of course, a response to the Depression of the 1930s. By the 1960s, however, the development of this line of policy was very much in accord with United Kingdom regional policy. The pattern that emerged was one whereby Northern Ireland, as a region of the United Kingdom, continued to offer grants and other assistance for industrial development broadly in line with those available in other United Kingdom regions. However, in recognition of the exceptional characteristics of Northern Ireland, these grants were generally available on more generous terms than elsewhere in the United Kingdom. Continuity rather than radical change has been the principal characteristic of Northern Ireland since 1960.

As part of its strategy to revitalise the industrial base of its economy Northern Ireland sought to attract new foreign investment as part of the United Kingdom economy. It offered new foreign firms access to the European Free Trade Association (EFTA) from the late 1950s. Up to 1973 the bulk of the employment created was in firms whose country of origin was the United Kingdom, the United States and West Germany respectively. During the early 1960s, Northern Ireland was particularly successful in attracting large-sized enterprises from overseas (including Great Britain), particularly in the engineering and metal goods sectors. However, from the early 1970s, Northern Ireland has had to rely increasingly on the expansion of existing firms to provide additional industrial employment for there has been comparatively few new enterprises attracted to the province.

The reduction of unemployment was the main objective of successive Northern Ireland governments, and this aim was central to a number of major economic plans produced during the 1960s, particularly the Wilson Plan of 1965. The Wilson Report set a target of a total increase in employment of 65,000 over the period 1964-70, of which manufacturing was to provide 30,000. However, the results proved disappointing. Between 1964 and 1971 total employment rose by a mere 8,000 of which just 3,000 came from manufacturing employment.

Since the early 1970s the intensity of the civil unrest has caused increasing problems for the Northern Ireland economy. Investment in particular has been badly affected, with the result that growth prospects are extremely poor. Assuming that civil unrest continues, it has been estimated that GDP may at best grow at a mere 1 per cent per annum up to 1993. The implications for job prospects are extremely serious in that, by 1993, almost a quarter of the civilian labour force could be unemployed. In recent years most attention, from an economic point of view, has focused on the rôle of the United Kingdom subvention, or financial transfers, to Northern Ireland. In 1970 this subvention amounted to 3.5 per cent of Northern Ireland's GDP but by 1976 it had increased to 28 per cent, and by 1993 it is projected to amount to 36 per cent. This subvention can be viewed economically as the equivalent of an external payments deficit, which at those levels could not be sustained by the Northern Ireland economy. The future of the Northern Ireland economy is crucially linked with progress towards restoring political stability and peace within its boundaries.

CHANGING SOCIETIES

In the Republic, economic transformation was associated with very significant changes in both demographic and class structures. The historical pattern of depopulation was reversed and the population increased from 2,818,000 in 1961 to 3,537,200 in 1986. Annual average declines of 14,000 persons in the 1950s gave way to annual increases of close to 50,000 in the 1970s. While rural areas benefited from the population increase, the highest growth was experienced within urban centres. The greater Dublin area in particular continued to increase its share of the national population. It became one of the fastest growing regions in Europe and by 1981 one person in three in the Republic was living there. The level of population growth in other cities such as Galway was also remarkable. The demographic factors which account for this resurgent population were the rise in the rate of natural increase and the virtual cessation of emigration.

During the 1970s there was a net inflow of population to the Republic of approximately 100,000 composed mainly of emigrants who had left during the years of economic depression in the 1950s. It should be noted, however, that the annual rise in population between 1981 and 1986 was 19,000 which represents a considerable reduction in the annual increases of the 1970s. In these five years net inflow of population has been replaced by net emigration of the order of 75,000. Natural increase is again being offset by emigration, and if the level of outflow increases even further, the Republic will shortly begin to experience a decline in population. During the 1960s and 1970s patterns of low marriage rate and late age of marriage altered, bringing the Republic into line with the general European pattern. Marital fertility still remains high but has declined noticeably. One very important outcome of these changes has been an unbalanced population structure characterised by large numbers in all age groups under twenty-five but with the age groups forty to sixty relatively denuded by the former heavy emigration.

The rising tide of economic prosperity did not raise all boats; some sank; others floated in comfort; while still others were all but lifted out of the water. The basis for 'getting on' and the relative advantages of resources altered. The nature of the change has been described in terms of 'a continuous contraction of employment possibilities for semi- or unskilled manual work and declining viability for small farm enterprises, . . . the converse was growth in employment prospects for those with credentials required for white-collar and service occupations and still more rapid expansion of opportunities for those trained in skilled industrial work' [Rottman and O'Connell, 1982, 69]. Property remained important but none the less gave way to educational qualifications as the major mechanism for allocating economic and social rewards. Despite the opening up of new educational opportunities in the 1960s and 1970s most of the advantages that accrued from the possession of educational qualifications were monopolised by the middle and upper classes. While more people than ever before were participating in the educational system, the possibility of social mobility was more apparent than real. Movement from the ranks of the skilled working class into the lower middle class occupations was not uncommon but professional and upper managerial positions tended to be socially exclusive and self-perpetuating.

By the 1980s the Republic had a substantial industrial base and the working class comprised more than 40 per cent of the population. Unlike their British and Northern Irish counterparts, the majority worked not in native industries but in factories that were in effect branch plants of multinational firms. In many factories, there were a small number of craft or skilled jobs and a larger number of semi-skilled positions. Many of the new industries located outside the large urban centres and employed a rural and farming labour force. A strong, united trade union movement did not emerge; rather,

201

organised labour was characterised by a large number of smaller unions. In the late 1970s it was estimated that there were over eighty unions in the Republic and more than half had a membership of less than 1,500. By contrast the largest, the Irish Transport and General Workers Union, acted for one union member in every three. The proportion of workers in the Republic who are unionised is high, as is the level of militancy. Many strikes, however, have been directed against other unions rather than against employers especially where skilled workers have endeavoured to maintain differentials between themselves and unskilled workers. The stronger and better organised craft unions often use their leverage to demand (and usually gain) pay rises for themselves rather than boosting overall levels of pay. Clerical workers' unions are also preoccupied with affirming their differences from the working class and preserving salary advantages. In these circumstances, the efforts of the trade union umbrella organisation, the Irish Congress of Trade Unions (ICTU), at unification and amalgamation of smaller unions have proved fruitless. On the other side of the table, employers also have a diversity of organisations to represent their interest but a degree of unity does exist. The Federated Union of Employers (FUE) looks after employers' interests in wage negotiations and industrial relations, while the Confederation of Irish Industry (CII) concerns itself more with general policy questions and directions. Employers, unions and farmers' organisations have increasingly been incorporated into the state policy-making process and are in regular consultation with relevant government ministers.

The proportion of the Republic's labour force employed in agriculture has continued to decline but is still very high by British or Western European standards. While all farmers did well out of the price increases that flowed from EEC membership, differences between farmers in terms of productivity and income have continued to grow. The Irish Farmers Association (IFA) with a membership of over 150,000 is regarded by many as the country's most effective interest group. It was among the first such groups to realise the significance of EEC membership by opening an office in Brussels before the Republic's formal accession.

The number of smaller (under 30 acres) farmers has continued to decline but at a much slower rate than many expected. State social security schemes, and Small Farmers Assistance (the 'rural dole') in particular, together with the opportunities of off-farm employment presented by rural industrialisation have proved important in ensuring household continuity. Many visiting anthropologists to the West of Ireland in the 1960s and 1970s found communities that were in varying states of decay and demoralisation, but these studies provide only a partially accurate picture. The reality is that while many households have been unable to survive the changes, others have accumulated, invested and diversified their activities to exploit new market opportunities. Again some of the best examples of self-help activity can be found in the West, including the pioneering work of Glencolmcille in Co. Donegal and the more recent achievements of Letterfrack in Co. Galway and Killala in Co. Mayo. In these and other areas, community development organisations have sought not only to resist the negative implications of change but also to take advantage of whatever opportunities it presented.

Changes in demographic, occupational and class composition led, as might be expected, to changes in social attitudes, values, behaviour and expectations. Contact with the outside world increased through holiday travel, and return migrants brought their experiences abroad back to Ireland with them. Above all, television (Telefis Eireann began broadcasting in 1961) proved to be a potent medium for the trans-mission of new and sometimes disturbing ideas. For example, issues that had been swept under the carpet for decades were openly dis-cussed on the country's most famous and longest-running pro-gramme, the Late Late Show. All the ills of Irish society have from time to time been blamed on television and one politician is reported as having said that there was no sex in Ireland before its introduction. The truth of course was that television and society fed off each other and the liberalisation which television both reflected and encouraged can be seen elsewhere. Censorship laws were relaxed and more infor-mation was available and consumed. In the midst of all this, com-mentators who had lived through the stagnant and conservative 1950s could be forgiven for writing that the Ireland they knew was becoming defunct. From the vantage point of hindsight, it is clear that this view was both premature and simplistic. A process of 'moder-nisation' did take place but it was grafted on to a social system which retained strong 'traditional' features. The outcome was not so much another addition to the club of urban, industrial countries but a complex society combining elements of the old and the new. The resulting mixture was both potent and confusing as becomes clear when we examine the role of religion, the position of women and the contrasting fortunes of Irish language and music.

Urbanisation and industrialisation are invariably associated with secularisation, that is, the diminishing importance of religious prac-tices and institutions. The Irish Republic would, at first glance, appear to be an exception to this thesis for survey research indicates that close to 90 per cent of Catholics attend Mass once a week. First- and second-level education remains very much in clerical control and while the number of vocations and the priest/people ratio may have fallen, the results of the 1983 abortion and 1986 divorce referenda are clear indicators that the Catholic church has a firm base of support and a loyal band of followers in every part of the country and particularly in rural areas. What is also clear, however, is that significant numbers of Irish Catholics are prepared to pick and choose from the menu of Catholic social teaching. For example, the reduction in marital fertility reflects the increased access to and use of family planning methods not approved by the church. Moreover, the rise in the illegitimate fertility rate (currently about 10 per cent of the total births) and the increase in the number of women having abortions in England (currently at least 4,000 per annum) indicate that more and more people consider sexual relations a matter of individual choice rather than clerical dictate. Both church and people have adapted to the demands of the changing society.

So far as women were concerned, the change in their position and status was taken by many as showing the extent to which the old mould had been broken. Certainly there were changes as Irish women began to infiltrate areas that were previously male preserves. They were no longer prepared to wait outside the pub or at home while their husbands consumed their quota and Irishmen were to be found committing such unnatural acts as changing nappies. Indeed, some Irish marriages became more modern in terms of shared rôles and decision-making while women's issues and equality were publicly discussed and as clearly articulated as elsewhere, and women's groups pressed for more egalitarian social arrangements. But none of these changes should be exaggerated and Irishmen and women, by and large, continued to inhabit their own social worlds and to have quite different experiences in such areas as work, religion and politics. For example, the proportion of women going out to work has hardly increased in recent decades; in 1951, 30 per cent of women participated in the paid labour force but in 1983 their participation rate was less than 32 per cent. Again, women in the Republic are much less likely to return to work after having children than their American or British counterparts and occupational segregation by sex continues to result in women working disproportionately in such traditional female jobs as clerical, health, educational and service employment. Irish women are still overwhelmingly working in occupations characterised by low pay, low skill requirements and low prospects for advancement. The success of the few has tended to obscure the fact that only a small proportion of women are to be found in top decision-making levels in trade unions, political parties, employer and professional organisations, or the civil service. Perhaps less than in the recent past, gender divisions none the less continue today to permeate every social relationship and every sphere of human activity.

In the mid 1980s more people than at any time since the 1920s are technically qualified to speak Irish but very few actually do so. The number of 'native speakers' continues to decline and the death of the *Gaeltacht* is a familiar theme. Individual attitudes and state policies on the Irish language remain confused and ambivalent. Surveys have shown that a majority of the population deem the language important for cultural and ethnic integrity; equally, these same surveys reveal that there is a low level of personal commitment to its use. Restoring the Irish language and preserving and developing the national culture remain two of the official national aims but how these should be achieved and whether they are worth the effort are contentious issues. In 1965, the Language Freedom Movement was formed with the objective of removing the compulsory elements of the Irish revival policy and it met with trenchant opposition from the pro-language groups. The second largest political party, Fine Gael, had included a proposal in its 1961 election manifesto to abolish the compulsory aspects of Irish in schools and when it formed a government in the early 1970s it carried out its promise. The requirement of a pass grade in the Leaving Certificate Examination Irish paper for entry to the civil service was also discontinued. Although a special *Gaeltacht* radio service was introduced in 1972, Irish revivalists could fairly point to the failure to provide adequate programmes in Irish on national radio and television. The survival of the Irish language may not be immediately in question but it has been more and more reduced to a minority interest and the situation has not been improved by the almost total lack of direction in state policy. However, if the future of the Irish language seems to be problematic, the same cannot be said of Irish traditional music: despite the mania for pop music which swept the Irish Republic, the 1960s witnessed an upsurge of interest in this aspect of Irish culture in all parts of the country. Irish music became an integral part of a youth culture and a market for recordings of traditional music emerged both in Ireland and in Europe. Irish music festivals have continued to attract crowds in excess of 100,000 and the revival of interest in Irish music crosses both age and rural/urban divisions. Irish music is among the best examples of how the old became very much a part of the changing society.

The 1960s and early 1970s witnessed a veritable explosion in the level of state provision of social services. This extension was greatly facilitated by rapid economic growth and it was deemed necessary because of the changing demographic structure and because of growing expectations that Irish society should be characterised by minimum levels of income and good housing, and free or near free education and health care. Some of the developments in education have included the introduction of free secondary education, the provision of a modest number of grants for higher education and the construction of third-level technical colleges. In health a choice-of-doctor scheme was introduced while other social welfare legislation included the introduction of benefits for deserted wives and unmarried mothers allowances, the constant widening of social insurance schemes and the maintenance of the real value of welfare payments.

Impressive as all this state intervention was, it did not eliminate poverty or crime and these have remained pressing problems. The poverty line has been variously defined but it is generally agreed that one person in five is born into or falls into poverty. Poverty is to be found in rural and urban areas but crime is predominantly an urban phenomenon. Between 1961 and 1984 there was a 600 per cent increase in recorded crime in the Republic. The most noticeable increase was in crimes against property with the number of burglaries increasing by 1,100 per cent, robberies by 4,000 per cent and larcenies of motor vehicles by 5,000 per cent. By contrast, the increase in crimes against the person was of a much lesser order. As in other western societies, 'criminals' typically came from working-class areas, were usually unemployed and had low levels of education. They benefitted little from official channels of advancement and chose unofficial means to get their hands on the symbols of affluence, cars and luxury goods. For many, the 'crime wave' as it was quickly dubbed, represented an extension of northern 'lawlessness' to the south. But it seems clear that its roots are to be found in the glaring and growing inequalities of southern society.

The level of social change in Northern Ireland since the 1960s was, in some ways, much less than in the Republic and in others, even greater. Northern Ireland had by 1960 many of the features of an urban industrial society and was benefitting from being part of the British Welfare State. By contrast, at this point the Republic was at a low level of socio-economic development and consequently the changes there appear all the more dramatic. Significant change did take place in Northern Ireland and few western societies have experienced the level of turmoil and disruption that followed on the commencement of the 'troubles' in 1968. Religion, as we have seen, is an important facet of many aspects of life in the Republic, but its influences are perhaps even more pervasive in the North. That religion is such a sensitive issue is perhaps indicated by the fact that 19 per cent of households did not answer the question on it in the 1981 census. It is estimated, none the less, that Catholics constituted about 38 per cent of the population in the early 1980s. The Protestant majority is, of course, divided amongst a number of groups, with Presbyterians and Church of Ireland being the largest. Again, parts of Northern Ireland continue to have considerable Catholic majorities, mostly in areas close to the Border, but also in West Belfast and parts of North Antrim.

Religious differences are reflected in demographic patterns, housing, occupations, unemployment rates and education. The population of Northern Ireland increased from 1,425,000 in 1961 to 1,534,000 in 1981 but this conceals a decrease between 1971 and

1981 caused by a reduction in the rate of natural increase and a substantial increase in the level of emigration. This was the first decrease in population since the foundation of the state and reflected in particular the degree of sectarian conflict in the society. Thus there were particularly high levels of emigration in the early 1970s at the height of the 'troubles'. Higher levels of natural increase for Catholics have tended to be offset by higher levels of emigration and consequently a Catholic majority is unlikely even in the distant future. Much depends, however, on emerging emigration patterns. The North's population continues to be heavily concentrated in the greater Belfast area. Like Dublin, Belfast's inner city has declined, while its suburbs and surrounding districts have expanded. While in some parts of Northern Ireland, Protestants and Catholics live alongside each other, increasingly in urban areas they live in streets and housing estates that are single-denominational.

Since the 1960s the occupational structure of the two Irish states has become more alike. The fall in the numbers employed in agriculture has been more severe in Northern Ireland, but the proportion employed in industry has lessened and actually has been surpassed by the Republic. The North is characterised by slightly more social mobility, but Catholics are disproportionately represented in low skill and insecure jobs. Like the Republic, Northern Ireland has experienced high unemployment in the 1980s and here again, religious differences are evident. In 1981, 12 per cent of Protestants were unemployed, compared to 30 per cent of Catholics. Religious differences have been very much reflected in the educational system with Catholics attending their own schools and Protestants attending state schools. The differences in the education experiences of Catholics and Protestants used to be evident in the emphasis on the teaching of Irish history in Catholic as opposed to its relative neglect in Protestant schools but this has changed of late. However, it is still reflected in extra-curricular activities such as sport, with few Catholic schools playing rugby or cricket whilst games such as gaelic football or hurling are never played in state schools. It has long been argued by Catholics that the difference between them and Protestants particularly in employment were not caused by chance but instead could be attributed to active discrimination. In 1969 the impartial Cameron Commission produced considerable evidence on the level of bias in favour of Protestants in job appointments and housing allocations. By then, however, these issues were being contested by organised and aggressive social protest.

The most recent chapter in the history of communal violence in Northern Ireland dates from around 1962-64. The IRA 'Border Campaign', in which eighteen people were killed, was ended in 1962. In 1963, Captain Terence O'Neill, a moderate Unionist, took office as

Prime Minister and was expected, not least by more hard-line Loyalists, to introduce a programme of modest social reform. In 1964, Ian Paisley began the current phase of his political career by being involved in anti-Catholic street demonstrations in Belfast. The final catalyst for the resumption of the 'troubles', however, was the emergence of the Civil Rights movement which first marched and demonstrated in 1968, though intra-Unionist conflict between hard-line loyalists and supporters of O'Neill had been accompanied by a steady increase in street violence in Belfast after 1965.

Those who wished to oust O'Neill consistently raised the political and sectarian temperature in an attempt to make his superficially more conciliatory position untenable. The single event that did most to transform the Civil Rights campaign into a mass movement, however, was the bloody end to the now famous Belfast to Derry 'long march' by students and other civil rights campaigners, beginning on New Year's Day 1969. The march was ambushed on the morning of 4 January 1969 by 200 loyalists, many of them members of the Ulster Special Constabulary, the hated 'B Specials'. That night, amid disorder in Derry, there is little doubt that the police went on the rampage. Even the Cameron Commission, set up by O'Neill to investigate violence in Northern Ireland, found 'no ... excuse ... for this unfortunate and temporary breakdown in discipline'.

O'Neill's credibility among Catholics evaporated as a result of police repression of civil rights demonstrations, while his standing among members of his own party plummeted as a result of his failure to curb street violence. In response O'Neill called a sudden election in February 1969 in order to renew his mandate, but his position was undermined by the success of more hardline loyalist candidates. He resigned in April 1969 and handed over to his cousin, Major James Chichester-Clark.

August 1969, however, may be said to be the month in which the Northern Ireland problem went past the point of no return. Following on from the traditionally aggressive Protestant celebration of the Apprentice Boys of Derry (who had slammed the gates of Derry against the forces of King James II in 1689, thus committing the town's Protestants to the long siege which still remains such a potent symbol for all northern Protestants), severe rioting broke out first in Derry and then in many parts of the Province. The B Specials were mobilised, and firearms and CS gas were widely used by the police. Barricades were erected to protect Catholic ghettoes in Belfast and Derry, leading to the famous 'no-go areas' for security forces. Finally on 14 August, British troops were deployed. Armoured cars and soldiers with guns first appeared on the streets. Since the IRA was unprepared for the violence and had failed to protect Catholic ghettos against Protestant and RUC attacks (leading to the famous 'IRA — I

Ran Away graffiti), British soldiers were at first welcomed by Catholics in Derry and Belfast — newsreel pictures of them being given cups of tea and were the order of the day. At this stage a group within the IRA, disgusted with the lacklustre performance of the parent 'Official' IRA, broke away and set up the Provisional IRA. They found it easy to organise behind the barricades that had been erected to seal off the no-go areas. Indeed the British Army enhanced Provisional IRA credibility by negotiating with them on relatively amicable terms for the removal of these barricades. The first real shoot out of the British Army's time in Northern Ireland was not with the IRA at all. Rather it came in October 1969, when a Protestant crowd attacked and fired on British soldiers. These returned fire with sixty-eight shots, killing two Protestants and wounding several more.

With increasing sectarian violence between Protestant and Catholic mobs, policed by the British Army, it was inevitable that relations between the Army and the Catholic community would become soured. As the IRA grew in strength and confidence and as the relationship between the communities sank ever lower, the situation drifted from bad to worse. Finally bowing to Unionist pressure, the British government agreed to allow the reintroduction of internment without trial — possible under the Special Powers Act. The result was a disaster. The army raids on Catholic homes and the 'lifting' and internment of 300 to 400 people without trial provoked a wave of outraged violence. The death rate soared and matters spiralled out of control. In February 1972 the 'Bloody Sunday' killings by the British Army in Derry showed the futility of a military solution and in March 1972 the British suspended the Northern Ireland parliament and introduced direct rule from Westminster.

British direct rule has continued since. This has been punctuated by sporadic attempts to find a constitutional formula, acceptable to all sides, that would allow the restoration of some sort of devolved parliament. This has proved quite impossible since 'all sides' in the Northern Ireland context must be taken to include paramilitary organisations of both hues which find considerable tacit support in the local community. After the early days of the troubles, the British refusal to negotiate (at least officially) with the Provisional IRA has meant that it has been forced into the very difficult task of defeating it. It faces a skilled and tenacious guerilla army operating among the civilian population. 'Normal' military methods used in places like Burma, Aden or Palestine have not been available, given that Northern Ireland remains formally a part of the United Kingdom and is under an intense international spotlight.

Attempts have been made by the British to 'Ulsterise' the security problem by replacing the Army with RUC police patrols and 'criminalising' paramilitary organisations through the ending of internment; by trying suspects before juryless, single judge 'Diplock' courts (so called because of the judge who recommended their introduction); and by removing 'special category' (political) status from paramilitary prisoners. The latter change provoked the republican hunger strikes in the 'H' Blocks of the Maze Prison over 1980-81. These arose entirely as a result of decisions taken by the prisoners themselves, in the face of opposition from Sinn Féin and the IRA. The first hunger strike collapsed in confusion just before Christmas 1980 (it had been designed to climax at this time). The second began in March 1981 led by Bobby Sands — who was elected MP for Fermanagh-South Tyrone from his death bed in April and who died on 5 May 1981, sixty-six days after he went on strike. The British Prime Minister, Margaret Thatcher, determined that the British government would take a hard line over the hunger strikes, and a total of ten prisoners died by 20 August, to the accompaniment of serious civil unrest. The strike was formally ended on 3 October after several strikers' parents had asked for medical intervention on behalf of their children. While, in this narrow sense, Margaret Thatcher 'won', the net result of the hunger strike was a dramatic increase in support for Sinn Féin, who had quickly endorsed the strikes despite their early opposition. Following the hunger strike, Sinn Féin began to develop its strategy of fighting elections, at the same time as supporting the armed struggle with the objective, as its spokesman Danny Morrison put it, of 'taking power in Ireland with a ballot paper in one hand and an Armalite in the other'.

Institutional experiments included 'power-sharing' in a Northern Ireland Assembly which took office in January 1974 and which was brought down four months later after British failure to take decisive action against a strike organised by the loyalist Ulster Workers' Council. A subsequent Constitutional Convention became a talking shop for unionists after refusal by the Catholic SDLP to participate. The most recent institutional initiative, after quite a long period of relative inactivity by the British, was the Anglo-Irish Agreement between the Dublin and Westminster governments, formalised on 15 November 1985. This offered Dublin a consultative rôle in Northern Ireland affairs, via the Anglo-Irish Intergovernmental Conference, the first meeting of which took place on 6 December 1985 amid vehement protest from Ulster loyalists. Rejected as irrelevant by Sinn Féin and as a sell-out by loyalists, the Agreement commands the active support in the north of the largely Catholic SDLP and of the Alliance Party (supported mainly by moderate Protestants). In the south, the Agreement is seen as the creation of the then leader of Fine Gael, Garret FitzGerald, has the active support of Labour and the Progressive Democrats, while it is not actively opposed by Fianna Fáil. It is presented as a framework for a solution rather than as a solution itself, but the continued and very determined opposition to it of a large part of the loyalist population does not augur well for its success. Certainly, the history of Northern Ireland since its formation is characterised by the singular failure of institutions to accommodate the volatile sectarian divisions. Attempts to 'solve' the 'problem' in recent times have concentrated on institutional arrangements and admustments, each of which has collapsed in turn, but the underlying social forces that sustaint he conflict remain substantially unchanged.

POLITICAL PARTIES IN IRELAND

Northern Ireland's 'troubles' have of course had a fundamental impact on party politics in the Province. The most obvious manifestation of this has been the highly sectarian pattern of party support and the almost total electoral failure of parties which have set out to appeal for support on anything other than the traditional religious/sectarian/constitutional cleavage. While remaining within the confines of this sectarian division, the pattern of Northern Ireland party politics did, however, begin to change in the early 1960s. Before this, the Protestant vote had typically gone either to official or unofficial Unionist candidates, or to Labour. The great success of the Unionist Party has been its ability to manage class disputes between its supporters who ranged from the richest to among the poorest in Ulster society. While Unionist dominance was occasionally challenged by unofficial Unionist candidates appealing to working-class Belfast Protestants, there traditionally had been no sustained and focused opposition at all to the Unionist Party in its social heartland among the Protestant middle class. From the early 1960s, however, there was a trend among some Unionist candidates towards evangelical Protestantism culminating in the emergence in the mid-1960s of the Protestant Unionists led by Ian Paisley. This movement had an altogether more evangelical and populist appeal than had traditional Unionism.

As we have seen (above p. 208) the early 1960s witnessed the emergence of a more liberal and conciliatory Unionism associated with the then party leader Terence O'Neill. This policy of conciliation led to a famous meeting between O'Neill and Sean Lemass, Taoiseach of the Republic, in 1965, a development that drove many Unionists into a state of fury and resulted ultimately in the splitting of Unionism into an official Unionist party and a variety of 'unofficial' brands. Anti-O'Neill factions within the party left in 1970 to join Paisley's Protestant Unionists, shortly to become the Democratic Unionist Party (DUP). Another faction formed around William Craig and ultimately left to contest the 1973 Assembly Election as the Vanguard Unionist

Party. Members of this faction probably had the closest associations with the newly-formed Protestant paramilitary organisations, including the Ulster Defence Association (UDA).

By 1973, therefore, the old Unionist coalition was shattered. The more liberal middle-class elements had stayed with the 'official' Unionist party under O'Neill, though some subsequently left to form the non-sectarian Alliance Party. Many hard-line and working-class Unionists left to form the DUP or Vanguard though the former soon became by far the most important focus for this strand of Ulster politics. Vanguard has since withered away.

By the time of the signing of the Anglo-Irish Agreement in 1985, the situation on the Unionist side had clarified itself. Two main parties remained: Ian Paisley's DUP and the Official Unionists led by James Molyneaux. Both were strong, and each reflected a clear strand of Ulster Unionism. On the one hand was the DUP, a political party which was more working-class, more evangelical and more uncompromising in its hostility to Dublin and which was deeply suspicious of any attempt by the British government to reach a settlement that involved the southern government. We might see this as reflecting one enduring strand of Ulster politics, made up essentially of those who maintain an aggressive and defiant allegiance to the traditions of Ulster Protestantism. On the other side was the Official Unionist Party, no friend of Dublin to be sure, but more inclined to enter into debate with Southern politicians, to send representatives south, and to make policy proposals involving a recognition of the rôle of Catholics within Northern Ireland. Above all, this strand of Unionism represents those who look to Britain for the future. In their eyes, while individual British governments might betray them, the link is an end to be valued in itself, not just something to be maintained in order to protect the Protestant position.

The two parties are in constant competition with each other for electoral support. Each claims to represent the true voice of Ulster Protestantism, though it would never be expressed in public in quite such terms. Their combined opposition to the Anglo-Irish Agreement, however, has forced them to act together and forced more liberal Unionists to take a back seat, though the two parties still watch each other very carefully and each would be very quick to take advantage of any weakness exhibited by the other. By the time of the 1985 local elections, the DUP was winning 24 per cent of the total vote, compared to the 30 per cent of the Official Unionists.

The Catholic vote in Northern Ireland had traditionally been gathered by the Nationalist Party, post-1920 successor to the old Irish Parliamentary Party. It was more a loose confederation of candidates and activists than a fully-fledged political party. Pursuing a policy of abstention, the Nationalists had consistently refused to become the official opposition at Stormont, leaving that rôle to Labour. After the O'Neill-Lemass meeting mentioned above, however, they did adopt this rôle and began to organise themselves more along the lines of a modern political party. An official manifesto was first issued in 1964 and a party conference first held in 1965.

The Nationalist Party, however, was completely outflanked by other organisations that sprang out of the troubles in the late 1960s, especially the Northern Ireland Civil Rights Association (NICRA), People's Democracy (PD) and, ultimately, the Social Democratic and Labour Party (SDLP). Moreover, some supporters left to join the Alliance Party when this was formed. By the 1973 election, the Nationalist Party was in ruins, gaining one per cent of the vote.

Its place was effectively taken by the SDLP, formed in 1970 from various strands of dissident Catholic opinion, notably within sections of the Labour movement. It rapidly rose to prominence as the main political recipient of Catholic votes. (Despite the fact that the SDLP might claim, as do most Northern Ireland parties, to be non-sectarian, it gets very few Protestant votes.) In the 1973 Assembly election, which led to a power-sharing executive in Belfast under the terms of the Sunningdale Agreement, the SDLP was the only effective parliamentary voice of the minority. The continuing search for a power-sharing solution has in practice meant the finding of an effective political rôle for the SDLP.

Recently the position of the SDLP as the sole 'Catholic' party has come under serious challenge. Building on the widespread Catholic anger produced by British handling of the H-Block hunger strikes in 1980–81, Sinn Féin, as we have seen, adopted its famous 'ballot paper in one hand and Armalite in the other' strategy. The SDLP, in a controversial decision, did not oppose Sinn Féin hunger striker Bobby Sands when he contested and won a Westminster seat from his deathbed. Since then Sinn Féin has pressed the SDLP hard for the right to claim to speak for the Catholic minority and has achieved a very solid level of electoral support.

The end result is a situation on the Catholic side of the sectarian divide that closely mirrors that on the Protestant side. There are now two main parties contesting for the Catholic vote. On the one hand is Sinn Féin, offering hard-line policies for those prepared to accept (or ignore) the connection of the party with the IRA and ready to capitalise on any sign of weakness from their main rivals. On the other hand is the SDLP, a party recognised by the British and Irish governments as the official voice of northern Catholics. The SDLP, under its popular leader John Hume, is so far managing to stay ahead of Sinn Féin at the polls. By the time of the 1985 local elections, the SDLP were winning 18 per cent of the total vote to the 12 per cent of Sinn Féin. Thus the existence of Sinn Féin as a very credible electoral threat acts as a powerful constraint on SDLP policy. Anyone who might be seen as being 'soft' on the British would almost certainly be punished at the polls, but the most important effect of Sinn Féin electoral strategy has been to ensure that the SDLP takes a tougher line than it otherwise might.

The centre ground in Northern Ireland politics has, to all intents and purposes, disappeared since the early 1960s. The Northern Ireland Labour Party (NILP) suffered from the first-past-the-post electoral system reintroduced in Northern Ireland after the 1925 election. In the 1962 Stormont election, for example, the party gained 26 per cent of the votes but only 4 of the 52 seats. (In contrast the Official Unionists got 34 out of 52 seats for 49 per cent of the vote, and the Nationalists 9 seats for 15 per cent of the vote.) This election, however, reflected the all-time high point of NILP support.

The long-term basis of NILP support was essentially Protestant. The result was that when the Nationalists took over the rôle of opposition in 1965 (thus removing a significant Catholic element in NILP support) and when Unionists launched a sustained electoral attack on NILP strongholds the party's vote declined steeply. By 1969 the NILP had slipped to 8 per cent of the vote and, by 1973, to 3 per cent and effective oblivion.

NILP's limited rôle in the centre of Northern Ireland politics has been taken over by the Alliance Party, also formed in 1970, this time from sections of moderate Unionist opinion and from the non-party-political New Ulster Movement. The Alliance Party set out to be non-sectarian and did indeed succeed in attracting votes from both sides of the divide. It is seen by the British government, who greatly encouraged its early development, as the 'official' non-sectarian party, though it has never done particularly well at the polls. It first contested the District Council Elections on May 1973, getting nearly 14 per cent of the vote and convincingly replacing the NILP in the centre. In the June 1973 Assembly elections, however, its share declined to 9 per cent of the vote and stabilised at this point or there-abouts. Thus in the 1985 District Council Elections, the Alliance Party managed to gain 7 per cent of all votes cast. The party, in a sense, has inherited the mantle of moderate Unionism from Terence O'Neill. It is now largely Protestant in its support, but remains con-ciliatory in tone. It is difficult, however, to see a long-term rôle for the Alliance Party in a situation in which parties in the North are now viewed by governments on all sides as spokespeople for one or the other sectarian interests.

Overall, of course, the future of Northern Ireland will not be decided by party politics. Despite the fact that the Province has as many elections as anywhere else in the world, none of the Northern Ireland parties will ever have a major voice in a law-making body that

214

will be able to take binding decisions. Northern Ireland MPs are a tiny minority at Westminster; Northern Ireland MEPs are an even tinier minority in the European Parliament. District Councils in Northern Ireland have no effective power. Thus the European, Westminster and local elections that take place really fulfil the function of opinion polls. No matter at what level the election is, the northern parties do not even attempt to pretend that the main issue is anything other than the constitutional future of the Province. Thus both local elections and European elections now reflect a contest between the Official Unionists and the DUP on one side, and between the SDLP and Sinn Féin on the other.

Party politics, in short, allows those involved on all sides to measure the pulse of the northern electorate. This has the important and destructive consequence that northern politicians are rarely confronted by the discipline that comes from the need actually to put their policies into practice in the real world. Furthermore at least one party or another has typically boycotted any forum designed to bring them all together. These two unfortunate features of the Northern political scene combine to provide one of the major reasons why the problem of finding a rôle for electoral politics in any practical constitutional solution has proved so intractable.

For outsiders looking at the party system in the Republic, the most puzzling thing is the fact that the battle lines drawn up in the Civil War (1922–23) still seem to mark the fundamental division between the main parties, Fianna Fáil and Fine Gael. Admittedly, a new party, the Progressive Democrats, proclaimed the 'end of Civil War politics' in 1986, but, after the 1987 election, Fianna Fáil and Fine Gael were still by a long way the two largest parties. The absence of a large communist, socialist, or even social democratic party sets Irish politics apart from those on mainland Europe. The main parties have Gaelic names with warlike translations: 'The Soldiers of Destiny' for Fianna Fáil and 'The People of the Gael' for Fine Gael. There remain few apparent policy differences between them, all of which helps to cloak Irish party politics in some mystery (or, at the very least, mist) when observed from the point of view of the innocent bystander. Writing in 1973, one author described Ireland as having 'politics with no social bases' and this view has since appealed to many.

The Irish party system has, in fact, changed substantially since the late 1950s, when Fianna Fáil under Sean Lemass adopted the First Programme for Economic Expansion (see above, pp. 196–7). This ended the era of economic isolationism and stated a clear objective of economic expansion and modernisation, achieved through the attraction of foreign investment, which was to become a staple of the modern Irish scene. Shortly after this, Fine Gael also made significant changes to its policy profile, adopting the 'Just Society' programme in 1965. This put forward more liberal and reformist social policies than Fine Gael's previous positions and marked the beginning of a concerted attempt to appeal to the younger vote in a society with an increasingly youthful electorate.

Throughout the 1960s, Ireland was governed by Fianna Fáil administrations, a situation that was made almost inevitable by the refusal of the relatively small Labour Party to consider entering a coalition government. Having lost votes as a result of previous experiences in coalition, Labour opted for an extended period in opposition, leaving the way clear for Fianna Fáil minority governments on those occasions when the party failed to achieve an absolute majority of TDs in the Dáil. This policy was reversed by Labour in 1972, opening the way for the Fine Gael-Labour coalition government of 1973–7 and ending sixteen years of unbroken Fianna Fáil government. The fourteen-year phase of Irish party competition that followed consisted of a regular, and often rapid, alternation of Fine Gael-Labour coalitions and Fianna Fáil single-party governments. Power changed hands in 1973, 1977, 1981, February 1982, November 1982, and 1987.

Between 1973 and 1982 the effective choice of governments offered to the Irish electorate was Fianna Fáil on one hand and a Fine Gael-Labour coalition on the other. Looking at the policies of the parties, the notion of a Fine Gael-Labour coalition may seem something of a paradox. There can be little doubt that Fine Gael typically had the most right-wing economic policies of the three traditional parties, emphasising a lean public sector and general fiscal rectitude. This was balanced to an extent by a more liberal policy on social issues, such as contraception and divorce, which formed the basis of a 'constitutional crusade' launched by Fine Gael leader Garret FitzGerald during the early 1980s and which was intended to make the Republic a more attractive place for northern Unionists. The liberal social policies of the 'Just Society' programme enabled Fine Gael and Labour to find some point of contact (indeed official Fine Gael policy on social issues was probably ahead of many Labour voters and it was certainly more liberal than that of several Labour TDs). Nevertheless, Fine Gael and Labour were often quite far apart on matters of economic policy, something which provided a continuing source of friction within their coalition governments.

Fianna Fáil, in contrast, is a populist nationalist party, very much in the same tradition as the Gaullists in France (with whom they form a bloc in the European Parliament). The party attracts significantly more working-class votes than any other, and has retained a Keynesian belief in the ability of government spending to generate

216

economic growth. In relative terms a big-spender on the economy, Fianna Fáil's social policies reflect the conservative rural Catholicism of its electoral heartland. Fianna Fáil TDs have recently campaigned to introduce into the constitution an amendment prohibiting abortion, and have campaigned against liberalisation of the laws on contraception and against the introduction of divorce. Notwithstanding this, there is a greater affinity, on matters of economic policy at least, between Labour and Fianna Fáil than there is between Labour and Fine Gael. There has, however, been no prospect of an alternative coalition, quite simply because Fianna Fáil has always seen itself as a single party of government and has refused to share power with anyone, even when faced with the prospect of minority government in a 'hung' Dáil.

However unsuitable as partners, therefore, Fine Gael and Labour were forced to the altar with one another for most of the 1970s and '80s if they were ever to keep Fianna Fáil out of office. During the period of coalition with Fine Gael, however, the Labour vote declined significantly. The loss of electoral support became so serious that, in 1985, the party set up a 'Commission on Electoral Strategy' to evaluate the options open to it. Predictably, the conclusion of this commission was that Labour should enter no further coalitions until it could do so from a position of strength. As an inevitable consequence of this decision, Labour withdrew from government in January 1987, forcing an election the following month. The former coalition parties attacked each other's policies during the subsequent campaign, have now distanced themselves from one another, and will not be going into government together for a long time.

Fianna Fáil has been able to pursue its go-it-alone policy while at the same time having its fair share of internal wrangles. In common with Fine Gael, the Fianna Fáil party is run on tightly authoritarian lines. A ruthless leader is able, in both parties, to maintain rigid discipline by summary expulsion of dissidents. This in turn has enabled Irish governments to function comfortably with what, in European terms, would be wafer-thin parliamentary majorities and even to form reasonably secure minority governments when faced with a divided opposition. None has wielded the authority of party leader more effectively than Charles Haughey in the early 1980s. The Fianna Fáil leader even survived one challenge to his position that was so close to success that one morning paper had already published his political obituary. This tough leadership stance did, however, provoke a major split from Fianna Fáil when Desmond O'Malley, who had twice challenged Haughey for the leadership and twice lost, was finally forced out and formed the rival Progressive Democrats (PDs) in 1986.

The formation of the PDs may have been a direct result of a split within Fianna Fáil, but the impact on the Irish party system has been rather more fundamental than this might suggest. From the earliest opinion polls it was clear that the new party would almost certainly damage Fine Gael more than Fianna Fáil. This was reflected in party policies, which echoed Fine Gael's monetarist goals of fiscal rectitude, and in the social patterns of party support, which high-lighted the PD's middle-class appeal.

So it turned out when, in the election of 14 February 1987, the main impact of the PD challenge was the collapse of the Fine Gael vote. While Labour's vote dropped, it held most of its seats. The PDs won 14 seats out of 166 with about 12 per cent of the vote in their first electoral outing. Almost all of this was at the expense of Fine Gael, who slumped badly from their position in the early 1980s when they had challenged Fianna Fáil for the position of largest party. But in 1987 they won a mere 51 seats to Fianna Fáil's 81. Ironically, while Labour feared the effects of coalition most, Fine Gael's participation in government left an opening for the PDs which was, in the short run at least, far more damaging.

In the aftermath of the 1987 election, it is clear that the era of Fine Gael-Labour coalition is over. Fianna Fáil have once more formed a minority government, which can be sustained in office by Fine Gael or the PDs, Labour or the Workers' Party if they choose to do so. This government faces opposition from the right (the PDs and Fine Gael) and the left (Labour and the Workers' Party). It is a situation that promises, if not exactly the breaking of the mould of Civil War politics in Ireland, at least the taking of a major step towards the more conventional left-right divisions in politics to be found in the rest of Europe.

Finally, in addition to the major changes which have affected the lives of all the citizens within the two states of Ireland since the early 1960s, these decades have also seen important changes in the inter-national setting within which the independent Irish state has sought to make its voice heard and its influence felt. (In the case of Northern Ireland as an integral part of the United Kingdom the question of a foreign policy does not arise.) Ever since the establishment of the Free State in 1922 a crucial aspect of the independent Irish state's claims to sovereignty was that it should be able to pursue — and be seen to be pursuing — an independent policy in international affairs. This it sought to do in every international forum to which it had access, including the International Labour Organisation and, most impor-tantly, at the League of Nations during the inter-war years.

The announcement and maintenance of a position of neutrality during World War II was a striking assertion and affirmation of the independent stance of the Irish state in international relations. Neut-rality, however, was not to be taken as a desire for isolationism; and in the period after 1945 the Irish state was active in seeking membership of a number of international bodies. These did not include NATO; in addition to the more general desire to avoid entanglement in military alliances, the obligation to accept existing United Kingdom boundaries (including Northern Ireland) effectively precluded the Irish state from involvement with NATO. No such factors existed to inhibit Ireland's applying for membership of the United Nations. However, the entry of Ireland to the United Nations was blocked until 1955 by a Soviet Union concerned that Ireland would be, in effect, a client state of the USA in the international organisation. As it transpired, the early years of Ireland's membership of the United Nations were notable for the substantially independent — or non-aligned — position taken by Ireland in respect of major international issues (e.g. Suez, Hungary 1956, the issue of Chinese representation in the United Nations).

This independent rôle was confirmed by Ireland's being invited, and being willing, to contribute soldiers to various United Nations peace-keeping forces in different trouble-spots throughout the world since the 1950s. This peace-keeping rôle has been maintained since the 1960s. However, during the 1960s — as foreign investment in Irish economic development increased significantly — Ireland's position in international relations came to be perceived as less independent, and more predictably 'western' in its orientation. The difficulty of maintaining a recognisably independent Irish voice in international affairs has increased since Ireland's entry to the EEC in 1973. As the European Community moves — however slowly or unevenly — towards common policies on foreign affairs and defence (particularly in the aftermath of the passing of the Single European Act in 1987), it has become increasingly difficult for successive Irish governments to reconcile this 'integrationist' European trend with the more traditional Irish policy of an independent and distinctive Irish voice in international relations.

REFERENCES
D. Rottmann and P. O'Connell, 'The Changing Social Structure', *Unequal Achievement*, ed. Litton, Dublin 1982.

FURTHER READING
Paul Arthur, *Government and Politics of Northern Ireland*, second edition, London 1984.
B. Chubb, *The Government and Politics of Ireland*, London 1983.
P. Clancy et al eds, *Ireland: A Sociological Profile*, Dublin 1986.
C. Curtin et al eds, *Culture and Ideology in Ireland*, Galway 1984.
C. Curtin et al eds, *Gender in Irish Society*, Galway 1987.
M. Gallagher, *Political Parties in The Republic of Ireland*, Dublin 1985.
N.J. Gibson, and J.E. Spencer eds, *Economic Activity in Ireland: a Study of Two Open Economies*, Dublin 1977.

J.N. O'Hagan ed., *The Economy of Ireland: Policy and Performance*, Dublin 1984.

M. Kelly et al eds, *Power, Conflict and Inequality*, Dublin 1982.

K.A. Kennedy and R. Bruton, *The Irish Economy*, Brussels 1975.

K.A. Kennedy ed., *Ireland in Transition: Economic and Social Change since 1960*, Cork 1986.

F. Litton ed., *Unequal Achievement*, Dublin 1982.

E. Moloney and A. Pollak, *Paisley*, Swords 1987.

M. Peillon, *Contemporary Irish Society: an introduction*, Dublin 1982.

B. Rolston et al eds, *A Social Science Bibliography of Northern Ireland*, Belfast 1983.

R. Rose, *Governing Without Consensus*, London 1971.

13
FROM MEGALITH TO MEGASTORE: BROADCASTING AND IRISH CULTURE

Luke Gibbons

THE development of the media in Ireland has been constrained from the outset by the competing forces of the *nation* and the *state*, the pleasure principle and the reality principle in Irish politics. Since the opening of 2RN, the first radio service, in 1926, the statutory legislation governing broadcasting has stressed the importance of maintaining and consolidating national identity, but the day-to-day policies of successive governments have worked almost as consistently to undermine these ideals. The media are often portrayed as modernising agencies, releasing society from the weight of tradition. Yet while television in Ireland did much to alter what are considered traditional values and other aspects of 'national life', there was nothing inevitable about this. One has only to look at the rôle of the media in perpetuating the cult of the monarchy in Britain to see that popular cultural forms, even television, have no difficulty in propping up, still less inventing, even the most venerable 'national traditions'.

It is tempting to suggest that the media only reinforce those 'traditions' which emanate from the heartlands of the culture industry, particularly those within the Anglo-American power bloc. But this does not happen as a matter of course. If we attend to the specific example of the monarchy, it is clear that its integrative function in British society is closely bound up with the public service ideal of broadcasting as it evolved under Lord Reith, the first director-general of the BBC. The 'high culture' aspirations of public service broadcasting made no secret of the fact that they were in the business of *establishing* a national consensus and projecting a symbolic image of 'the nation'. There was no illusion that the cultural brief of British broadcasting was to give the people back their own self-image: indeed with its emphasis on 'excellence' and 'high-seriousness', it was designed to combat the veryday culture of the masses and expose them to the 'higher self' of the nation. In the United States, faced with the problem of unifying a vast population of immigrants and different ethnic groups, there was even less pretence about *constructing* the nation. As Alistair Cooke has put it, 'America didn't inherit a nation: it invented one and boasted it would be better than everything that had gone before'.

Nothing could be further from the situation in Ireland. From the beginning, policy formation in Irish broadcasting has operated under the assumption that the *nation* was already in place: only the *state* awaited completion as part of the unfinished business of re-uniting the country. The state derived its legitimacy from the existence of an antecedent nation, and thus the function of broadcasting was not to establish but to revitalise this nation, releasing the cultural energies which, it was believed, had accumulated over centuries. It was the state, in fact, which needed building, given the fragility of the political settlement after the Civil War. To this end, broadcasting was brought under the direct control of the central administration, functioning as an extension of the civil service until 1953. Under direct state control, there was general agreement that the new radio service could hardly fail to preserve a distinguished national heritage, bringing it to wider audiences than ever before. As Dr Douglas Hyde stated in his speech at the opening of the station, underlining the difference between the cultural pedigree of the nation, and the artificial, political character of the state:

> A nation cannot be made by Act of Parliament; no, not even by a Treaty. A nation is made from inside itself; it is made first of all by its language, if it has one; by its music, songs, games, and customs. . . . So, while not forgetting what is best in what other countries have to offer us, we desire to especially emphasise what we have derived from our Gaelic ancestors — from one of the oldest civilisations in Europe, the heritage of the O's and Mac's who still make up the bulk of our country.

Initially this faith in the medium did not appear to be misplaced. The appointment of Seamus Clandillon, an ardent revivalist and music enthusiast, as director of the new station ensured that the Irish language and wider cultural concerns received comprehensive coverage. As a well-known traditional musician, Clandillon himself had no reservations about doubling up as a performer in his own station. In the area of Gaelic games, the station made broadcasting history by carrying the first live transmission of a sporting event in Europe when it covered the All-Ireland hurling semi-final in 1926. From the 1930s the voice of the sports commentator, Michael Ó Hehir, became synonymous with Gaelic games and so close was the affinity between the new service and official culture that a Dáil deputy in the early 1940s could welcome the appointment of a new director, Seamus Brennan, in the following convivial terms:

222

I should like to make a few suggestions to the Minister in this connection. I congratulate him on the appointment of Mr Brennan as director of Radio Eireann. Mr Brennan is a good friend of mine and was one of the best Gaelic footballers and stepdancers in the country.

All this is consistent with the earliest stages in the development of a new medium. As Bertolt Brecht has pointed out, radio did not come into the world with its own readymade subject matter but had to look to pre-existing cultural forms for its 'raw material':

> [Radio] looked around to discover where something was being said to someone and attempted to muscle in . . . . That was radio in its first phase as a substitute. As a substitute for the theatre, for the opera, for concerts, for lectures, for café-music, for the local columns of the press and so on.

Radio, in other words, had to adjust itself to the prevailing cultural dynamic, and in Ireland this was closely identified with nationalism. It would be mistaken, however, to conclude that in drawing on Irish culture in this way, radio was merely popularising a long-established native heritage. The idea that the media could act as an electronic museum, bringing the wisdom of ancient traditions to mass audiences, may have proved attractive to cultural revivalists such as Douglas Hyde but it seriously overlooked the fact that the media are themselves cultural *agencies*, actively shaping and reconstituting the material which passes through them.

The extent to which the media do not simply *transmit* but actively *transform* their content was a major preoccupation of the German critic, Walter Benjamin. In his influential essay 'The Work of Art in the Age of Mechanical Reproduction', published in 1936. Benjamin argued that the first casualty of the new media technology was precisely *tradition*, the shared experience of a continuous past. The endless proliferation of copies facilitated by mass production dispels any trace of 'authenticity', the 'aura' of the original, which is central to the concept of tradition. To compensate for this 'liquidation' of tradition, the media offers a new form of public identity, the sense of belonging which comes from being a member of a mass audience experiencing a national (or even an international) media event. In the case of media coverage of Gaelic games in the 1930s, for example, what is often interpreted as the 'handing down' of a sporting tradition to a new generation was in fact a fundamental restructuring of the whole basis of Gaelic games. So far from passively relaying the activities of a thriving sporting body to an already captive audience, both radio and the press contributed substantially to creating a *nationwide* audience for Gaelic games, thus establishing the Gaelic

223

Athletic Association as a truly *national* organisation. Radio broadcasts were augmented by the blanket coverage of Gaelic games in *The Irish Press*, the first daily newspaper adequately to represent nationalist public opinion. Within a year of its founding in 1931, no less than six correspondents were assigned to Gaelic games, and the *Irish Independent* had to increase its coverage tenfold to keep up with its rival. The GAA capitalised on its new national profile through the efforts of its dynamic General Secretary, Padraig Ó Caoimh (appointed in 1931) and by the end of the 1930s it had secured its reputation as Ireland's leading cultural organisation.

A similar situation obtained in the case of Irish music. While Radio Eireann's far-seeing archival policy saved whole repertoires of traditional music from extinction, it is again mistaken to construe this as preserving the native heritage in an unmodified form. The cultivation of a nationwide audience for traditional music did much to 'flatten out' variations in regional styles, and there is even a sense in which broadcasting may have 'invented' a key element in the traditional canon. According to some authorities, the ceili band, which was regarded as the distinctive sound of Irish music in the 1950s, was not an 'organic' development but was actually devised by Seamus Clandillon in the year of his appointment as director of the new radio service. Whatever about the origins, there is little doubt that this 'collective' approach to Irish music owed its popular currency to the 'alien' institutions of the electronic media and the dance-hall. It would seem, then, that the changes visited upon traditional culture by the media were not acknowledged as such but were considered to have maintained and even reinforced cultural continuity. Transformations and innovations, even of a substantial kind, are silently assimilated and accepted as indigenous once they make a positive contribution to an established tradition. It was easy for cultural revivalists to portray the media as exponents of some type of Socratic method, releasing the untapped cultural resources of the hidden Ireland. The rôle of the state was merely to provide a supportive environment for this form of national renewal.

STATE VERSUS NATION IN IRISH BROADCASTING

The first rift between broadcasting and its designated cultural rôle occurred in 1932–3 when the new Fianna Fáil government indicated that its main political priority was to strengthen the state, if need be at the expense of the more intangible nation. One of the anomalies in the financial structure of the new station — and one of the features which distinguished it from the BBC — was that even though it was under direct state control, the stage eschewed any financial liability for the service, insisting that it be self-supporting. Thus it was expected to live up to the ideals of public service broadcasting in an Irish context while maintaining its commercial viability at the same time. It was accepted in Britain that since the Reithian conception of public service broadcasting drew its bearings from high culture, this would not be commercially viable and hence would have to be funded like other uplifting areas of life from the public exchequer. In Ireland, however, the equation of public service broadcasting with cultural nationalism gave rise to the illusion that the media were simply giving the nation back its own birthright, promoting cultural values the population at large could readily identify with. If native culture was truly organic and 'of the people' there was no reason why it should not be commercially viable. The nation could look after itself: it was the state which was in urgent need of additional revenue and popular support.

In its initial phase, 2RN (as the station was called until the name Radio Eireann gained currency in 1937) derived its revenue from three sources: import duties on radios; licence fees; and advertising. Of these, import duties contributed by far the greatest portion to the station's finances. The number of radio licences increased from 2,805 in 1925 to 33,083 in 1933, and the import duties on these new radios accounted for almost two-thirds of total revenue, thereby acting as an efficient buffer between the station's public service remit and the commercial vagaries of the market. The prospects of a lucrative windfall, however, proved too attractive to the Department of Finance, and in 1933 the Minister, Sean MacEntee, directed that in future the revenue from import duties would accrue to the central exchequer. 'By this decision', Maurice Gorham writes, 'the government had at a stroke deprived the broadcasting service of one of its chief sources of income. ... But it still clung to the other half of the formula — that broadcasting should pay for itself and not get any help from the proceeds of general taxation.' As a result of this shortsighted measure, the station was compelled to fall back on advertising as a vital source of revenue, the immediate effects of which can be seen from the fact that whereas in 1932 advertising accounted for a meagre £220 in income, by 1933 it had increased dramatically to £22,827.

The new Fianna Fáil government saw no inconsistency between this reliance on advertising and the cultural objectives of the station: indeed, by stipulating that only native Irish companies were eligible to advertise, they were able to convince themselves that it was a positive advance on previous policy. However, the logic of the market was moving in a different direction, and the state's economic and political requirements began to diverge sharply from the path of cultural nationalism. Advertisers were extremely reluctant to sponsor programmes which catered for 'minority' interests such as classical music and the Irish language, and looked instead to a popular formula

225

of jazz, tin-pan alley and swing music to sell their wares. As Fr R.S. Devane wrote of the changing fortunes of the Gaelic revival in the first decade of the century.

> The soul of the nation was then deeply stirred by it. A mystic idealism spread throughout the land. A national messianism, the feeling that the nation had a secret mission, took possession of the people ... It is now sad to look back on those halcyon days ... Gone is the idealism; gone the mysticism; gone the messianism. They have been replaced by cynicism, fatalism and pessimism. Native music and song have given way to jazz, crooning, and the dances of African primitives.

In the early 1940s, the Minister for Posts and Telegraphs sought belatedly to reverse this trend by banning 'jazz and crooning' from the airwaves, as if it was only the false allure of popular music which was preventing Irish people from appreciating their true heritage. This crude protectionist measure was not accompanied by any change in the financial structure of broadcasting. The 'preservation' of national culture only proved attractive, it seems, when it added to the state's coffers. In 1932-3, for example, at the same time that the radio service was being deprived of import duties, a similar tax was imposed on 'alien' newspapers which netted the exchequer a substantial sum of £140,000. Patrick Pearse's famous dictum, that Ireland should be not merely Gaelic but free as well, was given a new literal meaning when it came to the question of funding Irish culture.

The increasing popularity of Anglo-American mass culture made it difficult to sustain the belief that the official national culture was a spontaneous effusion of the people. Accordingly, it is not surprising that the middle-class basis of cultural nationalism was thrown into sharp relief, and the centre of gravity in Irish culture shifted from a folk/cultural model towards a *rapprochement* with high culture. Thus, in the case of Irish music, the 1940s and 1950s witnessed what Seán Mac Réamoinn has referred to as 'the "waiting for our Dvorak" school' which entreated the Irish people to cherish their 'rich heritage of native melody and keep it safe for the great composer who, one day, will come along and make of it something which will take its place among the musical masterpieces of the world'. With the appointment of Dr T.J. Kiernan as director in 1935, Irish music on radio began to progress in an upwardly mobile direction from the Ceili House to the Concert Hall, and in the early 1940s a Light Orchestra was established to confer respectability on this and other forms of music.

This adoption of a high-minded Reithian outlook in Irish broadcasting was a major setback for cultural nationalism, for Irish culture on the radio began to shed whatever populist appeal it may have had in the past. Actors, readers, and presenters in the Irish language were recruited from a small coterie of teachers and civil servants, and the lack of diversity eventually took its toll. In 1949, Seamus Brennan (the well-known 'Gaelic footballer and step-dancer') could write more in sorrow than in anger of the failure of the station to inject new life into Irish culture during his tenure of office as director. (Brennan, it is worth noting, was recruited to the station from a post as Secretary to the Commission on Irish in the civil service):

> To me, I think the most disappointing aspect of broadcasting in Irish was the apparently complete lack of interest, the indifference, the apathy — call it what you will — of the listeners, so much so that I often wondered whether anyone listened to Irish ... let the programmes be very good, indifferent or bad ... there was complete silence. ... A remark Dr Kiernan once passed to me will illustrate the position, viz. 'You could get away with murder in Irish on Radio'.

Brennan's suspicions about the decline, if not disappearance, of an audience for Irish language programmes were borne out by an analysis of radio listenership figures in the late 1950s by Garret FitzGerald. This showed that while Radio Eireann had a virtual monopoly of the airwaves during news, popular variety and sponsored programmes (comprising over 80 per cent of the listeners), the figures plummetted drastically when it came to Irish language content. Only 1 per cent listened to the news in Irish at 6.00 p.m. (as against 41 per cent to the 6.30 English language news) while less than 0.5 per cent tuned in to the 7.30-8.30 slot in which a play in the Irish language was broadcast. The fact that 'Irish people seem to listen voraciously to variety and popular music', FitzGerald added in a revealing comment, should not be taken as a reflection 'either on Radio Eireann or on the Irish language [but] might, perhaps, be taken as reflecting on the Irish people'. Not for the first time the people were blamed for the parsimony and ineptitude of government policy.

FitzGerald's analysis of radio listenership is of interest as it proves an important corrective to the popular myth that it was television which brought about the demise of the cultural nationalist dream. Television is an obvious scapegoat for, as we shall see, it has been unduly reliant on imported products for its programming schedules. Yet it is clear that the problem long predates the advent of television. In the conclusion to his article, Garret FitzGerald warned that the crisis in Irish language programming on radio was a portent of what would happen if any attempt were made to combine commercial viability with a public service mandate in the new television service. His warning went unheeded and in both the establishing legislation for the television service and in subsequent policy formation, the rigid emphasis on balancing the books was accompanied by ritualistic incantations of the need to make programmes which 'would reflect traditional Irish values' [Radio Éireann, *Annual Report*, 1960-61], and promote 'a deeper appreciation of the intrinsic value of Irish language, history and tradition, [and] the development of a better public consciousness of national identity' [*A View of Irish Broadcasting*, RTE Authority, 1973]. In the meantime, as Seamus Brennan had observed as early as 1949, the subservience of broadcasting to the state was becoming more apparent, with the added proviso that the interests of the state were conveniently interpreted as coinciding with those of the government of the day:

> There is nothing the average Irishman loves more than a real live argument or discussion. My experience was that we had to be so careful for fear of offending anyone, or of allowing anyone to use the *government radio* for the purpose of criticising a government department or government policy of any kind that we had substantially to avoid open discussion. [my italics]

TELEVISION AND CULTURAL IDENTITY

The inauguration of the new television service on 31 December 1961 took place against a backdrop of immense social change in Ireland. The First Programme for Economic Expansion, devised by T.K. Whitaker in 1958 and implemented by Sean Lemass, opened up the economy to foreign investment, and membership of the United Nations (1956), the application for membership of the EEC (1961) and the reforms of the Second Vatican Council (1962-5) were seen by many as ushering in a welcome, outward-looking attitude in Irish life. Television played a major part in bringing the effects of these 'global' initiatives into the living rooms of Irish people, thus clearing away many of the cultural cobwebs which had accumulated since the founding of the state. Nor was television alone in this, for the appointment of Douglas Gageby to *The Irish Times* in 1964, and the facility with which both the *The Irish Press* and radio addressed issues raised by the women's movement also helped to redefine the relationship of the media to Irish society.

It is significant, however, that the liberalising trends promoted by the media were confined for the most part in areas outside the political and economic domain, and were most evident in precisely the realm of 'traditional values' that broadcasting was enjoined to protect in official policy statements. In the case of television, deference towards religious authority, the conservative sexual morality of the post-Famine era, the bias against urban life and many other conventional pieties came under critical scrutiny from programmes such as *The Late Late Show* (1962-   ), once-off plays such as *A Week in the Life of Martin Cluxton* (1971) and *Hatchet* (1974), and drama serials such as *Tolka Row* (1964-8), *The Riordans* (1965-79), *Bracken* (1980-81), and the six-part *Strumpet City* (1980). The most striking feature of Irish television is that it was *home-produced* programmes, not imported products, which posed the greatest challenge to traditional cultural values.

Of course there is a sense in which, notwithstanding their native origins, the 'formats' or 'genres' of many of these programmes (the 'chat show', the 'continuous serial', the 'slice-of-life' television drama) are of Anglo-American origin, and thus in the eyes of some critics represent a more insidious form of cultural domination. As Herbert Shiller expresses it with regard to the influence of Anglo-American programmes on indigenous production.

> Imitations of that material may appear when and if the indigenous broadcast/film/print industries demand a share in their home market. Directly or indirectly, the outcome is the same. The content and style of the programming, *however adapted to local conditions*, bear the ideological imprint of the main centres of the capitalist world economy.

The problem with this formulation is that *any* kind of influence from the metropolitan centres is evidence of cultural imperialism. On this reckoning, much of what is already taken to be traditional in Ireland — ceili music, Sean Ó Riada's adoption of jazz and classical formats during the folk revival in the 1960s, the foundation of gaelic games (an adaptation to Irish circumstances of the sports revolution which swept Victorian Britain), even cultural nationalism itself (which was, after all, a product of German romanticism) — all of these can be dismissed as examples of foreign cultural penetration. The interaction between dominant and subaltern cultures is considered entirely in terms of one-way flow, as if cultures on the periphery have no power to resist or assimilate external influences in ways which may prove positively beneficial.

The resilience of Irish television in the face of the Anglo-American culture industry is clearly evident in programmes such as *The Late Late Show* and *The Riordans*, perhaps the two most successful home productions. Both the cutting edge and popular appeal of these programmes derived from the manner in which they broke the conventions of their original models, reworking them in terms of local cultural idioms. The long-running serial *The Riordans* pioneered the use of outside broadcast cameras for television drama, an exigency which arose from its origins in a failed outside broadcast series on an Irish village. This innovation contributed a type of documentary realism to the action which helped it to investigate topical social issues, releasing television drama from the studio-bound approach which had dominated it up to then. The impact of the serial on Irish life was such that Raymond Williams was able to cite *The Riordans* in support of his argument that in some cases, the despised serial form could engage in a more subtle form of social criticism that the more prestigious once-off play. (Williams' article, written in 1969, appears to have been the first significant appraisal of the television serial as a dramatic genre.)

The Late Late Show, compered by Gay Byrne, also brought the American-style chat show out of the realms of light entertainment by using its open-ended format to probe and question some of the most deep-rooted traditional values. As if bearing in mind Seamus Brennan's statement, quoted above, that the Irish love nothing better 'than a real live argument or discussion', the show went out live (uniquely for a chat show at the time) and this, coupled with the active participation of an audience which frequently upstaged both the panel and the presenter, seemed to invite controversy from the outset. The apparently unscripted nature of the show, which moved abruptly from levity to gravity, from frivolous items to major social issues, without any advance warning, made it compulsive viewing for audiences. The paradoxical ease with which the programme combined a home-spun intimacy with 'Brechtian' television techniques (displaying studio technology, the presenter himself calling the shots at times including the show's catch phrase 'Roll it there, Colette',) gave it a place in Irish life not unlike that of the provincial newspaper: people watched it if only because they were afraid they might miss out on something.

Yet the show's penchant for controversy had limits, and these became obvious when it made incursions into politics and the area of current affairs. While it made deep inroads on what might be understood as 'the nation', it met an immovable object when it confronted the state. A turning point came in 1983 when it was prevented, on the direct instructions of the chairman of the government-appointed RTE Authority, from devoting a special episode of the show to a discussion of the constitutional referendum on abortion. Three years later, it did present a studio debate on the pros and cons of the divorce referendum but the discussion was virtually neutralised by adopting the stilted, legal format of a simulated courtroom. Open discussion is given free rein on television so long as it does not concern itself directly with politics. Affairs of state for the most part are confined to the tightly structured formats of current affairs programmes which leave little room for questioning the dominant political consensus.

The consolidation of the state's control of broadcasting was secured by a special provision, Section 31 of the 1960 Broadcasting Act. It was never invoked in the 1960s as government ministers felt free to interfere at will in the day-to-day operations of the station. The position was summed up in 1966 by the then Taoiseach (Prime Minister) Sean Lemass when, in a statement to the Dáil, he declared that RTE 'was an instrument of public policy and as such is responsible to the government':

> The government reject the view that Radio Telefis Eireann should be, either generally or in regards to its current affairs and news programmes, completely independent of government supervision.

Section 31 was not enforced until the escalation of the northern 'troubles' and from the early 1970s it has been used primarily to silence the voice of radical or paramilitary nationalist groups. The full rigours of censorship were first experienced in November 1972 when the RTE Authority was sacked by the Minister for Posts and Telegraphs for an alleged breach of Section 31. Following the appointment of Conor Cruise O'Brien as Minister in 1973, the provision of the section was refined by specifying the groups which were prohibited from the airwaves. The most prominent of these were the Provisional IRA and Provisional Sinn Féin (the political wing of the IRA), but the remit was extended to include any organisation proscribed by the *British* government in Northern Ireland. The gap between the state and the nation in Ireland could not be greater, for at the same time as he was implementing these new directives, Dr O'Brien was proposing to use the new television channel, RTE2, to relay the BBC signal to the entire country. The fact that the BBC did *not* prohibit interviews with paramilitary organisations apparently did not trouble him.

The attempt to place an Irish television channel at the disposal of a foreign television network highlighted a serious problem which had been developing for some time in Irish broadcasting. In the early years of RTE, approximately two-thirds of television programmes were home produced. By the late 1970s this proportion was reversed, and in 1980 almost 70 per cent of all programmes were imported, thus putting RTE into a 'Third World' category in terms of cultural dependency. The reason for this marked imbalance was not the lack of interest in home-produced programmes: on the contrary, they dominated the TAM (Television Audience Measurement) ratings throughout this period. The problem was the same as that which beset radio broadcasting: the stipulation that the television service had to be self-financing forced it to rely on cheaper imported products rather than more expensive home-produced material.

The solution to this is not to revert to a form of cultural insularity which seeks to defend a 'pure' native culture against foreign contamination. One does not counteract the one-way flow of cultural

231

imperialism by closing the ports and placing an embargo on all imported products. The dramatic revival of interest in the Welsh language in recent years is a standing rejoinder to such acts of cultural enclosure. Thus while Irish language activists such as Maolsheachlainn Ó Caollaí were pointing out the corrosive effects of soap opera or the television serial on Irish culture, their Welsh counterparts were noting its potential for attracting popular audiences to Welsh language programmes. As Harri Pritchard Jones expressed it, ironically citing on Irish example to drive home his point:

> One thing we must make sure of is that the native language channel does not become a ghetto. One certainly does not want a channel for penillion singing, rural crafts and customs and the problems of rural decline. One must produce a balanced diet of news and current affairs . . . a lot of sport and serial plays of the type of the O'Riordans [sic] . . . and a great deal of popular entertainment.

The strength of an indigenous culture does not lie in its ability to avoid contact with the dominant forces in the culture industry, but in the manner in which it appropriates the forms and products of the metropolitan centre for its own ends. In the case of film, for example, the French 'new wave' and recent German cinema have shown how Hollywood genres such as the thriller and family melodrama can be reworked and turned against the American culture that produced them. At their most astringent (for example, the films of Godard or Fassbinder) such cross-cultural offensives are no less critical of their own native culture, using the universal thrust of international culture to expand what are often constricting, local horizons.

The dynamism of these cultural initiatives does not derive from any 'national mystique' or ancient heritage but from the more mundane prerequisite of a secure *production base*, geared towards an indigenous film or television culture. It is precisely the lack of commitment by successive governments to establish the most basic resources in this area which has prevented Irish culture from making a sustained, creative engagement with popular culture. The insistence that culture is simply 'part of what we are', something handed down in tablets of stone from a prehistoric past, has helped the state to perpetuate the delusion that culture does need 'artificial', i.e. material, support. The myth of a homogeneous, continuous nation is also partly responsible for the state's hostility to *internal* criticism, to any form of cultural activity which explores the social *divisions* and *contradictions* concealed by the mists of the Celtic Twilight.

Since 1986, a new administration in Irish television has attempted to redress the imbalance between imported and home-produced programmes, making greater resources available for programmes aimed

232

solely at Irish audiences. In line with this, negotiations were opened with independent film makers to break the monopoly of in-house production in RTE, and bring a greater diversity in approaches to home production. However, no sooner had this discussion begun than the Fianna Fáil government under Charles Haughey abolished the recently established Irish Film Board, thus undermining the production base of the fledgling Irish film industry. At the same time, developments were taking place in Irish radio broadcasting aimed at deregulating the airwaves, thus paving the way for the proliferation of commercial stations dominated by play-listed, middle-of-the-road pop music. Once again, the state seems willing to leave cultural policy to market forces, as if the megastore is the custodian of a megalithic past. Writing about the decline of the Gaelic revival after the founding of the State the historian George Boyce has observed:

> The state was, in this most central aspect of Irish nationalism, modifying the nature of the ideology that inspired its birth. The very establishment of an Irish state created the widespread belief that such an act, by itself, ensured the preservation of the Gaelic League idea. . . . The task was, by implication, completed now that the state was a reality. And the Gaelic League, that most effective pressure group, was the victim of its own political influence: by helping to inspire political freedom it left the state with no really effective critic.

From its inception the state has tended to blame outside forces — Hollywood, Anglicisation, mid-Atlantic culture — for the erosion of Irish culture. Perhaps, like de Valera, it should look into its own heart to see the real source of the problem.

REFERENCES

Desmond Bell, 'Proclaiming the Republic: Broadcasting Policy and the Corporate State in Ireland', *West European Politics*, vol. 8, no. 2, 1985.

Walter Benjamin, 'The Work of Art in the Age of Mechanical Reproduction', in *Illuminations*, trans. Harry Zohn, London 1970.

D. George Boyce, *Nationalism in Ireland*, London and Dublin 1982.

Bertolt Brecht, 'Radio as a Means of Communication', *Screen*, vol. 20, no. 3-4, 1979-80.

Seamus Brennan, 'Seven Years of Irish Radio', *The Leader*, 25 December 1948 — 12 February 1949.

Citizens for Better Broadcasting, *Aspects of RTE Television Broadcasting*, Dublin 1976.

Rev. R.S. Devane, *The Imported Press: A National Menace - Some Remedies*, Dublin 1950.

Lelia Doolan, Bob Quinn and Jack Dowling, *Sit Down and Be Counted*, Dublin 1969.

Brian Farrell ed., *Communications and Community in Ireland*, Cork 1984.

Desmond Fisher, *Broadcasting in Ireland*, London 1978.

Garret FitzGerald, 'Radio Listenership and the TV Problem', *University Review*, vol. II, no. 5.

Maurice Gorham, *Forty Years of Irish Broadcasting*, Dublin 1967.

Richard Kearney ed., *The Crane Bag: Media and Popular Culture*, vol. 8, no. 2, 1984.

Martin McLoone and John McMahon, *Television and Irish Society*, Dublin 1984.

Seán MacRéamoinn, 'Traditional Music', *Radio Eireann Handbook*, Dublin 1955.

Micheál Ó hUanacháin, 'The Broadcasting Dilemma', *Administration*, vol. 28, no. 1, 1980.

Harri Pritchard Jones, *Wales/Ireland: A TV Contrast*, Dublin 1974.

Herbert I. Schiller, *Communication and Cultural Domination*, New York 1976.

Raymond Williams, 'Most Doctors Recommend', *The Listener*, 27 November 1969.

INDEX

235

236

238